RANCHERS' LEGACY

Ranchers' Legacy

ALBERTA ESSAYS BY LEWIS G. THOMAS

Edited by Patrick A. Dunae

Western Canada Reprint Series
The University of Alberta Press

First published by
The University of Alberta Press
Athabasca Hall
Edmonton, Alberta, Canada
T6G 2E8
1986

Copyright © The University of Alberta Press 1986

ISBN 0-88864-095-1
ISSN 0820-9561;4

Canadian Cataloguing in Publication Data

Thomas, Lewis G. (Lewis Gwynne), 1914–
  Ranchers' legacy

(Western Canada reprint series, ISSN 0820-9561)
Includes bibliographical references.
ISBN 0-88864-095-1

1. Alberta - History - Addresses, essays, lectures. 2. Ranch life - Alberta - Addresses, essays, lectures. 3. Ranchers - Alberta - Addresses, essays, lectures. I. Dunae, Patrick A. (Patrick Alexander), 1950– II. Title. III. Series.
FC3661.7.T56 1986   971.23   C86-0910709
F1076.5.T56 1986

All rights reserved.
No part of this publication may be produced, stored in a retrieval system, or transmitted in any form or by any means, electronic, mechanical, photocopying, recording, or otherwise, without prior permission of the copyright owner.

Typesetting by Typeworks,
Vancouver, British Columbia, Canada
Printed by John Deyell Company,
Lindsay, Ontario, Canada

Frontispiece: Line drawing by Edith Lucy Trotter, based on her memories of her father's Galloway Ranch, Millarville. See page 160 for a photograph of W. H. King's Galloway Ranch.

Cover: Cottonwoods Ranch, Okotoks, Alberta. Handpainted photograph used with the kind permission of L. G. Thomas's sister, Gwynydd M. Kelson.

PERMISSIONS

ONE   Lewis G. Thomas, "The Ranching Tradition and the Life of the Ranchers" (M.A. thesis, University of Alberta, 1935) is published here with permission of the author.

TWO   Originally published as Lewis G. Thomas, "The Rancher and the City: Calgary and the Cattlemen, 1883—1914," in *Proceedings and Transactions of the Royal Society of Canada,* Fourth Series, Vol. VI (Toronto: Royal Society of Canada, 1968), pp. 203—15. Reprinted with permission of the Royal Society of Canada.

THREE   Originally published as Lewis G. Thomas, "The Umbrella and the Mosaic: The French-English Presence and the Settlement of the Canadian West," in *Reflections of Western Historians,* edited by John Alexander Carroll (Tucson: The University of Arizona Press, 1969), pp. 135—52. Reprinted with the permission of the publisher.

FOUR   Lewis G. Thomas, "The Shires Transplanted—Millarville," is published here with the permission of the author.

FIVE   Abridged from Lewis G. Thomas, "Okotoks: From Trading Post to Suburb," *Urban History Review* 8, no. 2 (October 1979): 3—22. Reprinted with the permission of *Urban History Review.*

SIX   Originally appeared as L. G. Thomas, "Ranch Houses of the Alberta Foothills," in *Canadian Historical Sites: Occasional Papers in Archaeology and History,* no. 20 (Ottawa: National Historic Parks and Sites Branch, 1979): 125—45. Reproduced by permission of Supply and Services, Canada.

SEVEN   Abridged from Lewis G. Thomas, "Associations and Communications," in *Historical Papers/Communications Historiques 1973,* edited by Peter Gillis (Ottawa: Canadian Historical Association, 1973), pp. 1—12. Reprinted with the permission of the Canadian Historical Association, Ottawa, Ontario.

EIGHT   Originally appeared as Lewis G. Thomas, "Introduction" to *Pioneering in Alberta: Maurice Destrubé's Story,* edited by James E. Hendrickson (Calgary: Historical Society of Alberta, 1981), pp. ix—xxii. Reprinted with the permission of the Historical Society of Alberta.

NINE   Abridged from Lewis G. Thomas, "Prairie Settlement: Western Responses in History and Fiction; Social Structures in a Canadian Hinterland," in *Crossing Frontiers,* edited by Dick Harrison (Edmonton: University of Alberta Press, 1979), pp. 59—72. Reprinted with the permission of the publisher.

TEN   Originally published as Lewis G. Thomas, "Alberta 1905—1980: The Uneasy Society," in *The New Provinces: Alberta and Saskatchewan, 1905—1980,* edited by Howard Palmer and Donald Smith (Vancouver: Tantalus Research Limited, 1981), pp. 23—41. Reprinted with the permission of the publisher.

CONTENTS

Editor's Acknowledgements   ix

Introduction   xi

ONE   The Ranching Tradition and the Life of the Ranchers   1

TWO   The Rancher and the City: Calgary and the Cattlemen, 1883–1914   39

THREE   The Umbrella and the Mosaic   61

FOUR   The Shires Transplanted—Millarville   81

FIVE   A Ranchers' Community—Okotoks   99

SIX   Ranch Houses of the Alberta Foothills   117

SEVEN   Associations and Communications   139

EIGHT   Privileged Settlers   151

NINE   History and Fiction   169

TEN   Alberta 1905–1980: The Uneasy Society   185

Conclusion   213

Editor's Acknowledgements

I WOULD LIKE to thank Lewis G. Thomas for agreeing to this collection and for helping me to assemble the essays herein. Lewis wrote the captions to the illustrations and provided me with details of his family and early career. And I am most grateful for his stimulating discourses on Western history, which I enjoyed in congenial surroundings in Edmonton, Lake Wabamun, and Victoria. Those discourses were often enlivened by his kind and gracious wife, Jonesy; and I extend a special thanks to her for her friendship, encouragement, and hospitality.

Many of the photographs appearing in this book are from Lewis's private collection unless otherwise noted. The University of Alberta Press has asked me to thank Georgeen Klassen, Assistant Chief Archivist at the Glenbow-Alberta Institute, for her help in locating many of the other photographs used in this collection and Geoff Lester and the Cartographic Section, Department of Geography, University of Alberta, who made the necessary changes to the watercolour map from L. G. Thomas's thesis so that it could be reproduced in this book. The kindness of Stuart Sinclair-Smith for providing the picture of Viewfield Ranch is acknowledged. The photograph of the painting of Gate Ranch taken by Aileen Harmon is used with the permission of the late Elisabeth von Rummel.

This work is published in cooperation with the Western Canadiana Publications Project Committee of the University of Alberta with the assistance of a grant from the committee.

L. G. Thomas, Sub-Lieutenant, (S.B.), R.C.N.V.R., 1942.
L. G. Thomas recalls that Yousuf Karsh had the amiable habit of photographing service personnel for a nominal sum.

Introduction

LEWIS GWYNNE THOMAS has long been a major figure in the field of Western Canadian history. Alberta's senior academic historian, he was the province's first native son to be appointed head of the University of Alberta's History department. He is a Fellow of the Royal Society of Canada and past president of the Canadian Historical Association. He has written and edited four books, several dozen articles, and a great number of scholarly addresses and reviews. More important, he has taught, guided, and inspired at least two generations of students.

Throughout his career, Professor Thomas's interests have ranged widely—from fur traders and missionaries in Rupert's Land, to prairie horticulture and the Alberta Liberal Party. But today he is perhaps best known for his work on the ranching industry, particularly on the "privileged settlers" who gave a distinctly British flavour to the rangelands and foothills of southern Alberta between 1882 and 1914. His portraits of these well-born, well-educated settlers, and his picture of Alberta society during the "Golden Age of Ranching," are exquisitely drawn: precise, percipient, and evocative; they are among the most engaging works in the corpus of Western Canadian literature.

Professor Thomas's works are also provocative and controversial, for they challenge many widely-held notions of frontier society in Western Canada. His works demonstrate that the Canadian West was not the "wild and woolly West," so beloved of dime novelists. Nor was Western Canada the unstructured, egalitarian hinterland which many academic historians—especially those who subscribed to Frederick Jackson Turner's "frontier thesis"—imagined. Rather, Professor Thomas has argued, the pioneer society of Canada's West was generally peaceful, orderly, well-defined, and highly-structured.

His knowledge and understanding of the West was first demonstrated in his Master of Arts thesis, written in 1935. His views were subsequently developed and refined in a number of essays and in the addresses he gave to the Royal Society, the Canadian Historical Association, and other learned societies over the years. Yet while his scholarship is internationally known and respected, many of his important works are not easily accessible. His M.A. thesis, for example, which has provided the basis for several recent studies on the ranching frontier, was never published. Similarly, a number of Professor Thomas's most provocative, perceptive essays were delivered orally and afterwards were circulated among a select, but relatively small, audience. Other essays were published in specialized regional journals or were printed by university presses outside of the country. One of the intentions of this book is to bring some of these works together in a single volume, so as to make the works readily available and better known to students of Western Canadian history.

Bringing these works together serves to recognize Professor Thomas's scholarly activities and his contributions to our understanding of the Canadian West. Though not the first historian to lecture on the region, from the late 1940s until the late 1960s he was the only faculty member at any Canadian university to teach courses in Western history on a regular, continuous basis. His erudition in the field is patent in the essays which comprise this volume.

As the essays will show, however, Professor Thomas's concept of the West has been anything but static. While the main outlines of his thesis have remained more or less constant, his perspective on the region and on the forces which contributed to its character have altered over the years. The changes—some subtle, others substantial—are not simply the result of the changes which have taken place in Alberta since the Depression; they are more the result of assiduous research, coupled with that intuitive understanding of a subject which comes only from a career spent perfecting the scholar's craft. These changes are evident from the chronological arrangement of the essays herein—beginning with the chapter from his M.A. thesis, which even when it was written reflected some of the confidence of the early cattlemen, on through to the last essay in this book, an essay published in 1981 and entitled, significantly, "Alberta 1905–1980: The Uneasy Society."

It is true, nevertheless, that L. G. Thomas has not wavered in the emphasis he has placed on Alberta's "privileged settlers." Irrespective of the vogues and vagaries of Canadian historiography, despite the changing focus and fashions of other academic historians, he has continued to point to the importance of the well-educated, anglophile immigrants who helped to establish the ranching industry in the province a century ago. A prominent and vital part of Alberta society until the First World War, these settlers had a profound impact on the social, cultural, political, and economic life of the province.

This is not to say that the privileged settlers were an unmitigated blessing to Alberta. As Professor Thomas is the first to admit, they fashioned a society which some immigrants—notably those from eastern Europe and the United States—found to be stratified and somewhat elitist.[1] But by way of compensation, it was an orderly, well-regulated society; moreover, the stable character of the Alberta frontier facilitated greatly the establishment and success of those from other immigrant groups.

In any case, most of the institutions which developed because of the privileged settlers proved ultimately to be accommodating and enduring. The Anglican church and its many auxiliary organizations, the West's earliest literary and artistic societies, sundry athletic associations, various schools and colleges, and of course the venerable Ranchmen's Club and the celebrated Calgary Stampede were all established during the "Golden Age of Ranching" by the "privileged settlers" of the West. These institutions which still flourish today embrace Albertans of diverse ethnic stock. Accordingly, along with its basic objectives of honouring Professor Thomas's scholarship and making his essays readily accessible to students, this book seeks to recognize the contributions of Alberta's "gentle pioneers" and to acknowledge the "gentler tradition" in the history of the Canadian West.

II

"We see history, I submit, through the spectacles of our own experience and we write history so that we may share our experience of it with others."[2] L. G. Thomas's dictum may be applicable to the work of several Canadian historians, including Margaret Ormsby of British Columbia and the late W. L. Morton of Manitoba.[3] Certainly it is appropriate to his own work, for his perception of Alberta history has been coloured to a considerable extent by his family background and by the social milieu in which he spent his formative years. Although the Thomases were not one of the clans which comprised the influential "cattle compact," still they shared and enjoyed many of the interests and pastimes of the wealthy ranchers. By the same token, although they would not have described themselves as a prominent or influential family, the Thomases nonetheless subscribed to a set of values which has come to be associated with the "privileged settlers" of the province.

Lewis's father, Edward Harold Thomas, came from the town of Ruthin, North Wales. Eschewing a career as a civil engineer, he emigrated at the age of twenty in 1896. Briefly a "ranch pupil" in South Dakota, he worked on ranches in South Dakota and Montana, and made an adventurous but unremunerative foray into the gold fields of Alaska. About 1901 he settled on Sheep Creek, southwest of Calgary, acquiring a small herd of cattle, buying and selling horses and running a livery business in Okotoks. In 1908 he moved his wife and two daughters to Lloydminster but a year later returned to Britain. In 1910, in partnership with a young Manxman, he purchased a three-quarter section stock farm on Sheep Creek, eight miles west of Okotoks. The ranch house, called "Cottonwoods" after the trees that grew along Sheep Creek, commanded a superb view of the Rockies. It was here that L.G. Thomas was born in 1914.

L. G.'s mother, Edith Agnes Louise Lewis, was from the English cathedral city of Gloucester and came to Alberta as a governess in 1904. She and Harold Thomas were married in the Pro-Cathedral of the Redeemer in Calgary the following year. Gracious, well-educated, and adventurous, she adapted easily to her new surroundings. And while she did not regard equestrian pursuits with quite the same passion as did her husband, she had other interests which she pursued with no less ardour. One of

Introduction xv

Edward Harold Thomas, ca. 1903. A snapshot taken more to amuse than to impress his relatives in the United Kingdom.

Edward Harold Thomas, with his dog, ca. 1884. This is one of the earliest pictures that L. G. Thomas has of his father.

these was horticulture, an interest that found expression in the beautiful flower garden which is still to be seen at "Cottonwoods." She was also an eminently practical woman who took an active part in the management of the ranch and who, like her husband, developed a deep attachment to the land. What is more, in spite of their interests and deportment, their periodic visits to Britain and abiding affection for the Old Country, L. G.'s parents both regarded themselves as Canadians. They entertained no doubts as to their identity.

"Cottonwoods," as Professor Thomas has explained in one of the essays reprinted in this book, was not a large house. The two-storey structure consisted of a sitting room, a dining room, four bedrooms and a kitchen. Books accumulated year by year: classics like Walter Scott and the works of more modern writers sent out by bookish aunts in England. British periodicals such as *Punch* and the *Tatler* intermingled with the Montreal *Family Herald* and the *Farm and Ranch Review*. It was a happy home and as Lewis

The Thomas family at Cottonwoods, ca. 1916. From right to left: Lewis and his sister, Dorothy Gwynne (Gregg), on "Dimple"; his mother, Edith Agnes Louise, on "Marey"; his father, Edward Harold, on "Pat"; and his sister, Gwynydd Mary (Kelson), on "Tiny."

Haying at Cottonwoods, summer, 1914. From left to right: Lewis G. Thomas; his father, Edward Harold; his sister, Gwynydd; Lewis's father's partner and his god-father, Robert William Thompson; his sister, Dorothy; his father's elder sister, Ethel Gwynne Thomas; and his mother, Edith Agnes Louise.

has recalled "there was certainly no dearth of entertainment."⁴ From their mother, Lewis and his two older sisters, Dorothy and Gwynydd, learned to dance and—of no little importance at "Cottonwoods"—to play a respectable rubber of bridge. From their father, they learned how to ride. A tennis court adjoined the flower garden and there was ample space for more rumbustious outdoor games. Yet amid the merriment and activity at "Cottonwoods," a degree of formality and decorum was maintained. To offer but one example: Mr. Thomas's partner, R. W. Thompson, who lived with the family until his death in the 1930s, always addressed his friend's wife as Mrs. Thomas, never Edith. She, in turn, always addressed him as Mr. Thompson, never Bob. But such formality was not regarded as especially unusual. In fact, the ambience of "Cottonwoods" was not so different from that which characterized many homes in High River, Pincher Creek, and the other ranching communities in the Foothills.

In many of those communities the Anglican church held a prominent place. So, too, did it in Okotoks. As it happened, though, Lewis formed a stronger attachment to the parish in neighbouring Millarville. Completed in 1896, Christ Church, Millarville was built to minister to the spiritual needs of the well-to-do British ranchers and the less-affluent but no less genteel bachelors who first settled the area. Professor Thomas has described the log-built church at Millarville as possibly the most attractive of the pioneer churches in the Foothills and, among heritage sites in the Calgary area, as one of the most evocative of the "Golden Age of Ranching."⁵

There were other visible traces of that age, many of them close at hand. "Cottonwoods" itself had been built by a retired surveyor from Ottawa who had homesteaded in the district as early as 1885. The site of the Quorn Ranche, which had raised horses for the famous Leicestershire Hunt, was nearby, while even larger spreads such as the Cochrane were but a few miles distant. Buildings which had held the annual Sheep Creek Bachelors' Ball were still standing and the Millarville Races were still an institution during L. G.'s boyhood. It is hardly surprising, then, that he came to have such an interest in, and intimate understanding of, the pioneer ranchers.

Lewis's early interests extended far beyond the Foothills, though, thanks in part to his friendship with the indomitable Miss

Lewis G. Thomas standing in front of his mother with his sisters and his aunt Ethel, ca. 1917. The limed lines of the tennis court are in the foreground.

Jane Seymour, an elderly lady in Okotoks. Miss Seymour, who was something of a legend in the area, had been baptized by Bishop Strachan and had known MacKenzie King, Sir John A. Macdonald, Lord Dufferin, and a host of other historical figures. Her anecdotes sparked L. G.'s interest in Canadian history and British history—complementary subjects which he studied at Mount Royal College in Calgary and at The University of Alberta.

Lewis graduated with a Bachelor of Arts degree in 1934, having attained first class honours and the A. L. Burt Prize for the highest marks in English constitutional history. In completing his degree, he earned special praise from Professor Morden Long for an undergraduate Honours paper he had written on the early ranchers of Alberta. Though necessarily modest in scope, the paper proved to be the starting point for the many significant studies which were to follow.

Also important in retrospect was Lewis's first paid academic job—a contract he received from Professor G. M. Smith that summer to interview people in the Okotoks area on their attitudes towards Americans. The results (which Smith incorporated into an essay on Canadian-American relations)[6] reinforced Lewis's growing awareness that southern Alberta was not simply a northern extension of the American frontier. Historically and culturally, there were marked differences between the two frontier societies, a point he was to emphasize repeatedly in his later works.

Despite limited financial resources, Lewis returned to The University of Alberta in the autumn of 1934. He completed his Master of Arts dissertation the following spring. After a brief stint as an advance agent for a theatrical company that soon dissolved in Fort Macleod, he then registered as a doctoral candidate in History at Harvard. Interestingly, his choice of Harvard was determined in part by the presence of Frederick Merk, a noted authority on the fur trade and a disciple of F. J. Turner. However, Lewis was no Turnerian and rather than apply the frontier model to a Canadian region (as a number of his contemporaries were then doing) he set out to write a study of the Liberal Party in Alberta. That study, subsequently published by the University of Toronto Press in 1959, remains the definitive work on the subject.[7]

Although it was primarily a political study, Professor Thomas's Ph.D. thesis contained a great deal of social history; and, as one reviewer wrote when describing the published version, "for all its solidity, this is emphatically not a dull work."[8] Indeed, his Harvard dissertation was written with authority and verve, with a stylistic flourish which has come to be a hallmark of his ranching essays. That energetic yet graceful style also characterized the articles he wrote on church history, a topic always close to his heart and one which he pursued avidly in the early 1950s, following an extended visit to the archives of the major missionary societies in London. His distinctive flair is evident, too, in his introductions to the reprinted journals of Alexander Henry and the Earl of Southesk, in his articles on the fur trade, in his *Dictionary of Canadian Biography* entries, and in his introductory essay to the new edition of A. S. Morton's *History of the Canadian West.*[9]

Provincial politics, early fur traders, explorers, and missionaries—these were Professor Thomas's principal research interests during much of his tenure at The University of Alberta.[10] In fact, he did not return to the subject of his M.A. thesis until 1968, when he presented his landmark essay on Alberta ranchers and Calgary cattlemen to the Royal Society of Canada. His return to the field was prompted by two events. In the late 1960s, David Breen (then a post-graduate student at the University of Calgary) was completing an important study on the "cattle compact" of southern Alberta. Professor Thomas was greatly impressed by the study and a few years later had the pleasure of supervising Breen's Ph.D. dissertation on the ranching industry in Western Canada. At about the same time, Professor Thomas had accepted an invitation to join his long time friends Sheilagh Jameson (then Chief Archivist of the Glenbow-Alberta Institute) and R. H. C. King[11] in compiling a history of the Millarville area for a local history group. That project, which he described as "an exercise in filial piety,"[12] entailed a comprehensive study of the individuals and the institutions which had formed the fabric of pioneer society in southwestern Alberta. The labour he invested in *Our Foothills,* as his community history was entitled, plus the attention he devoted to David Breen's research, led him back to the field which he had first explored in the mid 1930s.

The interval between the completion of Professor Thomas's M.A. thesis and the publication of his address to the Royal Society may, however, be misleading. Throughout that period he maintained a working interest in the settlement of the ranching frontier; he was teaching courses in the history of the Canadian West all the while and in each of the courses he examined the impact of the early ranchers. Moreover, during these years he was developing and refining a theme based on what he called "social contiguity." This theme, which stressed the importance of order and effective communication between the leading social groups on the frontier, runs like a unifying thread throughout all of Professor Thomas's works.

Few historians would question the relationship between a stable frontier and orderly settlement. Nor would many question the social, political, and economic advantages of a peaceful and orderly frontier. Obviously, such a frontier is more attractive to immigrants and potential settlers, whose main purpose in coming to the frontier is to better themselves. For obvious reasons, a peaceful, prosperous, and progressive hinterland is also an asset to the metropolitan centres which control or depend upon the frontier. But what accounts for a stable frontier? What, or who, facilitates orderly settlement in the first place? In L. G. Thomas's view, responsible individuals—representing authority, established institutions, and traditional values—were key elements in the process. Such individuals acted as agents by bringing Old World ideas to the New Frontier. The success of these agents, who were often a minority among the frontier populace, depended on their ability to communicate with each other. For this reason, it was important for them to have certain attitudes and interests in common. It was equally important for the agents to maintain contact with older metropolitan centres, whence their authority and their cultural values derived.

Among the earliest representatives of authority and tradition in the Canadian West were the officers of the great fur companies, notably the Hudson's Bay Company; they established a network of small but stable communities throughout the prairies. The traders were followed by the missionaries—Roman Catholic and Protestant—who established their own series of communities and who, like the Hudson's Bay men, maintained an effective network of communication. Later in the nineteenth century, the North West Mounted Police played a similar role. In their official capacity the Mounties represented and enforced law and authority in such a way that Western Canada was spared much of the violence which characterized settlement south of the border. Recruited mainly from the middle classes of Great Britain and Eastern Canada, the Mounties also contributed to the social and cultural complexion of the region, by providing a link between scattered prairie settlements and distant metropolitan centres.

The privileged ranchers who came from the United Kingdom and the older provinces of Canada in the 1880s may be seen in the same light. They, too, were conduits through which certain Old World values were transmitted to the New Frontier. In the case of these settlers, the values included a faith in the church, a reverence for the monarchy, respect for property, and a belief in a conservative type of democracy: these were the basic elements in their system of social contiguity.

As Professor Thomas has explained, though, social contiguity involved "more than a cluster of attitudes, values, or convictions held in common." Social contiguity on the ranching frontier of Alberta "depended upon *some degree of education,* the *possession of some means* and, much more important, *some leisure.*"[13] The privileged ranchers were "privileged" because they met these criteria. Many of them—Britons and Canadians alike—had attended prestigious private schools and universities; many of them possessed a considerable amount of capital, in itself a requisite for stock-growing on a large scale. And in one way or another, they managed to devote a fair amount of time to leisure activities such as hunting, cricket, and polo.

The fact that the ranchers came from similar backgrounds, had undergone a similar kind of education, and enjoyed particular forms of recreation, ensured close contact and communication among them. It also accounted for the close relationship the ranchers enjoyed with many of the missionaries and N.W.M.P. troopers. This alliance and the community of interests which prevailed among the privileged settlers helped to ensure the survival of many of the values and institutions which were imported to Canada's western frontier.

There were other factors which helped the privileged settlers to maintain their distinctive and somewhat incongruous way of life on the frontier—factors which were related to outside communications. Put simply, it was relatively easy for the privileged ranchers to remain in contact with friends and families in Eastern Canada or the British Isles. A life-line always existed. The life-line helped to reduce the ranchers' social and physical isolation; it also fostered a feeling among them that they were still very much a part of the mainstreams of the Dominion and the Empire.

The ranchers' sense of security and confidence, which sprang directly from their ability to maintain contact with their homelands, was made possible because the period of rapid and decisive settlement in Alberta coincided with an age of rapid and relatively easy communication. Thanks to the railway, the steamship, and the telegraph, members of the ranching community were never too far from established metropolitan centres. Or, in Professor Thomas's words:

> The Alberta settler, and especially the settler who moved into positions of influence and power, could always maintain con-

nections with his parent society. This was particularly the prerogative of the relatively well-to-do. Letters, telegrams, cables, parcels, shipments of exotic commodities, newspapers, books, even concert pianists and theatrical companies, moved easily and comparatively rapidly. Visits back and forth were a simple matter of days, not a painful and tedious exercise of weeks or months.[14]

The channels which were maintained between the ranchers and their parent societies accounted for much of the European and Eastern Canadian money that flowed into southwestern Alberta during the late nineteenth and early part of the twentieth century. The financial infusions were important both to the local economy and to the local society, for they provided the ranching fraternity with the means to pursue their leisure activities. In addition, the channels and contacts which developed facilitated the settlement of the many young bachelors who came to the area during the quarter century prior to the First World War. Though not as wealthy or as influential as some of the ranching patriarchs, these younger gentlemen emigrants nevertheless added to the tone and temperament of the ranching frontier. And, of course, the ambience of the region owed much to the ranchers' wives, to the bachelors' sisters, and to those genteel women known in the Edwardian years as "lady helps." They were all important elements in the prevailing system which L. G. Thomas has identified as "social contiguity." The dynamics of that system, and its impact on the history and character of the Canadian West, are the subjects of the ten essays that follow.

Notes

1. See for example L. G. Thomas's comments in "Alberta Perspectives, 1905," *Alberta History,* 28 (Winter 1980), 5: "Quite apart from the normal rigours of the pioneer process, Alberta in 1905 was not an altogether comfortable society. In spite of its loudly voiced commitment to equal opportunity, it placed a heavy premium on being white, polite, and English-speaking."
2. L. G. Thomas, "The Shires Transplanted—Millarville" written in 1977, published in this book for the first time.
3. On the background and writing of two of L. G. Thomas's contemporaries,

see the introduction to Carl Berger and Ramsay Cook, eds., *The West and the Nation: Essays in Honour of W. L. Morton* (Toronto: McClelland and Stewart, 1976); and John Norris, "Margaret Ormsby," *BC Studies,* 32 (1976–77), 11–27. Their work is also discussed by Berger in his *The Writing of Canadian History: Aspects of English-Canadian Historical Writing, 1900–1970* (Toronto: Oxford University Press, 1976). L. G. Thomas's own view of the work of his Western Canadian contemporaries is outlined in his essay "The Writing of History in Western Canada" in David Jay Bercuson and Phillip G. Buckner, eds., *Eastern and Western Perspectives. Papers from the Joint Atlantic Canada/Western Canadian Studies Conference* (Toronto: University of Toronto Press, 1981).

4. Lewis G. Thomas, "The Harold Thomas Family," in *A Century of Memories, 1883–1983: Okotoks and District* (Okotoks: Okotoks and District Historical Society, 1983), pp. 593–596. Further information on the Thomas family is to be found in L. G. Thomas, ed., *Our Foothills* (Calgary: Millarville, Kew, Priddis, and Bragg Creek Historical Society, 1975).
5. L. G. Thomas, "The Shires Transplanted—Millarville."
6. G. M. Smith represented the prairie provinces in H. F. Angus, ed., *Canada and Her Great Neighbour. Sociological Surveys of Opinion and Attitudes in Canada Concerning the United States* (Toronto: The Ryerson Press for the Carnegie Endowment for International Peace, 1938).
7. L. G. Thomas, *The Liberal Party in Alberta, 1905–1921* (Toronto: University of Toronto Press, 1959). An earlier version, also based on the author's Ph.D. thesis, was published in the *Canadian Historical Review,* 28 (December 1947).
8. Review by J. T. McLeod in *Canadian Journal of Economic and Political Science,* 26 (August 1960), 494.
9. Among L. G. Thomas's articles on church history are: "English Missionary Records and the History of the Canadian West," Canadian Historical Association *Annual Report* (1954); "The Church of England and Higher Education in the Prairie West before 1914," *Journal of the Canadian Church Historical Society,* 3 (January 1956); and "Mission Church in Edmonton: An Anglican Experiment in the Canadian West," *Pacific Northwest Quarterly,* 49 (April 1958). L. G. Thomas's works on the fur trade include "The Historiography of the Fur Trade Era," in Richard Allen, ed., *A Region of the Mind: Interpreting the Western Canadian Plains* (Regina: The Canadian Plains Research Centre, 1973) and "Fur Traders in Retirement," *The Beaver,* Outfit 310:3 (Winter 1979). His essays on Edward Ermatinger, Donald Gunn, and William Henry Taylor appear in vols. 9 and 10 of the *DCB.* Other works include introductions to new editions of Alexander Henry's *Travels and Adventures in Canada and the Indian Territories* [1809] (Edmonton: Hurtig, 1969) and the Earl of Southesk's *Saskatchewan and the Rocky Mountains* [1875] (Edmonton: Hurtig, 1969). The introduction and extensive notes L. G. Thomas provided for the second edition of A. S. Morton's *History of the Canadian West to 1870–71* [1929] (Toronto: University of Toronto Press, 1973) were based on research at the Public Archives of Canada in Ottawa and the Hudson's Bay Company Archives in London.
10. Lewis G. Thomas was first appointed to the History department staff at the University of Alberta in 1938. He continued on staff until 1942, when he left for service with the Royal Canadian Navy Reserve. He rejoined the University as Lecturer in History in 1945 and the following year was appointed Assistant Professor. In 1951 he became Associate Professor, and in 1958 was

promoted full Professor. In 1958 he was also appointed Head of the History department, a position he held until 1964. He retired in 1975. For an account of his academic career, see the *festschrift* edited by his friend and colleague, the late Lewis H. Thomas: *Essays on Western History. In Honour of Lewis Gwynne Thomas* (Edmonton: University of Alberta Press, 1976).

11. R. H. C. ("Dick") King was the grandson of Chief Trader William Cornwallis King of the H.B.C. and his wife Charlotte Flett of Fort Chipewyan. "My friendship with the Kings was particularly close and gave me, I am convinced, a valuable perspective on the relationship between the fur trader, the natives of the Northwest, and the missionaries... I think this friendship with the Kings... has been very important in forming my view of the West" [L. G. Thomas to the Editor, 19 April 1984].

12. L. G. Thomas, "Millarville: A Personal Memoir," [unpublished manuscript in the possession of the author].

13. L. G. Thomas, "Associations and Communications," Canadian Historical Association, *Historical Papers/Communications Historiques* (1973), 5 [emphasis added].

14. L. G. Thomas, "History and Identity: Perceptions of the Past in Alberta," 5. [Unpublished paper delivered to a Trent University History Department colloquium in 1977. Excerpts from the paper were published as "Missing Links to Alberta's Past" in the Edmonton *Journal* (14 April 1978)].

ONE THE RANCHING TRADITION AND THE LIFE OF THE RANCHERS

Lewis Thomas's Master of Arts thesis was entitled "The Ranching Period in Alberta." It was supervised by Professors Morden H. Long and George M. Smith and was submitted to the History department of the University of Alberta in April, 1935. The first half of the thesis dealt with the historical geography of southern Alberta, the economic factors which led to the establishment of the cattle industry, and with leasing arrangements and other legislation introduced by John A. Macdonald's government to encourage large-scale ranching in the early 1880s. Also considered were the settlement and immigration policies of the Laurier government and the subsequent decline of the large ranches in the early 1900s.

The second half of the dissertation dealt with social issues. As the author's friend and colleague, the late Lewis H. Thomas, noted, the social history of the cattleman's frontier was a "congenial theme" to the young Okotoks scholar, while the study itself was executed "in the best tradition of English literary style."[1] The social history of the ranching frontier was indeed congenial and topical for L. G. Thomas. His thesis was written when the "Golden Age of Ranching" was less than a generation removed, when vestiges of the great ranches were still to be seen in the Foothills, when the memories of the ranching fraternity were still fresh. He was, accordingly, able to draw upon a great deal of first-hand information, including the memoirs and reminiscences of some of the pioneer ranching families.

On the other hand, many important primary sources were not then available. Alberta did not possess a provincial archives and the Glenbow-Alberta Institute—today the principal repository for documents pertaining to the ranching frontier—was many years in the future. Consequently, the author had to use *Sessional Papers* and contemporary newspapers as primary documents. Moreover, relatively few secondary sources were available at the time: aside from L. V. Kelly's *The Range Men* (1913), C. M. MacInnes's *In the Shadow of the Rockies* (1930), and John D. Higinbotham's *When the West Was Young* (1933), there were no book-length studies of the early ranchers.

Despite the limited resources available to him, Lewis produced an admirable study. Detailed and authoritative, it represented the first comprehensive examination of the cattle industry in Western Canada. And, though written half a century ago, it has endured remarkably well. It has, in fact, provided the foundation for several recent works by scholars who had at their disposal far more resources than were available to Professor Thomas. What is more, the recent works tend to confirm the picture which he offered in his post-graduate dissertation.[2]

The essay that follows is excerpted from chapter VI of the thesis. It comprises vignettes of the ranchers, their domestic lives, their attitudes and interests, their involvement with their communities. The thesis chapter from which the following is taken introduces the concept of social contiguity, the value of leisure, and several other ideas which Professor Thomas was to develop in later years.

For the sake of clarity and uniformity, the original footnotes have been amended to include bibliographic details of works cited. For the sake of continuity, letters and numerals which originally accompanied subheadings in the thesis have been omitted. In a few instances, supplementary notes have also been added; in such cases, the notes are indicated by a bracket, thus [1]. Otherwise, the text is as it was first written in the spring of 1935.

Notes

1. Lewis H. Thomas, ed., *Essays on Western History. In Honour of Lewis Gwynne Thomas* (Edmonton: The University of Alberta Press, 1976), p. 4.
2. Among the recent works which are indebted to L. G. Thomas's dissertation are David H. Breen's highly-acclaimed book, *The Canadian Prairie West and the Ranching Frontier 1874–1924* (Toronto: University of Toronto Press, 1982) and the editor's *Gentlemen Emigrants: From the British Public Schools to the Canadian Frontier* (Vancouver & Toronto: Douglas & McIntyre, 1981).

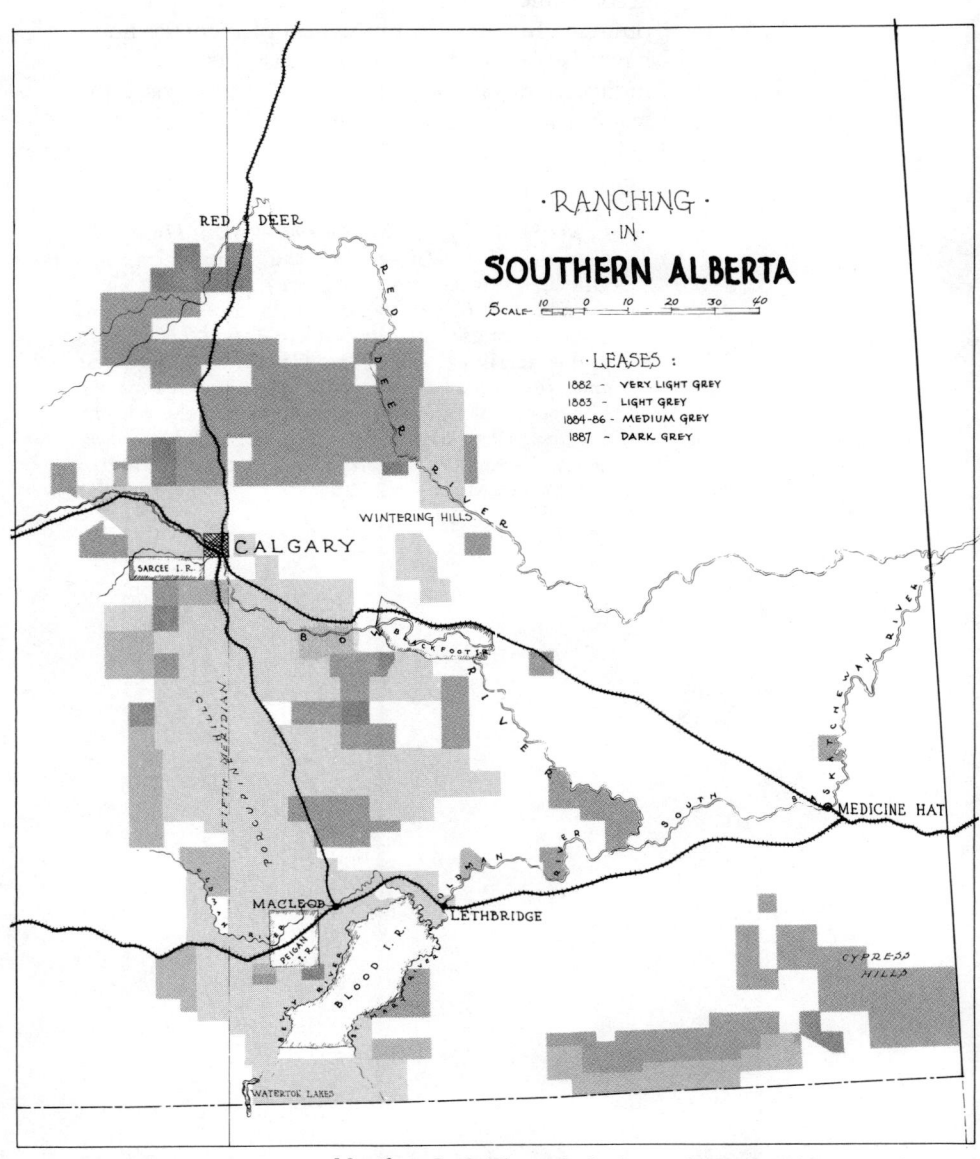

Map from L. G. Thomas's thesis was drawn by John A. ("Jack") Cawston who did the original in watercolour for a bottle of rye. (In this book, the watercoloured areas have been replaced with shaded grey areas and a new legend by the Cartographic Section, Department of Geography, University of Alberta.)

ONE The Ranching Tradition and the Life of the Ranchers

IN THE United States the ranching community developed a folk-lore, a tradition and a way of life which has been profitably absorbed into the national culture. If we examine the history of everyday things in Southern Alberta we may find evidences of a similar contribution by the ranching community there to the Canadian culture....

The National Origins of the Ranchers

The first white settlers, or more properly, residents, in Southern Alberta were the traders and missionaries. The country was a preserve of the free-traders, mostly Americans, who had drifted in from the neighboring territories and states. The first missionaries to settle down were the MacDougalls who were established by 1870 at Morleyville on the northern edge of the range country. After the Mounted Police arrived in 1874, settlement increased. A number of the traders remained and a few farmers came into the country to supply the Force. The new lease regulations of 1881 greatly stimulated settlement in spite of their alleged effect upon it. Indeed it is from 1881 that the population begins to assume its eventual composition.

More than any other agency the Mounted Police influenced the complexion of early settlement in Southern Alberta. Many members of the force, after their term of service had expired, settled in the country which they had helped to open. The makeup of the force during its early years has been frequently described and its retiring members stamped their impress upon the country in which they settled. Letters and visits to their homes gave free advertisement to the South-west and attracted still more young men of their own type. They in turn influenced their friends and relatives until Southern Alberta was filled with young men from the middle and upper classes of Eastern Canada, the British Isles, and even the Eastern United States, who found or hoped to find in the less restricted life of the West a welcome escape from the prosperous but rather stuffy life which several generations of commercial success had produced. To Southern Alberta came the young men who have been generally credited with the building of the British Empire: healthy, well-educated, usually possessed of a little capital, adventurous and devastatingly well-bred. Men of the same variety coming to Southern Alberta to-day might find it difficult to credit the fascination which that land exerted upon the younger sons of the seventies and eighties; in 1874 the virgin prairies and inviolate mountains must have had their own charm. It was for the time the last frontier and not, for a last frontier, unattractive.

The peculiar instinct which leads young Britons to remote and unlikely corners of the earth, led them in large numbers to the ranching lands of Alberta. The Eastern provinces and states had not reached the saturation point in 1874: they could still absorb most of their younger sons. The older lands sent more of their young men so that until 1895, that is during the "Old Days," during the "Golden Age" the ranching community was predominantly British and predominantly upper-class. This applied especially to the ranch-owners and to the superior officers of the British cattle-companies. The ranch foremen and the stock-hands were frequently Americans from the ranching states, especially Wyoming and Montana.

There seems to be justification for accepting the view that the early ranching community was predominantly British. It is recorded in the Journals of the Legislative Council of the North-West Territories that in 1885 "the Provisional District of Alberta (had).... received a very important addition to its population, consisting principally of wealthy families, whose future occupation will be chiefly that of stock-raising."[1] L. V. Kelly's book on the ranching period, *The Range Men,* is inclined to suggest that immi-

Bradfield College. Established ca. 1909 at Priddis, Alberta, by an English clergyman, Dr. H. B. Gray, as a training school for young Britons interested in an agricultural career in the Canadian West. Glenbow Archives NA-639-7.

grants of this sort were with few exceptions drunken and dissolute remittance-men, tolerated for the ready money they brought into the country.[2] It seems odd that a community such as Kelly describes, with its strong resentment of Britain and the British, should have sent as its first representative to the Territorial Council, Viscount Boyle, who, during the eighties, ranched at Macleod.[3] Professor MacInnes, in his excellent book, *In the Shadow of the Rockies,* regards the British immigration as of the utmost importance, and indignantly refutes the suggestion that all British immigrants were wasters and drunkards.[4] Most of them were "remittance-men" in the sense that they had allowances or capital from the Mother Country, but that all should share the blame which rightly attaches to a few of their number, is absurd.

Naturally the ranch-owners during the first years, whether individuals or companies, knew nothing of ranching methods. They may have known something about agriculture as it was practiced in Eastern America or in the British Isles, but they had never dealt with stock upon the open range. Practical assistance could be obtained from the range country of the United States, where by 1880 the ranching industry had achieved a certain maturity and developed a definite practice. The new range inherited the experience of the old. The limitation of the American range had begun, and American ranchmen and stock hands, who loved the life with an abiding passion, were glad to come to the new land which offered continued freedom from barbed wire and civilization. The close contact which had existed between Alberta and Montana since the first fur-traders had brought in whiskey from Fort Benton made it natural that during the early years, while the owners of the ranches were British or Eastern Canadians or Americans, the stock-hands or cowboys, and many of the ranch-managers, should be American Westerners.

This difference in nationality between employers and employed was a temporary condition. The ranch-owners, except those who were absentees, learnt their new business rapidly and many of them became quite as capable practical stock-hands as their employees. A native-born stock-hand class gradually evolved, although it remained essentially American in its personality. A number of the smaller ranchers became good stock-hands since their interests were not large enough to require all their energies for executive work. Some large ranches employed young Britons, who learnt the business from the ground up. At the same time a number of American ranchers appeared. In spite of the tempering influence of time this cleavage remained, that while the owner-class was British, even English, in its outlook, the employee-class was strongly American and Western. There was little friction, for a strong practical sympathy existed and each class was secure in the consciousness of its own superiority. As the years passed the ranchers drifted out of the country, or proved themselves capable, and the good points of the stock-hands were revealed to their owners. What little friction there had been, disappeared in mutual admiration and in mutual antagonism to the "dirt farmer."

After 1890 the settlers who came into Southern Alberta were of all races and classes. Those who were drawn from the upper reaches of European and Eastern life, and they were numerous, were inclined to identify themselves with the "ranchers," although they were economically more akin to the "farmers." They reinforced the ranching class so strongly that it remained a noticeable section of the population long after the ranching industry as it was understood during the "Golden Age" had been submerged. These new settlers helped the older-established ranchers to give the industry the new lease of life which has been called the "New Ranching." They changed it from a particular method of economic subsistence, to a way of life against an economic background almost indistinguishable from mixed farming. To those who were ranching in the "Golden Age" their order seemed to end in 1895: actually it survived until 1914. Here and there it still lingers but it has been absorbed, a valuable leaven, into the life of the province.

Southern Alberta was fortunate in her early settlers. They were, with a few regrettable exceptions, the best an old country had to offer to a new. In breeding, education, ability and spirit, Southern Alberta's pioneers excelled those of almost any other community. Their adventurous youth brought them there and enabled them to overcome the country's hardships. The solid qualities which developed with age kept them there. A few passed on, perennially adventurous, to new frontiers; a few were misfits in any country, they had their day and vanished; the majority remained, a reliable foundation. The ranchers had the defects of their qualities but the defects can be forgiven in view of their services.

Daily Life

Nowhere in Alberta are pioneer days very far in the past; many of the communities are still in the first stage of development and some seem permanently arrested therein. The ranchers of Southern Alberta were pioneers but their hardships were slight compared with those of the people who hewed homes out of the forests of Upper Canada a century before. The country to which they came offered a living with little preparatory effort. It is easier to turn cattle onto the range than to grow wheat in the heart of a virgin forest. The pioneer ranchers often had some capital and a good deal of influence. A little social pressure at Ottawa must have eased the passage of a good many younger sons.

Perhaps the most striking characteristic of the pioneer rancher as of the pioneer elsewhere was his failure to emphasize the hardship of his life. There were hardships, difficult and unfamiliar work, long exposure, bitter cold and disappointing results for the men, inadequate houses, more hard and unfamiliar work, and long periods of isolation for the women. Yet when the pioneers recall their early years, hardships are merely recounted as incidental, negligible, amusing. Certainly they did not dominate life. Perhaps it is the vagary of memory. Perhaps it is the spirit in which they had been trained at home. Perhaps it was because everyone was young —a little girl who had come to Pincher Creek in 1881 as a baby, wept when she saw old men and women for the first time when she was taken to Eastern Canada.

When conditions in a country which has not long since passed out of the pioneer stage are being described it should be remembered that advance is piece-meal, that at the same point in time there are parts of the country in every stage of development. Although this is to an extent true of Southern Alberta, its natural endowments permitted it to attain a unity and homogeneity which make generalization possible. The pattern of life in one river-valley was repeated again in the next, with only slight individual differences. Everyone, it was said, knew everyone else. Certainly, everyone's cattle ranged free and that was a great unifying influence.

Work and Working Conditions of the Men

It was the work of the ranchers which gave their community meaning. Their work was the foundation of the life of the ranches, the reality behind it. Their economic usefulness depended upon the way in which they looked after the livestock they owned or of which they had charge. Not all the work was done by the ranch-owners and the company-managers; they planned, and the brunt of the execution of their plans fell to the stock-hands and the ranch foremen. The small rancher did much of his own work and naturally a thorough knowledge of the practical technique of the business was essential to success.

The everyday care of the stock was in the hands of the cowboys and the foremen under general orders from the owner or manager of the ranch. Ranching did not mean merely the acquisition of a large lease and a proportionate herd of stock and the placing of one in convenient juxtaposition to the other. The general routine was not particularly onerous, but there were special practices, of which the "roundup" has been most frequently described.

The roundup was the gathering of the cattle from the range, at first from all southern Alberta, and then, when this proved impracticable, from various well-marked natural districts. There were two roundups, one in the spring for branding, etc., and one in the fall for the selection of beef. The cattle were divided according to their owners, calves were branded and culling was done. The same procedure was applied to horses. Sheep were always herded and their owners had no need of roundups.

When the practice of district roundups was adopted, it became customary for districts to send representatives to other roundups to claim stock which had strayed from its home district on to the foreign range. The roundup bore heavily on the small man, with five hundred cattle or less. On the roundup the large ranch of the district usually "sent out a wagon," probably several wagons, and usually the representatives of other ranchers paid board. Branding was done on the range, with the minimum apparatus it required. A big roundup lasted several weeks; it was the most characteristic institution of the ranch and one of the most picturesque, with its great herds of cattle, its wagons, its fire, and the sight of difficult work accomplished with efficiency and speed. The canvasses of C. W. Russell illustrate its intricacies better than they can be described.

As we have seen elsewhere, the ranchers after several cold winters, began to put up hay to carry their stock through this trying season.[5] At first only calves and weak cows were fed, later the practice was widely extended. As the country developed, grain and forage crops supplemented the wild hay. The later phase of ranching devoted itself more and more to the winter feeding of cattle. A certain amount of agricultural labour supplemented the purely pastoral efforts of the stock-hands. The men of the old school scorned such work as fit only for farmers and on most of the ranches except for the small ones, cultivation remained at a minimum. The ranchers preferred to buy feed from homesteaders rather than raise their own. Haying-time, however, rapidly became the busiest season of the year, lasting for about six weeks. Fencing was another indignity which the old-fashioned cow-hand suffered with blasphemous reluctance. The increase in settlement, the necessity for preserving winter ranges and hay and forage crops made fences essential. Much of the fencing was in the river-bottoms and the eccentric habits of the mountain streams compelled annual attention to the miles of barbed wire.

During the winter some of the herds had to be fed on the home ranch. It was the custom to hold breeding-cows near the home ranch all year round while the rest of the herd ranged abroad. This required constant line-riding. Cattle on the range had to be looked after during severe weather and turned onto the choicer ranges which had been reserved for winter pasture. Water had to be kept open, for cattle, unlike horses, cannot quench their thirst with snow. A very severe winter meant hard, cold work in an effort to save the lives of stock by guiding and forcing them to distant but better pastures. Winter, however, was usually the slack season.

The rancher required very little equipment. At the home-ranch there was the usual quota of stables, store-houses, granaries, corrals, etc., and on outlying leases or ranches there might be cabins for the men and a shed or two. Buildings were simple, generally of logs where logs could be obtained, but might, if well built, be warm and comfortable. Stock was wintered outside, even around the home ranches, although there was usually shelter for exceptional cases. The agricultural implements used were those of the Eastern farm, although in later years ranchers tended to lag behind farmers in their use of up-to-date machinery, simply because machinery was of secondary importance.

The most important item in ranch equipment was the horse. The stock-hand usually owned his own saddle or saddles—stock-saddles of course—lariats, and other equipment. Frequently he owned his own horse. Most of his working hours were spent in the saddle and this is the aspect of ranching most popularized. Without good horses and capable riders the industry would have been like a locomotive without wheels. A good stock-horse and a good stock-hand were inseparable, and to the rancher indispensable.

Work on the ranches was not inhumanly hard. It was not nearly as hard as work on farms. At certain seasons hard work was expected, but there was no weary level of back-breaking toil. It was healthy work, with plenty of exercise in the open air. The only risk to health was frost-bite in the winter. Of course the element of physical danger was seldom absent but it was regarded as part of the day's routine. Hours, long at certain seasons, were not consistently so. Plentiful leisure seems to have been the rule; long hours and hard work were seasonal rather than permanent. Ranch work conferred independence on the employee. General orders were given but their execution depended upon the energy, initiative and skill of the individual. Skill was essential to the success of the stock-hand; he was a skilled worker, member of an old, exclusive and jealous craft.

The workers on the ranches liked their life, whether they worked for themselves or for another. They believed that the life of the ranches was the finest in the world, were they stock-hands or ranch-owners. Such a life appealed only to a certain type. There were miserable misfits. Lonely suicides and hasty flights from the range proved that ranching was not a universally suitable profession. The transports of enthusiasm which it evoked from its practitioners, even those who found it financially hopeless, suggest that working conditions, if occasionally poor, were not uniformly wretched.

Work and Working Conditions of the Women

Well-deserved tribute has been paid to the pioneer women of Alberta and the women of the ranches have received their share. Their hardships and privations have been celebrated, not perhaps in song, but certainly in story. To them fell multitudinous duties. They were the home-makers and on their shoulders fell much of the responsibility of raising their families. Most of the ranch-women came from homes of comfort and luxury, they were accustomed to the ample leisure which the plenitude of servants in middle-class Victorian England permitted, and their training had not been one to inculcate sturdy self-reliance. When they came to Alberta, especially to the Alberta of the eighties, they found a very different existence. It is strange that there were so few complaints of the bitter toil of the new life but apparently these women bore their burdens with praiseworthy equanimity. Why?

Perhaps it was the very difference of their new environment. It must have seemed an adventure, and before the feeling of adventure wore off, comfort had arrived. They were young and the young are supposed to be more tolerant of discomfort than the old. Their wants seemed unimportant, for behind the ranchwoman was a solid tradition which made possessions second to origin. The bitterness of competition was absent. No one had more than the other of the materials of comfort. The shadow of success was over their enterprise; they remembered their past lives and they would model their future lives after the past. Present discomforts seemed negligible.

For most of the ranchers early discomforts did not endure. Even those who came before the railway did not live for long in their mud-floored, mud-roofed cabins. Solid and watertight log houses replaced them, small but eminently liveable. By 1890 almost everywhere money could secure most of the less perishable luxuries of life. The wholesale importation of young and eligible female friends and relatives as governesses, housekeepers and companions, which was almost an industry in the nineties and the nineteen-hundreds, considerably relieved the burden of work which fell to the rancher's wife.

The actual work which the women of the ranches had to do was very much the same as that of housewives everywhere who are without servants. Sometimes assistance was available from the source aforementioned, ephemeral but helpful, but usually the housewife worked alone or with the assistance of her daughters. Primarily the house had to be kept in livable order and the meals prepared. The former duty was conditioned by the size of the house and the ability and convictions of the housekeeper. It was not an arduous duty, for simplicity was the rule. The preparation of the meals was more difficult. Food was plentiful but it was difficult to achieve variety, especially at a distance from the railway. The personal factor was equally important here for individual ingenuity, skill and vigour counted heavily under pioneer circumstances. The hospitality of the ranches made the preparation of meals, simple though they were, the chief duty of the housewife.

The ranch women had other duties. They made their own clothes, their children's and many of their menfolk's. This duty took up a good deal of spare time. Their house-furniture was a matter of their own resource; men might be trusted with the

The churn and other butter-making equipment, most of it still at Cottonwoods, was a relic of an early venture into dairy-farming of the original owner.

foundation work but the women supplied the draperies so fashionable in late Victorian days. There was always washing, ironing and mending to be done and the various seasonal duties like preserving. Butter-making was left to the women. Frequently women taught their children when no other education was available. They were usually the letter-writers and the keepers of accounts and diaries. Sometimes they had to act as dentist or doctor when such services were not otherwise available and they were frequently in demand as nurses.

The ranch women rarely did much outdoor work. The English tradition was strong enough to make it difficult for men to believe that the woman who was too weak to pass a tea-cup in the drawing-room was strong enough to milk a cow in the stable. On many of the ranches very little of the work which on farms is traditionally the task of women was done at all, as may be inferred from the small numbers of fowls and milch cows, and the small yield of dairy products in the Macleod census district in 1891. On many ranches no cows were milked, simply because the men regarded such labour as beneath their dignity. It must have annoyed housewives to use tinned milk while thousands of cattle roamed outside their doors. On some of the ranches where these duties did exist, they fell to the women, but because they enjoyed the work or preferred to do it rather than do without its products. However the typical ranch woman did little outside work except for occasional flower-gardening, which was held to be a suitable occupation.

Since ranch-women did most of their work about their homes, their working conditions may be conveniently considered in connection with their houses. Considering the newness of the country, they were not unsatisfactory and the work was little harder than work in the same houses to-day. The ranch women worked hard and long at unaccustomed labours, but with a few exceptions they seem, like their menfolk, to have found happiness in the new life.

[Ranch] Houses

The houses of the Victorians may have been stuffy, tasteless, over-ornamented and over-draped but to their occupants they were the acme of beauty and comfort. Whatever their faults they were large. The houses which the ranchers occupied in Alberta must have offered a strange contrast to their former homes, but with pioneer adaptability, they made the best of it and produced dwellings which were far from unpleasing.

Elsewhere in Western Canada the pioneer has often had to be content with a sod shack or a dug-out for the first years after arrival. The rancher was generally more fortunate. The very early ranchers and those who settled later in isolated and uninhabited districts sometimes lived in a tent or camped outside until the first rude log shack was built. Otherwise it was only the men who occasionally roughed it thus. The women and children of the rancher's family were left in town or with friends until adequate shelter was available. As the country developed it was possible to provide a more finished article as the "first house" and the hardship of mud floor and sod roof was rare.

The dwellings of the first ranchers were very primitive. Logs were the earliest building-material as they had been in other pioneer communities. Plenty of logs were available in the foothill country and spruce and pine were most popular. On the prairies, unless spruce and pine could be floated down the rivers, cottonwood logs were used. The log cabin, built without finished lumber, nails or shingles, mud floored and mud roofed, was the rudimentary ranch-house. It was not long endured, but with improvements it remained the typical dwelling until saw-mills were established.

The size of these houses varied according to the length of logs used. Frequently there was only one room, but where the rancher had brought his family with him the cabin was typically divided into three sections. At one end was the men's quarters, at the other, usually the north end, was a store-room and in the middle the family quarters. These rooms did not communicate with one another but had only one door each which opened outside. The central room was kitchen and dining room as well as living-room and sleeping room for the family and contained most of the sparse furniture.

The walls of this primary dwelling were of logs, hewn square or left in the round and chinked with mud. The logs were laid in horizontal courses and the finish of the corners varied with the discretion of the builder. Upon the skill of the latter the whole structure depended, for the erection of a log house is a complicated task. The cabins were usually on sills rather than on a more solid foundation. Doors were made of hewn planks and various and ingenious hinges and fasteners were contrived. Such hardware could be imported from Fort Benton and these complicated mechanisms were a proof of ingenuity rather than necessity. Windows were few and small, with glass from Fort Benton, which was very expensive. The floors were mud, puddled and tramped to the consistency of concrete, and fairly satisfactory except in rainy weather. Roofs were made of split rails, covered with grass and mud. Roofs were the most unsatisfactory feature of these houses and the need for shingles or even sawn lumber was felt most acutely at this point. Such houses offered shelter but they must have been very uncomfortable.

For the houses, the establishment of saw-mills was the critical event. By 1883 four saw-mills are recorded as established in Southern Alberta.[6] This meant that much better houses could be built and finished with sawn and planed wood. Doors and windows, frames, wainscoting, floors and roofs or the materials to make them, could be obtained. Even in those leisured days, to make such articles out of logs entirely by hand would have been impossible. There were not many carpenters available and the cost of transporting such a bulky article as finished lumber was prohibitive. These products of the first saw-mills were rough and ill-finished but infinitely preferable to the hand-hewn logs and planks of the immediate past. When they became available a marked improvement took place in the construction of the ranch-house.

By about 1884 the ranchers were moving into their new houses. Most of the old ones, with new roofs, were converted into stables, store-houses or bunk-houses, and served their purposes well. Many of them still exist but few are used for human habitations. The new house was on a considerably more ambitious scale. Log houses allow for almost unlimited additions and the average ranch house as it stands to-day was seldom built all at once. The first beginnings, even of the new house, were very unpretentious. Sometimes it was the old house with the new improvements. More usually a square structure formed the nucleus. The square plan has many advantages. It is easily built, simply roofed, and gives a maximum cubic content for material used. The square was divided into living-room and bedrooms. Single-story houses were commonest although a loft was often arranged to give extra bedroom space.

Once the first unit was complete additions could be made at leisure. Since space and materials cost little and the ranchers were accustomed to large rooms, the rooms were of good size. A typical ranch sitting-room would be about sixteen feet by twenty-two and kitchens were usually of similar dimensions. Bedrooms were much smaller. The kitchen frequently served as dining-room as well. Store-rooms were the rule and summer-kitchens were popular. As a few of the new houses had stone foundations, although most of them were still built on sills, good cellars were to be found. Otherwise the cellar was merely a hole in the ground reached by a precarious ladder and a dangerous trap-door. A good many ranches had spring-houses to keep their perishables cool and some had root-cellars. Bunk-houses for the men employed were almost always separate from the main body of the house and sometimes at a considerable distance from it. Occasionally, and usually on large ranches in later days, the men had their own cook and the lady of the house was relieved of responsibility for their physical welfare. Verandahs were popular additions to ranch-houses, keeping them cool in summer and "affording pleasant auxiliary sitting-rooms." Unfortunately they made the house dark. Adequate plumbing, always rare in the country, was, until the last decade almost unknown. The water-supply was the local stream, a nearby spring or else a well. As by the very nature of the industry the ranch-houses were rarely far from water, lack of that necessity was infrequent.

Bricks were unobtainable during the first years of settlement and chimneys were made out of oil-cans which are indispensable to the modern pioneer community. They would hardly have been acceptable to fire-insurance companies and the fire hazard arising from their use was an accepted feature of everyday life. The North-West Council even went so far as to pass an ordinance stating definite requirements as to chimneys. Stone chimneys may have been attempted by the ingenious, as they certainly were later, but there is no record of their use before 1885. By 1890 the main chimneys were usually of brick, but auxiliaries were still made of metal. Ranges and heaters were freighted in from Fort Benton. In a two-story house of eight rooms, one range and one heater were regarded as sufficient. Coal was often used where it was locally available and it was mined very early. Sherar's mine near Lethbridge was operating in 1880. Elsewhere wood was used, for ranch-houses were rarely located far from wood supplies.

During the eighties, the log house flourished. As the ranchers prospered and their families increased, their houses grew larger and more comfortable. Some of them were very beautiful and all of them had the charm which comes from native material used functionally. All through the ranching country, along the edges of the rivers and the streams, among the trees which grew there, lay these houses, simple, solid, comfortable, secure in the knowledge that they were pleasant places to live in and that they could, with suitable adaptation, grow old gracefully.

Unfortunately fashion was growing in strength upon the last frontier. During the "Golden Age" the ranchers cared little what capers she cut in the remote world. Log houses were comfortable and there appeared to be no reason for a change. Fashion as usual prevailed over common-sense. Log houses were discovered to be dusty, hard to keep up, draughty, almost indecent. They were old-fashioned. Everyone should have a frame house, a nice modern house with a balcony, some coloured glass and plenty of tortured wood work. Everyone of consequence who built a house now built a frame house, except for those who were so unfortunately poor that they could afford nothing but logs. This momentous change in Alberta's tradition of domestic architecture came at slightly different times according to locality, but 1890 may be selected as a convenient point of divergence. Until 1890 an indigenous style was developing, attractive, comfortable, simple, inexpensive and as admirably suited to its purposes as the landscape its simplicity adorned. After 1890 the ranchers joined in the last throes of the Battle of the Styles and an average successful rancher was as likely to erect a Moorish villa or a Swiss chalet as a log house.

The frame era brought a new series of ranch-houses; ugly, expensive and devoid of individuality, but indicative of their owner's social prestige. After 1890 ranch-houses resembled town-houses in general plan and construction although grudgingly adapted to rural use. No acute distinction could after that date be made between rural and urban houses although a few isolated die-hards still experimented with logs and native stone.

It is hard not to regret the change. Their style of building was one of the ranching period's most concrete contributions and it seems sad that it could not have been allowed to develop further. There are still people who are experimenting with log in relation to new methods of building and at the same time trying to preserve the old tradition. Unselfconsciously a style had developed, of which the characteristics were large, irregular masses, long, low lines and large roof areas. Beyond this there had been no crystallization, for the style was still in an experimental stage. It may form the root of a style of domestic architecture, unpretentious but beautiful and peculiarly suited to certain rural localities.

Furniture and House Fittings

The construction and general aspect of the ranch house in its various phases has been considered. Its interior appearance and its furnishings and fittings also require treatment. Considerable individual differences exist here as well, differences of wealth, of taste and of necessity, and the most we can hope to obtain is a sort of composite picture of what some of the rooms in a ranch-house looked like. Many of them have existed almost unchanged from the eighties and nineties, a few draperies removed, a little new furniture added, but substantially the same. The Briton abroad has an aptitude for unchanging preservation which simplifies the problem of reconstruction. If Victorian drawing-rooms held too many ornaments in 1883, sitting-rooms on Alberta ranches still preserved them twenty, thirty, forty, even fifty years later.

The pre-railway ranch houses were furnished and equipped with extreme simplicity, as only the barest necessities could be freighted in from Fort Benton. The first houses with their leaking roofs and mud floors were not designed to encourage the introduction of fine furniture. Much of the furniture was home-made although as early as 1882 Fort Macleod possessed a furniture store. Tables, chairs and benches could be made by anyone with a few tools and an aptitude for cabinet-work. A cooking-range was usually the important purchase and beds and springs were purchased rather than made. Chests of drawers and the ubiquitous American rocking-chair sometimes appeared in homes where a feminine influence was felt. As in the first dwellings most of the furniture was in the family quarters, space was at a premium and various devices were adopted for its full utilization, truckle-beds for example, which could be wheeled underneath more permanent resting-places.

Very few families endured these discomforts for long, and after 1883 most established ranchers and their families had moved into the more commodious dwellings described elsewhere. Better interior finishing was one of the greatest improvements. In the old houses the logs had been left bare, a practice which, although it gave an attractive appearance, was trying to the house-keeper. The new houses were either lined with stained or varnished matchboarding, or else they were lath-and-plastered and distempered. This made a warmer and cleaner house, although the walls were less picturesque than the bare logs had been. Some of the new houses even had built-in cupboards, closets and linen-presses, especially if the builder happened to be of an ingenious turn. The new houses offered a better background for furniture as there was no more danger from leaking roofs and there was more space to display it. The houses were not overcrowded for freight rates still existed, but there was more furniture and much more comfort.

The decorative instinct asserted itself. When the first settlers had freighted in their belongings they had brought only the barest necessities, such things as flat-irons, table-silver, linen, bedding and cooking utensils. Larger furnishings were purchased at the nearest store, home-made substitutes were used or the article dispensed with altogether. Books, pictures, ornaments and fine table-furnishings were non-existent. As the settlements grew older these luxuries slowly drifted in, remained and accumulated. They were the appurtenances of the life which the ranchers had known and they were quickly absorbed into the new life. The arrival of the railway stimulated the importation of these trifles, although in the more remote districts during the eighties they were still rare and precious.

Taste and ingenuity were valuable assistants in the furnishing of the ranch house. Much of the furniture was home-made, the dining tables in the kitchens, the settees against the wall, the cupboards and the chairs. Packing-cases, decked out with muslin and covered with the excellent linens with which Victorian trousseaux were so amply furnished, made sideboards and dressing-tables and wash-hand-stands. A little furniture, usually American, was purchased. The last decades of the nineteenth century were nowhere noted for their excellence in furniture design and the American industry was far from famous for the quality or workmanship of its products. Suitably disguised by the yards of drapery which the Victorians adored, the few pieces fitted well enough into the general scheme.

Like the furniture, windows were generously draped. Floors were covered with skins. Cattle and horse hides were commonest,

L. G. Thomas's aunt Ethel arranging flowers in the sitting room at Cottonwoods. One of his mother's experiments in taking interior shots with only natural light.

with bear, wolf or coyote for variety. Poorly tanned, these skins were hard and odorous, and one lady, more ingenious than her friends, covered the floor of her sitting-room with a rug made from her family's accumulated rags by the Mormon settlers on Lee's Creek. Heating arrangements have already been described. As for lighting, even very early settlers obtained kerosene lamps at the stores at the Police posts. These were frequently supplemented by tallow candles home-made from beef fat.

After the railways arrived, the ranchers made considerable importations from Great Britain and Eastern Canada. Family possessions were brought out and many new settlers brought all the furniture and household equipment from their old homes. Some of it looked a little out of place but a great deal of fine furniture and household gear found its way into the ranch-houses of Southern Alberta. The general atmosphere changed little with the new additions, indeed interiors seemed to have changed much less than exteriors. Packing-case makeshifts rubbed shoulders with family Chippendale in a general atmosphere of good taste, a little obscured by draperies, but solid, comfortable and refined. It was hard to change such an interior. Half the ornaments could disappear and there would still have been a good many. New furniture was lost among its predecessors. With all their faults and odd, amazing inconveniences, the ranch houses were pleasant places, homes, as Mr. Staveley-Hill might have remarked, from home.[7]

Foods and Cooking

Except for the Indian women, the wives of the Police officers and a few hardy pioneers like Mrs. Armstrong and the famous "Aunty," Southern Alberta was in its first years an exclusively male community and its food was characteristically simple. After 1881 the influence of women who began to come into the country transformed the simple diet of the plains.

A varied diet cannot be completely sustained by importation but depends on a measure of agricultural development. The Police found a large native meat supply available. It had to be supplemented by freighting in staples such as flour and salt. To avoid the prohibitive costs and to give more variety the Government established police farms near the posts to raise vegetables and cereals for animal as well as human consumption. The Police were thus the pioneer farmers and gardeners of Southern Alberta.

An enterprising Montanan, Olson by name, brought in a herd of dairy cattle and sold his produce at excellent prices. Domestic fowl were unknown until a later date. Other supplies were obtained through I. G. Baker and Company, whose stores were also the chief sources of goods for the early ranchers. Their stocks, which were freighted in from the United States, included almost everything which could possibly survive the journey, and were sold at very high prices.

The diet of the first ranchers was much the same as that of the Police. If anything it was less varied. After the buffalo had disappeared in 1878, beef replaced buffalo-meat as the staple food. By the Census of 1880–81 there were only 346 sheep in the North-West Territories so it seems unlikely that mutton appeared very often on Alberta tables. There were no hogs although salt pork and bacon were imported. The country fortunately teemed with game and its streams with fish. The hunter could take all he wanted as game laws and closed seasons were unknown. Game and fish formed an important addition to the rancher's diet well into the nineties. Game was often sold in the towns. In Calgary in 1889 a brace of prairie-chicken fetched thirty-five or forty cents. The proceeds formed a welcome addition to the settler's ready cash. The eggs of wild fowl were a popular delicacy and ranchers, remembering the past, compared them favourably with plover's eggs.

Like the Police, the ranchers grew vegetables, or purchased them from those who did. Potatoes were most important, followed by vegetables such as carrots, turnips, cabbage and onions, which could be kept all winter. At those ranches which had gardens the various vegetables were enjoyed in season. The ranchers do not seem to have been adventurous gardeners but followed beaten paths in their choice of varieties. The women were of a more inventive spirit. In 1888 tomato plants were being raised at a ranch near Gleichen and presented to neighbors. Many of the ranch women canned and otherwise preserved the more exotic and perishable vegetables, to the enrichment of their winter menus.

Flour, as well as other staples and luxuries had to be imported. Prices were high at first but sank to normal levels after 1885 in regions near a railway. All varieties of tinned stuff were obtainable at centres like Macleod and Calgary. Following the tradition of the Hudson's Bay Company the merchants stocked the best brands obtainable. Cost of transport made prices so high that the very best cost comparatively little more than inferior varieties, so the pioneers who could afford them enjoyed the best imperishables.

There were deficiencies. Butter, milk and eggs, dear to the housewife's heart, were during the early eighties rare and costly. Since by 1888 in the Gleichen district butter sold for twenty-five cents a pound and in 1889 turkeys sold for $1.25 a bird, it would appear that the high prices for such products were neither universal nor permanent. Fresh fruits, except for those that grew wild, were almost impossible to obtain. A barrel of Eastern apples purchased at Pincher Creek in the middle eighties cost fifteen dollars. Dried and tinned fruits were substituted.

In post-railway days it was possible to obtain most edibles at a price; although even in the first decade of the twentieth century out-of-season vegetables and fresh fruits were rare outside the cities. Even after 1885 most of the ranching country was remote from the railway and not until the middle nineties did the southwesterly areas come into close contact with outside markets. The ranch housewife, unlike her urban sister, had only a limited range of foodstuffs available and she had to wait to replenish unexpectedly diminished supplies. In early years she was compelled to order all her special requirements for the year at one time, and this problem, although it progressively lessened, always remained.

Ranch meals were simple, meat, vegetables and bread, followed by puddings or cake. Cooking was very cosmopolitan and recipes were constantly exchanged in an effort to secure variety. For great festivals Mrs. Beeton's monumental handbook was produced and the glories of English cookery attempted and, one gathers, achieved. Tea and coffee, with the advantage to the former, were the most popular beverages. Beer, and other slightly alcoholic drinkables were very often made at home. The men consumed a great deal of brandy and whiskey. Meals in the grand ranch manner were great occasions reminiscent of Dickensian banquets. They were served with the utmost informality but a dim reverence brooded over them as if the ghost of not-quite-forgotten Victorian mahogany sanctified the rougher boards of the last frontier.

Clothing

Skins and furs were not the only materials available to clothe the pioneers of Southern Alberta. The Hudson's Bay Company had initiated a commendable policy by importing only the best cloths. Men's work-clothes could be obtained at the stores of the posts although many men preferred to equip themselves in Montana, where prices were lower and stocks more varied. Many of the settlers who came to the ranches brought extensive wardrobes with them, more notable for completeness than for suitability to the new life. One legendary lady, a later arrival, had eighteen trunks. It must have cost a good deal to freight them from Fort Benton.

When women began to come into the country they found the stores ill-equipped for their needs, and mothers wept as they fitted their daughters with copper-toed boots. Ready-made clothes were obtainable, but in limited variety, and ready-made clothes were indeed a little suspect to the generation which was settling in Alberta.

Those ladies who could afford to do so continued to have their clothes made "at Home." The less fortunate majority had to be content with making their own clothes from the excellent materials available. This practice had its disadvantages, for in Pincher Creek early in the eighties needles cost twenty-five cents apiece, a price attributed by the vendors to the freight. Trips to the East, or to the "Old country" were usually occasions for the purchase of a good many clothes. The women made some of their menfolk's clothing but the men bought more ready-made clothes and their English wardrobes lasted longer. Tailors and dressmakers appeared at Macleod and Calgary and their services assisted the amateur seamstresses. Some of the professional clothes-makers were excellent, especially in the later years, and their cut was admired we are told, in London and New York. But during the whole ranching era women continued to make most of their own and their children's clothes themselves.

Fashions on the ranches during the "Golden Age" seem to have been rather insensitive to the changes in the prevailing mode decreed elsewhere. The excellent English stuffs wore well and descended through the family from the eldest to the youngest. Few of the ranchers' wives, until the railway brought civilization, cared whether their hat or bonnet was outmoded or stylish, since no one knew anyway. They were much too busy to be bothered with such trivialities. Competition, the life-blood of fashion, was unimportant in a land where unmarried women were so rare and eligible and young men so common-place.

An increase in leisure and wealth and the improvement in communications during the nineties and the nineteen-hundreds ended this happy state of affairs. Women still made their own clothes, or on special occasions had a dressmaker make them, but they reflected more faithfully the modes of London and Paris, although not with the photographic accuracy of to-day. For the majority, clothes were very simple, and the elaborate toilettes of Edwardian England were seldom paralleled in Canada. A few die-hards, secured against criticism by their early arrival, continued to ignore the changes of fashion, and complacently wore clothes made along the same general lines as those in vogue when they had left their native land for the West.

There is a parallel between the attitude of the ranch-women to clothing and their attitude to house-decoration. They used their native taste and ingenuity to make the best of limited materials and against heavy odds they achieved a good appearance. The influence of fashion appeared in both fields at about the same time and in both their houses and their clothes the ranch women showed an aptitude for preserving without change the styles to which they had been accustomed.

Associations and Organizations

During the ranching era in Southern Alberta, although the population was small and scattered, associations and organizations flourished. Political, fraternal, cultural, social and business organizations were built up, had their day and either languished or were absorbed into the general fabric of provincial life. The very smallness of the population created a need for these organizations and associations, for without them few of the aims and ambitions of the community could be accomplished. The desire for rapid development, the "Booster Complex," from which the ranchers were not entirely free, the desire for a fuller social and cultural life, and the evident benefits of co-operation in the ranching industry itself, led men into combination.

The Stock Associations were the most important of all the organizations. They brought the ranchers into contact with each other, enabled them to organize their work to prevent wasteful duplication of effort, disseminated information and enabled the ranchers to combine for various useful purposes, ranging from the improvement of the breed of range-stock to the placing of bounties on timber-wolves. They developed the corporate spirit of the ranchers and gave weight to their representations to Dominion and Territorial governments. Indeed, without the Associations, the industry would have suffered partial paralysis or even death.

Political organizations had their origin at the first elections. Politics was a lively game and the ranchers' interests were at stake. Instinctively Conservative, the rancher cynically believed that all governments alike were quite indifferent to his plight. His frequent victimization "to protect the credit of Canada"[8] suggests that his belief had foundation. Even as early as 1883, at the meeting for the organization of a stock-association, when it was proposed to place some matter before the North-West Council the reply was, "the Council never meets: there is no money in it."[9] In spite of this attitude of disrespect for the governing bodies, the ranchers, or some of them, occasionally took a hand in election fights. During the campaign of 1896, an enterprising group of amateur politicians and newspaper-men published *The Outlaw* at Scott's Coulee, near Pincher Creek.[10] The frank and vigorous personalities of this organ would have done credit to professional journalists.

Southern Alberta had its intellectuals, or at least its intellectual interests. One of her scholars shot himself, perhaps unable to find consolation in either the volume of Plautus or the bottle of whiskey which were found beside his bed. In Macleod, on December 14, 1884, a Literary, Scientific and Historical Society was founded. It had ten charter members and others were to be elected by ballot. The first officers were the Reverend John Maclean, Captain Cotton, F. W. G. Haultain and J. D. Higinbotham. On December 22 the President, Dr. Maclean, delivered the inaugural address, which dealt with "Indian Literature."[11] Such a society was a remarkable phenomenon in a pioneer community.

No account of ranchers' organizations would be complete without mention of their activities during the Rebellion of 1885. Although the Southern Alberta Indians remained loyal, tension was high. Harnessed teams waited day and night near each isolated ranch house to convey the women and children to the nearest police post at the first sign of trouble. Many of the men joined [Major-] General [Thomas Bland] Strange's little expeditionary force [the Alberta Field Force]. The rest organized into patrols to keep watch. Perhaps the most famous was "Stimson's Rangers," formed by Fred Stimson, manager of the Bar U, which operated south of High River. Although no outbreak occurred, and the "Rangers" were deprived of opportunity for heroism, their organization illustrates the remarkable power which a very small and scattered group of people possessed, of co-operation in the face of common danger.

Fraternal organizations duly appeared. By 1894 five lodges were advertising in the Macleod *Gazette,* a medley of initials and symbols. They were the I.O.O.F., I.O.F., A.O.U.W., L.O.L. and the A.F.&.A.M. The "Joiners" had arrived. In so obviously gregarious a community, it would have been strange if a good many other social clubs had not existed. All through the ranching areas, but especially where settlement was well-established, as at High River, Calgary and Macleod, cricket, polo and race clubs flourished. Some clubs were more purely social in intention and with the athletic clubs they formed convenient centres for the life of the neighborhood and performed a successful function in the clear articulation of society.

Sports and Pastimes

People's pastimes reveal their group personality even more frankly than their serious occupations. The ranchers held their leisure dear, and they filled it with the amusements which they had enjoyed at home. Cricket, polo, tennis and horse-racing played as large a part in the new life as in the old. There were new sports, by-products of the new business, which they found diverting, at first as spectators and later, in the next generation, as performers. The feats which professionals perform at stampedes and rodeos to-day had in the ranching era a real utility. In England the squirearchy was committing "slow, gentlemanly, unintelligent hari-kari before its trinity of the fox, the horse and the pheasant."[12] Fox and pheasant found adequate and less expensive substitutes; horses were plentiful and cost little to keep in the new country. Even quite poor people could now indulge the tastes of gentlemen.

The Ranching Tradition and the Life of the Ranchers 31

Tennis ca. 1915 at "the Alexander place," where a tennis court laid out among the cottonwoods near Sheep Creek was a popular meeting place. L. G. Thomas and his mother, Edith, occupy the democrat seat. The court may have been originally the achievement of the Church brothers and one of the earliest on Sheep Creek.

There is a tradition that polo was played for the first time in America, near Pincher Creek in 1886 when a rancher brought the first real sticks and balls from England.[13] As the game had only been introduced into England fifteen years before, the claim may be justified. In the years following its initiation, polo enjoyed great popularity. Stigmatized elsewhere as a rich man's game, it could be played by Alberta ranchers with a minimum of expense. Clubs were formed in almost every ranching centre. There were several teams near Pincher Creek and Macleod and at High River, Millarville, Calgary and Cochrane. Tournaments were arranged and cups were donated. The Beaver Creek trophy, over which many hard-played games were fought, was an ordinary tin mug mounted on miniature polo sticks carved by members of the club.[14] The polo matches and the tournaments were great occasions; the former of course attracted fewer spectators than the latter, to which came crowds from every district. Polo was a very social game and the onlookers were almost as important as the players. The standard of play was high and Alberta produced some world-famous players, notably Major George Ross of High River. Polo continued in favour in Alberta until the war when it languished for want of players. Afterwards it recovered and teams appeared in unlikely places. Depression struck it a bitter blow but it survives, although its chief support comes no longer from the ranches but from the cities.

Horse-racing was another popular diversion. Informal races between the favourites of two or three proud owners were very frequent and race clubs were organized early in the period and held frequent meets. Horse-races formed an inevitable part of the sports days which were held to celebrate national holidays and other great occasions. Many horse-lovers imported and bred racing-stock and, although by the nineties there were already protests that the sporting spirit of the West was declining, very good races were run on Alberta tracks. Every village and town had a track of some sort, and there were many tracks where there were no towns. Racing was in the early years an almost exclusively amateur affair, with owners, jockeys and trainers who lived in the neighborhood. Racing was "straight" in those days, thanks to the British tradition.

Everyone in the country who could, attended the meets, driving or riding for miles. Sometimes they stayed with friends in the vicinity; sometimes in their enthusiasm they camped. Everyone met everyone else, for the race-meetings were like large family parties. Sometimes the meets were one-day affairs, often they lasted longer. Almost invariably the Race Club held a Ball which everyone attended. Until the War the character of the "races" changed little, but most of the Clubs disappeared then. There are very few rural race-meetings to-day, but the one or two which survive have lost little of the atmosphere which characterized their predecessors of thirty, forty, even fifty years ago.

In spite of their predilection for the horse-sports, the ranchers had time for other diversions. Cricket and the Mounted Police appeared simultaneously on the Western plains. When the ranchers came they organized with zest. Cricket Clubs flourished everywhere and matches were regular features at Sports Days and other gatherings. Lawn tennis was a popular game with both men and women and showed the same notable tendency to tournaments.

Many of the ranches had courts and the gentle sport was everywhere enjoyed.

Obviously the ranchers' games reflected very faithfully the English scene. Enthusiastic sportsmen, with excellent athletes among them, the ranchers played at everything, whether at the games they had imported themselves, or at the new games which cowboys from the old ranges introduced. Perhaps no pioneer community ever devoted quite so much time to amusement. The ranchers had both leisure and an exemplary training in its use.

Tournaments and race-meetings alike usually ended with a Ball and dancing was always a favourite amusement, even in Mounted Police days: ".... a new social life was unfolding in the land. Band practice was held daily at Fort Walsh and Fort Macleod and for what was a band if one did not dance? Dancing raged. During January and February 1880, at Fort Walsh, thirteen police dances were held. ... either the half-breed women were exceptionally interesting or. ... girls had followed Mrs. Macleod and Mrs. Winder and Mrs. Shurtleff in some profusion."[15] After settlement began the Police posts remained the centres of social life and their Balls were the great events of the social calendar.[16] As settlers came in they too entertained on a scale commensurate with the size of their houses. Their clubs and organizations all gave Balls as well. In 1882 at Macleod "there were one or two dances every night during Christmas week," which was the high point of the year's gaiety.

The evidence suggests that the ranchers were well amused. Most of the dances of the seventies and early eighties were quite informal, held wherever a floor was available and with whatever music could be improvised. The dance-figures themselves were those of the England of the seventies, with a few American jigs and reels introduced for variety. As the years advanced newcomers brought the latest innovations and the informality of the pioneers was modified. Balls during the late eighties and after were modelled after similar functions in England. Evening dress became the rule, the ladies strove after more elaborate toilettes and the music, the decorations and the refreshments—these latter somewhat complicated by the liquor laws—were matters of consequence to be considered by Committees. People still came miles to attend the dances, staying with friends or at hotels. Those days

A picnic party at the gymkhana at the Roo Dee ranch, Pincher Creek, May 24, 1899. The gymkhana was a useful fund raiser at Millarville as late as the 1930s. Glenbow Archives NA-184-72.

of leisured transport were the hey-day of the small town hotel, since in the later years the centre of social life had in large measure moved to the towns.

Cards and theatricals were other indoor diversions only less popular than dancing. Poker was the men's game; few ladies played it, although other card games were approved. Whist had its day and by the nineteen-hundreds auction bridge was becoming popular. Longstreth records what must have been one of the first theatrical productions in Alberta, a performance by the Mounted Police in 1880: "... The men, instead of a society drama.... presented 'Dick Turpin' as their first play, although the actors had just come in from making the arrest of Four Jack Bob for assaulting an Indian."[17] Men and women shared both indoor and outdoor games—women shot, rode, fished and played tennis with vigour and skill. So much progress had the New Woman made in Alberta. All kinds of expeditions were popular, picnics as well as longer camping expeditions such as that Craig described at the end of his book *Ranching with Lords and Commons*.

The ranchers enjoyed themselves. Life was easy enough to allow plentiful leisure and they used it pleasantly without the conscientious scruples which might have troubled those who had known a harder pioneering. Every occasion was seized for entertainment and the ranchers foregathered upon the slightest excuse. Sometimes work was neglected for a more attractive diversion, but very rarely; haying meant staying at home and gaiety ran highest when work was slack. It would be unfair to call the ranchers a lazy people, equally unfair to stigmatize them as over-industrious. They were not always financially successful; but they did introduce into Alberta a tradition of leisure, a more graceful mode of living, in welcome contrast to the glorification of labour as an end in itself which has been so characteristic of the Canadian and American way of life....

The Ranch and Intellectual Life: [Literature]

Some of the ranchers had intellectual interests. They were men with good minds, good educations and good memories, who brought a few books with them and had more sent out. Many of them, moulded by the educational system peculiar to the British upper and middle classes, were excellent classical scholars who found in their new life a new appreciation of classical wisdom and wit. Not all the ranchers were classical scholars; the majority had probably shed their hardly-acquired knowledge of Greek roots before they saw the foothills of the Rockies. For those who had the inclination, the new environment was favourable to scholastic indulgence, for the ranches offered ample leisure, sufficient solitude and a disposition to accept the rights of others to gratify their peculiar tastes. As long as his cattle were reasonably well cared for, the intellectual rancher who preferred converse with Catullus to discourse upon cows was regarded as odd rather than offensive. Literary enthusiasm was usually genuine; as a pose it would have been ridiculous in a country where, since most people were preoccupied with cattle, there was more honour to the stock-man than to the scholar.

The ranchers who were inclined towards things of the mind

were appreciative rather than creative, and their literary output was negligible both in quantity and quality. A few jingles in the local papers and an occasional travel-book or novel comprise almost the entire production of the period. There was nothing of real literary value but much that is interesting to any collector of Canadiana. These writings reveal, however, that in Southern Alberta there had settled a very odd pioneer community, for few pioneers have the time or the inclination to read books, let alone write them.

In the first column of the first issue of the Fort Macleod *Gazette,* published on July 1, 1882, there appeared above the initials R.O.F. what must have been Southern Alberta's first published poem, "A Valentine." It was hardly a poem, little more indeed than three eight-line verses of doggerel. Its subject rather than its technique is its claim to interest. It is an attempt to satirize the aesthetic tendencies peculiar to the last decades of the nineteenth century in England, and especially their most famous representative, Oscar Wilde. True, the "fin-de-siècle" school received rough treatment, but that such a composition should appear in the first number of a pioneer paper in a pioneer country is surprising. The literary interests of the *Gazette* were not limited to verse, for in the same issue there was a very caustic article on "Boy's Western Stories." The *Gazette* was destined to become more Philistine in its tone for in the issue of June 23, 1883 we read, "We received a contribution of poetry for insertion in the 'Gazette.' No doubt the poem had merit, but then we don't know much about poetry, and so did not want to take the chances of getting mobbed. We shall always be glad to receive contributions which will be of interest to our readers, but at poetry, unless above the average, we must draw the line. We need all our space for more important matters."

Apparently the Press was adamantly low-brow. In the meantime, however, the *Gazette* ... had given a "puff" to the Rev. [John] Maclean's *Lone Land Lights* [1882] that book of allegorical essays with a double motive, to further the cause of religion and to raise funds for the [Methodist] Mission. The price, neatly bound, was fifty cents. In 1886 Alexander Stavely Hill, not really a rancher, but an English M.P. who was part owner of the Oxley Ranch, had published *From Home to Home,* descriptive of his Canadian travels and experiences, especially in the ranching West. The sometime manager of the Oxley Ranch, John R. Craig, also wrote a book, published in 1903. *Ranching with Lords and Commons* is a rather one-sided account of the experiences of the Canadian ranch-manager for an English ranching company. General Strange, the moving spirit in the Military Colonization Company's ranch on the Bow below Calgary (near Gliechen) wrote a diverting semi-autobiographical novel, *Gunner Jingo's Jubilee* [1893], in which he recounts his Canadian adventures. Members of the Mounted Police as well made occasional literary excursions. There was even a poetess of the ranches, Mrs. Walter Skrine of High River who, under the pseudonym of Moira O'Neile wrote a good deal of verse dealing with the North-West, some of which is to be found in *Songs of the Glens of Antrim* [1910]. Her verse was certainly not of a distinguished greatness, but she must have caught a measure of the spirit of the days, for there are frequent affectionate references to her poetry in the reminiscences of pioneer ranchers.

In none of the arts did any of the ranchers rise above the level of mediocrity. They were amateurs in execution as well as in spirit. None of the innumerable water-colours, oils and sketches, which the women of the ranches, like their English sisters, delighted in making ever equalled the works in which C. W. Russell depicted so vitally the life of the American range. Painting, like writing, was for the ranchers a pleasant hobby, very suitable to men and women of taste and refinement but not for a moment to be taken seriously. The artist would have been a little out of place in the ranchers' scheme of things, a little unreal, a little unrestrained. Their culture was the prerogative of their class, inseparable from it and essential to it. It did not make for great artistic achievement but it did make for a very agreeable and balanced way of life.

Notes

1. Lieut. Governor Edgar Dewdney, Address to the Eighth Session of the North-West Council (13 October 1886), *Journals of the Council of the North-West Territories* (Regina: A. E. Forget, 1886), p. 8.
2. L. V. Kelley, *The Range Men. The Story of the Ranchers and Indians of Alberta* (Toronto: William Briggs, 1913), pp. 240–242.
3. *Journals of the Council of the North-West Territories,* 7th session, 1885 (1886), p. 3.
4. C. M. MacInnes, *In the Shadow of the Rockies* (London: Rivingtons, 1930), p. 329.
5. The depredations of severe winters on livestock are discussed on pp. 45–47 of Thomas's thesis. His discussion was based on Kelly, *The Range Men,* p. 201 and Dorothy Diller, "The Early Economic Development of Alberta" (unpublished B.A. thesis, University of Alberta, 1923), p. 92.
6. Canada. *Sessional Papers.* Vol. XVI, no. 10 (1883), paper 23, p. 126.
7. Alexander Stavely-Hill, *From Home to Home: Autumn Wanderings in the North-West, in the Years 1881, 1882, 1883, 1884* (London: Sampson Low, 1885). [Hill and the Earl of Lathom were the principal owners of the Oxley Ranche, located on Willow Creek, south of Calgary.]
8. E. H. Maunsell, "Memoirs: Part II," (manuscript written for the Southern Alberta Old Timers' Association, 1922), p. 6.
9. Macleod *Gazette* (14 April 1883).
10. Emma Lynch-Staunton, *A History of the Early Days of Pincher Creek* (Lethbridge: Herald Publishing, [1920]), pp. 42–44.
11. John D. Higinbotham, *When the West Was Young: Historical Reminiscences of the Early Canadian West* (Toronto: Ryerson, 1933), p. 317.
12. Alan John Bott, *Our Fathers, 1870–1900. Manners and customs of the ancient Victorians* (London: Heinemann, 1931), p. 6.
13. Lynch-Staunton, *Early Days of Pincher Creek,* p. 36.
14. *Ibid.,* p. 10.
15. T. Morris Longstreth, *The Silent Force. Scenes from the Life of the Mounted Police of Canada* (New York: Century, 1927), p. 115.
16. Macleod *Gazette* (15 July 1882; 14 December 1882; 13 January 1883).
17. Longstreth, *The Silent Force,* p. 117.

TWO THE RANCHER AND THE CITY: CALGARY AND THE CATTLEMEN, 1883–1914

The essay that follows marks Lewis Thomas's return to the subject of the ranching industry in southern Alberta. The essay is interesting on several counts, one being that it shows the way in which the author's ideas had developed and matured since he first looked at the subject some thirty years previously. Noteworthy, too, is the wide range of primary and secondary material he had at his command in the late 1960s. Clearly, resources for the study of Western Canadian history had increased considerably since the 1930s.

"The Rancher and the City" was originally delivered to a meeting of the Royal Society of Canada, held in Calgary in 1968. The essay was written at the request of the Society, who asked the author to prepare a paper which would relate to the Society's interest in social history and to its meeting place. Professor Thomas was subsequently elected a Fellow of the Royal Society of Canada in 1979. He was the first Alberta historian, since Professor Morden Long was elected in 1949, to be so honoured.

TWO The Rancher and the City: Calgary and the Cattlemen, 1883–1914

WHEN THE STEEL of the Canadian Pacific reached Calgary in 1883 only a few settlers had squatted in the vicinity of the North-West Mounted Police post to which Commissioner James Farquharson Macleod had given the name of his family's Scottish home. Fort Calgary lay on the periphery of Alberta's potential ranching country and the geographical centre of the most favoured region was closer to the original police post at Fort Macleod. The force, established there because of the proximity of the American border, provided with its Indian wards the pioneer ranchers' first market. Until the building of the Canadian transcontinental Fort Benton in Montana was its most convenient point of contact with the eastern world.

The railway was Calgary's opportunity. It opened to the rancher the prospect of a more than local market. The ambitious hamlet that was all that was left when the steel passed by was quick to recognize the possibility that it might become the market centre for the ranching country.

This was not Calgary's only goal, for its pioneers thought also in terms of mining, farming, and industry, but control of the ranching empire was indefatigably pursued. At the same time the ranchers made use of Calgary's facilities and imposed upon the aspiring city a character that has not entirely disappeared today. It is the purpose of this paper to explore some aspects of the relationship between the two. This involves some description of the pattern of settlement of the ranching country.

The golden age of the ranchers extended from the early eighties to the middle of the nineties, when settlers began to arrive in such numbers that the open range, fragmented by their fields and fences, to all intents and purposes disappeared. As early as 1890 and 1891 many leases were being cancelled and few new leases granted. Though as time passed there were more ranches, individual leases became steadily smaller.[1] The day of the great companies who had played so prominent a part in the establishment of industry in the eighties ended when the Cochrane Ranch Company sold its Waterton holdings, purchased outright during the nineties, to the Mormon church. Yet the number of ranches continued to increase and as late as 1914 more land was under grazing leases in Alberta than ever before.[2] The pattern had, however, changed and many of the ranches of the first decade of the present century were little more than stock farms, though stock farms with an unusual way of life.

The relationship between large and small ranching enterprises has been by no means adequately explored. To what extent did the companies, for example, dominate the stock-growers' associations? How effectively did the two groups combine or oppose each other in bringing pressure upon government? To what extent was the pattern of relationships established with Calgary dictated by one group or the other or by both? It would be rash to attempt categorical answers to these questions, but there is evidence to suggest that the relationship between the two elements in the ranching community cannot be accurately represented by any stereotype of the rancher-settler relationship drawn from the real or imagined experience of the American frontier.

An understanding of the relationships within the ranching community itself and also between the ranchers and the city of Calgary depends, I suggest, upon an appreciation of the nature of settlement in the ranching country, not only in its earliest days but in the whole period from 1874 until 1914. Though the large ranching companies were by the nineties rapidly declining in relative importance, the ranching community, and the way of life it nurtured, continued to play a prominent part in the life of the region.

Superficially southern Alberta may today appear to be the most Americanized part of Canada, and Calgary its most American city, but this is by no means the impression they would have made upon an observer sixty years ago. The attraction the region exerted upon a particular kind of immigrant produced a society that, though by no means in every sense unique in North America, does not fit easily into the patterns elaborated by the followers of Frederick Jackson Turner. Nor does it conform to the popular mythology of the Canadian west. The city of Calgary has the amiable habit of presenting to its distinguished visitors white stetson hats. The generosity of the gesture is unquestionable, but as a symbol of Calgary's historic connection with the ranching industry it is perhaps misleading.

Many of the first ranchers were former members of the North-West Mounted Police. No close analysis of the composition of the force in its early years exists, but traditionally it attracted the young and adventurous from eastern Canada and the United Kingdom, men often drawn from families of some means and education. Among those who remained in Alberta some attained positions of importance in the ranching community or in the business and professional life of the region. The Irish-born Edward H. Maunsell, for example, served in the force until 1877, was among the first to place cattle on the open range, and with his brothers operated for a time the largest ranch in Alberta.[3] Leverett George De Veber, son of a prominent New Brunswick family, for some years staff surgeon to the force, became a member of Alberta's first provincial cabinet and a senator.[4] George C. King, an Englishman, and a prominent merchant who was for many years Calgary's postmaster, was the first member of the founding police detachment to set foot on the city's site.[5] Colonel James Walker, Ontario-born, resigned from the force to become first manager of the Cochrane Ranch Company and was for many years one of Calgary's leading citizens.[6]

The police were effective propagandists for southern Alberta and the pattern of immigration they established was to be persistent. Southern Alberta, and especially the foothills country along the Rockies, had peculiar attractions for a particular species of immigrant. It was admirably suited to the raising of livestock on the open range. Though its rainfall was light, it produced excellent grass which, curing on the stalk, provided winter forage. The winters were not generally severe and snow cover was generally light, especially where it was subject to the influence of the chinook, the warm wind from the west that could melt what snow there was with breathtaking rapidity. In the foothills the valleys of the creeks and rivers provided water and shelter. Above all the land was virtually unoccupied, now the buffalo had disappeared and the Indians had been more or less confined to the reserves, and it was easily available to those able to make even a relatively small investment. Not the least of the region's attractions was the charm of its landscape. "God's country," the Marquis of Lorne, vice-regally unselfconscious, called it when he paid it a visit in 1881, and the phrase recurs again and again in the documentation of the period. There is physical as well as literary evidence for the ranchers' response to landscape. With an almost unerring eye they built their houses to command the finest possible prospect available, whether of the Rockies, the river valleys, or the spreading plains. At the same time they and their ladies recorded their impressions in oils, water colour, pastels, pencil, charcoal, and pen and ink and, in one case at least, burnt them into cowhide.

In the three decades preceding the outbreak of world war in 1914 the United Kingdom and continental Europe provided a rich source of immigrants to whom the ranching country might be expected to appeal. Their upper and middle classes enjoyed a degree of affluence but the opportunities for their sons and daughters, privileged though they were, were not unlimited. In the United Kingdom particularly the life of the landed gentleman, to which many were accustomed and more aspired, required a substantial capital backing. To many business and the professions, where careers were certainly open to talent backed by a private income, made little appeal. Sheer love of adventure or its promise and the lure of the distant were less easily definable but nevertheless effective compulsions. The world beyond the limits of western Europe and eastern America was full of travellers, some of whom at least found what they sought in southwestern Alberta. They reinforced an element already present and gave substance and structure to a social framework established in the early eighties. Though the great days of ranching as the economic basis of southern Alberta might be over by 1900, or even by 1895, the way of life they fostered and the immigration they attracted survived until dealt a shattering blow by the impact of the war.

As early as 1884 her first newspaper suggested that Calgary had no ordinary destiny. It was

> a western town, but it is not a western town in the ancient use of the word. It is peopled by native Canadians and Englishmen ... citizens who own religion and respect law. The rough and festive cowboy of Texas and Oregon has no counterpart here. Two or three beardless lads who wear jingling spurs and walk with a slouch ... [but] the genuine Alberta cowboy is a gentleman.[7]

Two years later the establishment of railway communication had only strengthened the *Herald*'s conviction that Calgary would attract English settlers. "This is much more of an English district than Scotch or even Canadian, and the chances are it will presently become even more so."[8] Lieutenant-Governor Dewdney, speaking to the territorial Legislative Council, referred to "a very important addition" in 1885 to the population of the District of Alberta, "consisting principally of wealthy families, whose future occupation will be chiefly that of stock-raising."[9] The evidence of the census is not especially helpful but Professor C. M. MacInnes, himself a son of the ranching country, in his admirable account of early days *In the Shadow of the Rockies,* stresses the importance of this aspect of southern Alberta's settlement.[10]

Professor MacInnes is also a staunch defender of the remittance man. The latter's role in the mythology of southern Alberta needs no elaboration. Popular writers have dwelt lovingly but uncharitably upon their picturesque follies, their wild extravagance, their epic drinking. Soberer historians like Paul F. Sharp[11] have examined their eccentricities with mild surprise but the myth-makers have been less discreet.[12] The remittance men of legend formed a small though spectacular minority among those the ranching country attracted. The remittances were, however, the firm foundation upon which the ranchers developed their way of life.

Though "English" is the word conveniently used to describe the ethnic origins of the group with which this paper is concerned, it may be misleading. Again no definitive study has been made but the evidence available suggests that ranching times had a singularly cosmopolitan flavour. There was at Trochu Valley, far from the foothills but socially closely affiliated with Calgary and the ranching community, a colony dominated by former officers in the French army, disenchanted with the anticlerical and antimilitarist atmosphere of post-Dreyfus France.[13] French, Belgian, and occasional Swiss and Italian names occur in the records of the foothills ranching country and German names are not uncommon. A few Hungarian families are represented, but I have found no Russian names prior to 1914. Almost all these names bear prefixes that suggest that social congeniality rather than national origin was a critical factor in the decision to settle, however briefly, in the ranching country. Some means and a degree of education made identification with the community comparatively easy. Another group that the word "English" tends to conceal is the Irish, who in some of the ranching communities were close to predominance. Most of them were Irish of the Ascendancy, Protestant almost to a man, often with close ties to England but consciously Irish nonetheless and sharing to the full the national passion for the horse. The connection between "Home Rule" and the pattern of settlement in southern Alberta before 1914 ought to be more fully explored.

Calgary in its social and institutional as well as its commercial life consciously and unconsciously catered to its ranching constituency. Its first newspaper proclaimed itself not only the *Herald* but *Mining and Ranche Advocate and General Advertiser*. In its columns "ranche cards" played a conspicuous place. Editorially the *Herald* under its original ownership viewed the large ranches and the whole leasing system with some scepticism, though it seems to have been more concerned to reassure prospective homesteaders than to attack either ranchers or the lease system.[14] Under the new editorship of H. S. Cayley in December 1884 it proclaimed itself Conservative and showed a cautious warmth towards the federal government's land policies.[15] After Cayley became proprietor[16] the interests of Calgary and the cattlemen are increasingly identified.

The ranchers' activities provided some of the *Herald*'s earliest social notes and the style of their reporting is a revealing blend of formality and the frontier. This account of Calgary's first "society" wedding seems worth extended quotation. The announcement followed the canon of the *Morning Post;* "At Bonny Blink, near Calgary, on the 28 January, Adriana Bell Irving, youngest daughter of the late Henry Bell Irving, Drumfreshire [*sic.*] Scotland, to William Dupean Kerfoot of Big Hill."[17] The news story, which had appeared a week previously, proceeded up to a point with the utmost decorum: "Mr. W. D. Kerfoot, manager of the British American Ranch Co., was married yesterday to Miss Bell-Irving, of Calgary. The wedding took place at Mrs. Bell-Irving's ranch on the Elbow, Rev. E. P. Smith, of the English church performing the service." So far so good, but the Texas touch was irresistible. "The wedding cake, a symphony in chocolate and cream composed for the occasion by F. J. Claxton, was the largest ever made in this country . . . "[18]

Calgary's business community was as alert as its first newspaper to cater to the rancher's needs. Its hotel keepers rose handsomely to the opportunity provided by the arrival of this relatively affluent group, whether they made Calgary their headquarters while they surveyed their prospects or used it as a convenient place in which to do business, shop, or, as time went on, to amuse themselves or to educate their children. The Royal, generally conceded to be the leader among Calgary's pioneer hotels, seems, from the evidence of registrations, to have had the best of the ranchers' business. After 1889 the more pretentious Alberta Hotel, still standing today on the southeast corner of 8th Avenue and 1st Street West, built of the local sandstone and with a bar of majestic proportions, replaced it in their favour. Neither had, however, quite the distinction of Braemar Lodge. Though it was not opened until 1906, Braemar Lodge[19] was unique among the facilities Calgary offered to existing ranchers and their affiliates. The house was built originally in 1892 by D. W. Marsh, the Calgary manager of the Hudson's Bay Company store, with a view to renting it to the Anglican Diocese of Calgary as the residence of the bishop. As Bishop's Court it proved too expensive and the bishop and his family moved to a less pretentious establishment. It was purchased in 1906 by Miss A. S. Mollison of Macleod, who operated it for many years as a residential hotel, the elegance of its appointments exceeded only by its unchallenged respectability. Its registers establish its immediate popularity with the ranchers and particularly their wives and daughters, who found it a welcome refuge against the rigours of the ranch-house and the

The Ranchmen's Club, Calgary, first building, on the corner of 7th Avenue and 2nd Street West, ca. 1910, which was occupied from 1892 until 1914. Prior to 1892 the club leased rooms over Mariaggi's restaurant on Stephen Avenue. Glenbow Archives NA-1791-8.

The Ranchmen's Club, Calgary, 1211 6th Street S.W. soon after the new building was opened in 1914. Glenbow Archives NA-4462-9.

vulgarities of less well conducted hostelries. Many of its guests are identifiable as visiting relatives of ranching families, who must have found Braemar Lodge reassuring if they had any doubts of the wisdom of settling in the wild west.

Braemar Lodge has vanished, but the Ranchmen's Club survives; no more impregnable bastion guards Calgary's tradition of gentility.[20] Founded in 1891 it modelled its constitution on the St. James Club at Montreal. Although this was not the first attempt to form such a club in Calgary, it was to prove highly successful and extremely durable. The names of its early members include many ranchers as well as most of the leaders of Calgary's civic life, many of whom had ranching interests. Its rules reflect a desire to cater to more than a merely local constituency; the annual subscription was reduced for non-residents, who were defined as those having no business or residence within seventy-five miles of Calgary. It admitted as "privileged members" officers of the Imperial government, civil and military, militia officers, and officers of the North-West Mounted Police, and it is evident that from the first these gentlemen availed themselves of its facilities.

Even in the not very prosperous early nineties the Ranchmen's Club flourished, though in 1896 the construction of the clubhouse seems to have brought it into dire straits. An extraordinary general meeting was convened to consider measures to "continue the club as a running concern or to close the Club House and wind up its affairs, [or] to consider the resignation of the Committee."[21] This crisis successfully surmounted, the club settled down as a focal point of the social life not only of Calgary but of the ranches. The use the latter made of it affords an interesting contrast with the Cheyenne Club, an institution established in another western town whose aspirations to greatness were based on the glittering prospects of the cattle kingdom.[22] In the case of Cheyenne the cattle kings actually lived in the town and excluded all but a few of the other townspeople from the precincts of what Owen Wister called "the pearl of the prairies." The Alberta ranchers who used the Ranchmen's Club lived, with few exceptions, on their ranches. Though a few might also maintain establishments in Calgary, the ranchhouse was for most of them their real home. The ranchers did not dominate the Ranchmen's Club, as the Wyoming cattlemen did the Cheyenne Club; they shared it with Calgarians of congenial social and cultural outlook. The club made life more comfortable for the ranchers; it was also a factor in establishing a close and intimate relationship between Calgary's elite and the city's rural hinterland.

One of the strongest bonds between the two elements who coalesced so happily in the Ranchmen's Club was a common passion for sport, especially for those sports in which horses play a major role, racing, hunting and, particularly conspicuous in the southern Alberta tradition, polo. That the club played an active part in nurturing the development of these activities is indicated by its application in 1895 for a license to sell on August 22 "ale or lager beer upon grounds known as the Queen's [Owen's?] Race track near Calgary rented and occupied for the time being by the Ranchmen's Club, an incorporated society, for the purpose of holding a meeting for the encouragement of manly sports and exercises, to wit, to enable the Calgary Polo Club to hold horse races and athletic sports."[23] A year later a further application was made for a license to a local publican to sell liquor at retail at Elbow Park Race Track in order that the Polo Club might hold a race meeting and gymkhana.[24] Evidently the club sought not merely to encourage manly sports but also to mitigate the rigours of their practice in a society where the prohibition laws of early territorial days had left their imprint.

Polo may have been played in southern Alberta as early as anywhere in North America; Pincher Creek claims to have had the first polo team on the continent.[25] Certainly it was well established by the late nineties, and it reached its height in the decade before 1914. There were teams not only at Calgary and Pincher Creek but at Macleod, Standoff, Millarville, Fish Creek, Cochrane, and at particular ranches like the Roo Dee. Southern Alberta teams competed in tournaments in eastern Canada and in British Columbia, defeating teams from Rochester, Buffalo, and Toronto, and on one memorable occasion almost defeating the English Ranelagh team, which included players as famous as the Grenfells and Lord Rocksavage. Polo in southern Alberta survived the war of 1914–18 and even the depression but today Calgary's club is the sole survivor in the province.

Horse-racing was a sport of greater popular appeal than polo and more or less organized from an early date. The Indians figure

Ladies' nomination race at gymkhana, Calgary, Alberta, 1895.
Glenbow Archives NA-3620-11.

prominently in early accounts and "Indian races" remained a feature of southern Alberta meets. The police, the cowboys, and the ranchers were all by the very nature of their occupations horsemen and, although cattle outnumbered horses on the range, there can be little doubt that a love of horses was a most important element in the creation of a sense of community in southern Alberta. There is no more surprising entry in the minutes of the Ranchmen's Club than that which records the defeat of a motion "that some sort of shed be put up at the back of the club house for horses and dogs to be tied in, in inclement weather."[26]

In the fall of 1885 elaborate plans were laid for a week of racing at Mosquito Creek, a conveniently central point between Calgary and the southern ranching centres of Fort Macleod and Pincher Creek.[27] The committee was widely representative of the ranching community, and race-horses from Calgary competed.[28] Those attending were expected to bring their tents and bedding and the meet was to end with a grand ball. Mosquito Creek had a social reputation to maintain for a ball the preceding February had a great success, with the legendary negro cowboy John Ware acting as caller and the festivities lasting until ten the next morning.[29] The ball had attracted a number of people who were willing to make the fifty-six mile trip from Calgary. Perhaps this encouraged the organizers of the race meeting in their hopes that it "would make this place the Derby of racing, which will do an incalculable amount of good for this country and its popularity." Local race meetings were so deeply entrenched in the Alberta tradition that several survived the war of 1914–18. Perhaps most characteristic was that held at Millarville, about twenty-five miles southwest of Calgary. Formally established in the 1890s, the Millarville Race Club until quite recently happily operated an informal and wholly illegal parimutuel under the very noses of the dignitaries of the law, the bench, and even the church who were among the faithful racegoers.

Hunting was not as formalized as racing or polo, but there were attempts to reproduce this aspect of English country life, with the coyote cast in the role of the fox. The fleetness of the coyote brought at least one such run to a rapid conclusion, after about fifty seconds, but this did not discourage further attempts. In 1886 one of the Critchleys, a name that figures prominently in the horsemen's lore of Alberta, was hunting coyotes with greyhounds in the vicinity of Calgary. The hound indeed had a place in the rancher's affections only second to that of his horses, and it is not surprising that the managing committee of the Ranchmen's Club was obliged to remind its members that under no circumstances might they bring a dog into the club-house.[30]

Not all the games in which Calgarians and ranchers competed were exercises in horsemanship. Cricket and lawn tennis, as much a part of the late Victorian and Edwardian picture as point-to-point or hunt, had ardent followers. The cricketers of Calgary were organizing in April 1884 and Frank Hardisty, a member of a well-known fur-trading family, had sent to Winnipeg for "a complete cricket outfit."[31] In their first match, played against the Mounted Police, a bountiful reservoir of cricketing talent, they lost by an inning and twenty runs. The Calgary team included two of the ubiquitous Critchleys, one identifiable remittance man, and an enterprising Englishman who had recently arrived in Alberta to establish a woollen mill on Fish Creek, but was more successful in founding one of the ranching community's most widespread kinship groups.[32] The Macleod team had already suggested a cricket week and later in the season Calgary sent a team southward which included the recently arrived Anglican missionary, the Reverend E. Paske Smith, on what appears to be his first recorded expedition outside the immediate environs of the town. At Macleod they confronted an eleven which included the Reverend Samuel Trivett, the Anglican missionary there, ranchers like E. H. Maunsell and Lord Boyle and C. D. Wood, first editor of the Macleod *Gazette*.[33] Cricket clubs were organized in a number of ranching centres and the game was widely played, in spite of the difficulty of maintaining a cricket green through a southern Alberta summer.

Alberta turf proved equally adaptable to tennis. When the game was introduced has not been satisfactorily established, though it was popular in Calgary in the 1890s and tennis racquets surviving into the 1920s suggest an earlier origin. Certainly it achieved a wide popularity and in at least one foothill valley it would be possible to draw an almost straight line fifteen miles in length which would pass through the sites of at least fifteen tennis courts. These were extremely sporting courts for only a few, even by 1914, had any surface other than that provided by the native grasses. In one case at least, where a cattle path had crossed the most promising available space, the court owed some of its peculiar qualities to the turfs with which the path had been filled by a mother determined that her children should not be deprived of this amenity.

Sports events were often an occasion for dinners and balls where the intimacies fostered on the cricket pitch or the tennis court could be prolonged and intensified. Such entertainments were an engaging mixture of Victorian formality and the light-hearted improvisation of the frontier. A nephew of Colonel Macleod recalls that when spending Christmas with his aunt and uncle at the fort all except himself were in evening dress at dinner.[34] Ladies were seldom seen away from home in anything but an evening gown or a riding habit. "As they had to ride everywhere and rode side-saddle, the habit was a necessity. If invited out for the evening they rode for miles, carrying ball dresses along if it were to be 'an occasion.' "[35] One of the earliest and most spirited of ranchers' wives rather charmingly records her pleasure in having not only a plaited quirt for her daily use on the ranch but "a lovely crop" for church.³⁶ Along with their taste for formality the ranchers and their wives brought attitudes that might have seemed mildly scandalous in Barrie or Orillia. Ladies smoked cigarettes in southern Alberta in 1884 although even quite dashing young ladies thought it unbecoming in a public place.³⁷ Some of the tension that later existed between the ranchers and some of the small towns of the region, a tension no more than social but nevertheless present, was not eased by such a difference in the concepts of propriety. Calgary, on the other hand, was large enough to accommodate an influential group who had both social and economic reasons for maintaining an amiable relationship with the ranchers.

It would be unwise to exaggerate the measure of elegance and decorum introduced and maintained by the ranchers and their Calgary friends. That the pleasures of early Calgary were not always as refined as the balls in Boynton Hall is suggested by an 1884 account of an "old-time half-breed dance" at Ellis's restaurant, apparently an establishment going back to police-post days, at which Hank Forbes, late a detective for the Southwest Stockgrowers' Association, shot and grazed the Black Kid, one John Bertrand, and rode for the border.³⁸ At the log-built Rancher's Hall at Millarville, where in the 1890s evening dress and white kid gloves, champagne cup, and imported bands were supposed to set the tone, it was still considered appropriate regularly to provide a hogshead in which the younger son of one of England's ducal families could be deposited upside-down when his conduct upright became unduly obstreperous.

The ranchers were not without influence on the educational and religious life of Calgary in the part of Alberta where their influence was strongest. The education of their children presented real problems; the sparseness of settlement did not encourage the establishment of rural schools. Many parents taught their own children or employed governesses. Of the latter, the mother country offered a plentiful supply but eligible young men were equally plentiful in Alberta and the rate of attrition among governesses was high. Some parents could afford the expense of private schools in eastern Canada, British Columbia, or further afield but apart from cost this involved extended separations. Private boarding-schools in a centre like Calgary were an obvious solution and several were established. The churches, and particularly the Anglican church, which claimed many of the ranchers as adherents, took an interest. In the 1890s Bishop Pinkham made efforts to provide a school for girls and in 1905 St. Hilda's Ladies' College opened. In 1903 Western Canada College was founded by J. C. Herdman and A. O. MacRae, both Presbyterian ministers and the latter its first principal. In 1908 Bishop Pinkham College began as a school for boys on English public school lines. Mount Royal College, a Methodist foundation, opened in 1911.[39] All these schools, but particularly Western Canada and St. Hilda's, found a constituency among the ranchers and carried into the next generation the personal associations that bound Calgary and the ranching country so closely together.

Although the ranching community included representatives of many religious positions, it was predominantly Anglican. Colonel Macleod, himself a staunch churchman, appealed as early as 1878 to Bishop McLean of Saskatchewan to place an Anglican missionary at Fort Macleod, where most of the members of the force were Church of England.[40] Paske Smith, founding priest of what was to become Calgary's Anglican cathedral, soon after his arrival reported the presence of a group of well-to-do old country ranchers on Sheep Creek and before long was holding regular services in three ranch houses about ten miles apart in that delightful valley. This was the beginning of one of the prettiest of the ranchers' churches, Christ Church, Millarville, which was almost named St. Patrick's, Sheep Creek, an instance of the influence of the Irish Ascendancy. Paske Smith was also the founder of St. Paul's, Fish Creek, which still stands on the Macleod trail within Calgary's present civic limits and which in its early years was reputed to have a larger and more faithful congregation than Calgary's Church of the Redeemer. Farther south W. F. N. Scobie, one of the first police officers to turn to ranching, played the leading part in the building of St. John's, Pincher Creek, one of the oldest church buildings still in use in southern Alberta.

Not all the ranchers were as devoted churchmen as Macleod and Scobie but there were enough of them to exercise a strong influence on the Anglican church in Alberta, especially in the foothills country. They played an active part in diocesan affairs for the first

Bishop of Calgary, the Right Reverend W. Cyprian Pinkham, had through his wife, a sister of Mrs. Macleod's, family connections with the ranching society. The horse played almost as important a part in the mundane affairs of Anglican churches in the ranching country as on the ranches themselves, for not only did he provide an essential means of transport for clergy and laity alike but sports in which he figured afforded a useful means of raising church funds.

If any individual can exemplify the relationship between Calgary and the ranching tradition it is Alfred Ernest Cross. Born in Montreal, the son of a judge of the Quebec Court of Queen's Bench, educated there and at an English public school, he came to the west in 1884 as bookkeeper and assistant manager of the British American Horse Ranch, a subsidiary of the great Cochrane ranch. He homesteaded on Mosquito Creek, one of the foothills streams, and built up one of the largest ranch holdings in the province. During a convalescence in Montreal from a riding injury, he studied brewing and in 1892 organized the Calgary Brewing and Malting Company, which became one of Calgary's largest industrial enterprises and until quite recently remained under his family's control. In 1912 he became a member of Calgary Petroleum Products Limited, a company which was ultimately responsible for the establishment of Alberta's pioneer Turner Valley oilfield. Cross was a founding member of the Ranchmen's Club, an active polo player, and one of the four men who provided financial backing for the first Calgary Stampede in 1912. He married a daughter of Colonel Macleod, who, as the niece by marriage of the bishop, was appropriately active in the affairs of the Anglican church.[41]

Calgary achieved its early ambition and became the ranchers' metropolis. In the process its social and institutional life was affected as much as its economic basis. The ranching society this paper examines was a small minority, and after 1895 it declined rapidly in number relative to the total population of the region. By assimilating to itself many smaller stockmen and some urban elements, particularly in Calgary, it was able to maintain a way of life they found congenial. It was a vulnerable society, for it depended heavily upon financial transfusions from outside. It was a snobbish society, though it imagined itself to be highly egalitarian. It was a society based on values that traditionally do not survive in a frontier environment, though in southern Alberta they have proved remarkably durable. Many who were originally attracted to the life found it less to their taste after a brief experience and either returned home or moved on to softer climates like that of British Columbia.

The war of 1914 almost completely destroyed its basis. Even after thirty years it was still a youthful society and its most recent recruits were quick to enlist. Many indeed had some service connection. The French colony at Trochu, for example, practically vanished. Many were killed; of those who survived some did not come back to Alberta. The institutional basis of the way of life they had created was severely dislocated and an Alberta in the grip of the post-war recession was not likely to attract the excess youth of a Britain whose wealth was no longer to be taken for granted. Life for the ranchers and their friends was not again to be the gay and decorous picnic of the golden generation before 1914.

Notes

1. *Sessional Papers of the Dominion of Canada, Report of the Department of the Interior, 1892.*
2. L. G. Thomas, "The Ranching Period in Southern Alberta," unpublished M.A. thesis, University of Alberta, 1935, pp. 66–7.
3. John Blue, *Alberta Past and Present: Historical and Biographical* (3 vols.; Chicago, 1924), vol. II, pp. 102f.
4. Archibald O. MacRae, *History of the Province of Alberta* (2 vols.; [Calgary], 1912), vol. II, pp. 783f.
5. Lawrence H. Bussard, "Early History of Calgary," unpublished M.A. thesis, University of Alberta, 1935, p. 23.
6. MacRae, I, p. 475f.
7. *Calgary Herald*, 2, 11 (63), Nov. 12, 1884; also *C.H.* 1, 3, 5, Apr. 30, 1884 "... we can easily foresee a population of Britain's best blood following the life of the ranchman."
8. *C.H.* 3, 24 (129), Feb. 14, 1886.
9. *Journals of the Legislative Council of the North-West Territories*, 8th Session, Oct. 13-Nov. 19, 1885.
10. London, 1980, pp. 328–30.
11. *Whoop-Up Country: The Canadian-American West, 1865–1885* (Minneapolis, 1955), p. 241.
12. See, for example, L. V. Kelly, *The Range Men, The Story of the Ranchers and the Indians of Alberta* (Toronto, 1913), pp. 239–48; Robert E. Gard, *Johnny*

Chinook, Tall Tales and True from the Canadian West (London, New York, and Toronto, 1945), pp. 140–52; Grant MacEwan, *Eye Opener Bob, the Story of Bob Edwards* (Edmonton, 1957), pp. 45–59.
13. S. R. Mealing, "Old France in Alberta," *The New Trail* V, 2, April, 1947, pp. 78–80.
14. *C.H.* 1, 5, Sept. 28, 1883; *C.H.* 1, 4, Sept. 21, 1883; *C.H.* 1, 11, Nov. 9, 1883.
15. *C.H.* 2, 19 (71), Jan. 8, 1885.
16. *C.H.* 2, 14 (66), Dec. 3, 1884.
17. *C.H.* 2, 23 (75), Feb. 16, 1885.
18. *C.H.* 2, 22 (74), Jan. 29, 1885.
19. Glenbow-Alberta Foundation Archives. Braemar Lodge Registers, 1906–1910, 2 vols. See also *C.H.* July 31, 1959, "Passing Parade." Glenbow has all the original registers.
20. Ranchmen's Club, Calgary. First minute book, 1861 [sic], 1904. A photostat copy is in the Glenbow Foundation's collection. It begins with the meeting in 1891 to establish a constitution and includes minutes of committee, general, and special meetings.
21. Ibid., 144.
22. Gilbert A. Stelter, "The Urban Frontier: A Western Case Study, Cheyenne, Wyoming, 1867–1887," unpublished Ph.D. thesis, University of Alberta, 1968, pp. 436f.
23. Ranchmen's Club, Calgary. First minute book, 125.
24. Ibid., 140.
25. Glenbow Foundation. Pioneer Interviews by Edna Kells, ca. 1935. Miss Kells was a staff member and women's editor of the *Edmonton Journal*, 1910–33. The original manuscript was loaned to Glenbow for copying by William Fleming, Curator, Fort Macleod Museum, August, 1960. Interview with Mr. Plunkett of Pincher Creek. See also, in Glenbow, a manuscript account of polo in western Canada by Eleanor Luxton.
26. Ranchmen's Club. First minute book, 199.
27. *C.H.* 3, 2 (106), Sept. 9, 1885.
28. *C.H.* 3, 4 (108), Sept. 23, 1885.
29. *C.H.* 2, 22 (74), Jan. 20, 1885. Also *C.H.* 2, 25 (uu), Feb. 19, 1885.
30. Ranchmen's Club Minute Book. May 5, 1891.
31. *C.H.* 1, 31, April 2, 1884.
32. *C.H.* 1, 38, May 21, 1885. Also *C.H.* 1, 39, May 28, 1884.
33. *C.H.* 1, 50, Aug. 13, 1884.
34. Glenbow Foundation. Kells interviews. Interview with Norman Macleod of Lethbridge.
35. Ibid. Interview with Mrs. Alfred Wilson of Pincher Creek.
36. Glenbow Foundation. Mrs. Charles Inderwick papers. "Hope" to "Dearest," 4.
37. Ibid., 20.

38. *C.H.* 3, 24 (131), Feb. 27, 1886.
39. MacCrae, I, 473.
40. Archives of the United Society for the Propagation of the Gospel. London, England. Letters Received (o) Saskatchewan. Bishop McLean to the Secretary, S.P.G., May 3, 1878.
41. Blue, III, pp. 362–4. Also Mary Julia Dover, "Alfred Ernest Cross," in *The Story of Calgary, 1875–1950* (Calgary, 1950), pp. 132–3.

THREE THE UMBRELLA AND THE MOSAIC

Originally delivered as a conference paper to a meeting of American historians, "The Umbrella and the Mosaic" is one of Lewis Thomas's most eloquent essays. In it he suggests that the cultural diversity of Western Canada owed much to the liberal policies of land settlement pursued by the federal government during the last century, and to the "French-English" presence in the Dominion as a whole. The bi-cultural "fact" of Canadian history served as a kind of "umbrella" which protected the vibrant ethnic mosaic in the prairie West.

Among the groups which constituted the mosaic were Icelanders, Mennonites, Mormons, and Ukrainians, all of whom were able to maintain distinctive cultural communities. Also sheltering under the umbrella were people who were nominally a part of the two dominant language groups, the French and the English. The privileged ranchers from the United Kingdom were members of the latter group. Their pastimes, homes, values, and interests were as distinctive as those which characterized other ethnic communities. Yet while their culture was distinctive, the privileged ranchers, like many other settler groups, were a minority and under a set of different circumstances their culture might not have survived beyond the first generation. That it did survive was due in part to the "cultural permissiveness of Canada's prairie West."

This essay was written during Canada's centennial year, when Canadians were expressing great pride in their past and great faith in their future. Nineteen sixty-seven was a year when Canadians were united and soon to be excited by the cultural visions and liberal ideas of their new prime minister. Temporarily at least, it was a time on the prairies when demands for regional autonomy were muted, when the West did not feel so antagonistic towards, and alienated from, the East. The same kind of nationalistic pride and purpose is not as prevalent today. Still, there was a certain nobility in the sentiments which prevailed at the time and those sentiments have not disappeared completely. Nor are they likely to, for as Professor Thomas makes clear in this centennial assessment of Western settlement, historically the umbrella and the mosaic are complementary and enduring.

THREE The Umbrella and the Mosaic

The settlement of Canada's prairie west coincides, though not exactly, with the century of Canadian development that has elapsed since Confederation in 1867. Confederation served two major purposes. The first was to create out of a number of British North American colonies a political entity capable of an existence separate from the United States. The second was to accommodate within that entity the presence of two major groups, one French-speaking, the other English-speaking. The purpose of this paper is to suggest that the arrangements necessary for this accommodation of the French-English presence, and the national policies and attitudes that grew out of these arrangements, influenced the Canadian pattern of prairie settlement.

The "mosaic" of the title is, of course, the pattern of prairie settlement; the "umbrella" is the French-English presence. The implication is that the "umbrella" has protected the "mosaic" from the fading, blurring, chipping, breaking and scuffing that would have reduced its pattern and its color to a dull and unexciting homogeneity, without either aesthetic interest or physical durability.

If this suggestion is acceptable, it seems to indicate a direction that research in the history of Canadian prairie settlement might profitably take. Though much has been done for particular ethnic groups, less has been said of the impact on them of the national policies under which their settlement took place. National policies are obviously of the first importance, since immigration, railways, agriculture, and, for the most significant period, public lands were all matters of federal concern. Such policies have been extensively discussed, but more from the point of view of the creation and maintenance of a political and economic than a cultural entity. It is conceivable that out of the operation of national policies in relation to prairie settlement, cultural values have arisen that, though regional in origin, are significant for Canada not only in her internal but in her external relationships.

There is in Canada a widely held view that in the United States the processes of history have produced a national character that can be recognized as distinctively American, as distinctive as the national character of the English, the French, the German, or the Greek. While it is recognized, even by the naive, that there are regional differences—that the southern Californian is distinguishable from the Vermonter—these differences are seen as much less than the sum of the resemblances that constitute being an American. It is also held that the establishment of this American norm took place fairly early in the history of the United States; and that its existence permitted the assimilation of an exceedingly polyglot immigration, mainly of European origin, into the distinctively American community. The crudity of this view will be instantly recognizable, but the point is that something like it is held by many Canadians of varying degrees of sophistication.

Many Canadians also hold that the existence of such a national norm is essential to national survival, and a great deal of time and thought has been devoted to the search for a norm of Canadianism. There are obvious difficulties, the most obvious of all the fact that a very large minority exists with a history, a cultural tradition, and above all a language that differs substantially from those—and the plural is important—of the majority. This minority, although widely dispersed throughout Canada and with an historical presence in every part of the country, has an extremely strong geographical base in the province of Quebec, a vitally important part of the country from the point of view of physical and human resources. There the minority becomes an overwhelming and even an aggressive majority. The norm of Canadianism, if it is to have any meaning as the core of Canadian nationhood, must be acceptable to this minority. It seems perfectly clear at present that a

The Umbrella and the Mosaic   65

Emigrants for Canada on board *The Empress of Ireland*, ca. 1910. Glenbow Archives NA-1960-1.

Ranch house in Millarville that was originally owned by Count Georges de Roaldes. Glenbow Archives NA-1858-4.

Canadianism analogous to what many other Canadians regard as the American norm, essentially assimilative as that is, is not acceptable to the vast majority of French-speaking Canadians.

Assimilation to a single Canadian norm poses other problems than the obdurate, but entirely comprehensible, distaste of a substantial element in the Canadian population. Some Canadians, outside the French tradition, believe that a single norm of Canadianism would be for all practical purposes undistinguishable from that which they believe to exist in the United States, and that the achievement of such a norm would make nonsense of the continued existence of Canada as a separate political entity. Those

The John Ware Ranch at Kew, Alberta, ca. 1896. John Ware, the celebrated black cowboy, had early associations with Sheep Creek but is better known as a rancher on the Red Deer River, where he moved in 1902 with his neighbor Charles Linzee Douglass. Glenbow Archives NA-266-1.

who hold these views differ as to whether this is desirable. Some Canadians undoubtedly regard the swallowing up of Canada by the great republic to the south as inevitable and, consciously or unconsciously, do not look upon this as a fate worse than death. Others, while considering the disappearance of a political Canada as inevitable, still hope, rather vaguely perhaps, that the whale will, when the time comes, either be a more socially acceptable whale or perhaps benefit in health and temper from its ingestion of the northern Jonah.

A third group regards the continued separate existence of Canada as desirable and is consciously opposed to what is called Americanization, although there are marked differences within this group as to which aspects of the American way present the greater menace to Canadianism. This group is not necessarily made up entirely of aging Colonel Blimps and their ladies. At one time it surely would have included a majority of French-speaking Canadians; nowadays this is not so sure. Certainly, however, anti-

Americanism in the sense of hostility to political absorption into the United States has been historically a very powerful force in Canadian development. There has nevertheless been a wide, and perhaps an increasing, recognition that such a negative sentiment is an uncertain foundation on which to build a sense of nationality—this in spite of the numerous and illustrious precedents which exist in other countries whose national identities are no way in doubt.

The process of settlement in the Canadian West, from the Bay to the Pacific, has been conditioned by the tensions suggested here. Prior to confederation the Hudson's Bay Company fought a skillful holding action against settlement, a holding action primarily economic in motivation but with important political overtones. To the Hudson's Bay Company the preservation of British sovereignty north of the Great Lakes and the forty-ninth parallel was a desirable, even an essential, condition for the preservation of its trade in furs. Settlement was inevitable in the future, as the Company fully realized, but it could scarcely be expected to encourage or hasten the process. The fate of the Company in the Oregon country after 1846 made obvious what it might expect elsewhere if the United States rather than Britain became sovereign throughout the western part of the continent. Insofar as the Company encouraged, or at least gave assent to, the processes of settlement, it was settlement that was as little as possible American in origin and continental in outlook.

The Dominion of Canada, as the heir of the great company, pursued after 1870 policies that differed radically as to the degree to which settlement was encouraged, but which were not unlike those of the Bay insofar as they sought to avoid the situation that arose in Oregon—or, if we wish to draw on the earlier history of the Canadian heartland, the situation which the Loyalist element feared was arising in Upper Canada prior to the War of 1812. It was consistent with the national purposes of the new Dominion in the first decades of its life that undue pressure should not be placed on immigrants to conform to any Canadian pattern. The resulting transformation might go too far and issue, not in Canadianism, but in Americanization.

The future of the new Canada depended not only on the avoidance of absorption by the neighboring republic but also on the rather more positive necessity of maintaining the cooperation between the French and English speaking elements, upon which the very existence of confederation was based. When the new Canada assumed control of the Northwest not quite a century ago, what settled society existed in the prairie region was not merely bi-cultural but multi-cultural. The Red River settlement itself showed a great variety of social patterns; but, and this was true generally of the tiny pockets of settlement that were growing up around the Hudson's Bay posts, they could be roughly divided into French and English speaking, Roman Catholic and Protestant. Both groups had a close relationship with the Indians through intermarriage, but even as late as 1871 racial mixture was less important than economic and educational status.

Indeed it may be suggested that by 1871, thanks to the comparative isolation which the *régime* of the Company had provided for nearly half a century and to the educational efforts of the missionaries, British Northwestern America had taken important steps toward the assimilation of the Indian to something like a settled pattern of living which was European in many respects but very much part of the new world. This western society had affinities with the two cultures of eastern Canada, but it was only tenuously linked with them. The majority of the English-speaking, of whatever racial mixture, looked generally to the United Kingdom; the slightly larger French group had, as far as those of mixed white and Indian race were concerned, come to think of themselves as *Métis,* the New Nation of Louis Riel.

The vigor of the reaction in eastern Canada to the disturbances of 1870–71, commonly called the first Riel rising, made apparent the dangers that would be involved in a rigorous policy of assimilation to a single Canadian norm, even assuming that such a norm existed. There were, of course, some eastern Canadians who assumed that it did. Among the English-speaking, the movement called "Canada First" saw assimilation to the patterns of Ontario, the old Upper Canada, as the happiest possible fate for all inhabitants of the Dominion. The French-speaking were more modest, putting forward the view that the bicultural nature of central Canadian society should be reproduced west of the Great Lakes.

The federal government, treading gingerly between the two positions, actually inclined toward the latter. The constitutional foundation it laid for the province of Manitoba and for the North-west Territories was rather more appropriate to a new Quebec than to a new Ontario. The rights of the two languages and the two religious positions were entrenched, though it was apparent that it was the French and Roman Catholic position that was expected to need constitutional support.

The power of numbers, rather than constitutional safeguards, determined the issue, and Manitoba became, according to her most distinguished historian, not a new Quebec but a new Ontario. When Manitoba became a province, the balance of population inclined slightly towards the French and Roman Catholic element; but the boom of the early 1870s, and the substantial settlement upon which it was based, changed the picture. Not all the settlers came from Ontario, but the majority were English-speaking and Protestant and, even though they came from the United Kingdom, from the Maritime provinces, or from the United States, they identified themselves with the newcomers from Ontario and soon formed a majority.

In the next twenty-five years the new majority eliminated in Manitoba the constitutional safeguards for a bi-cultural society, though not until a French-speaking and Roman Catholic prime minister, Wilfrid Laurier, had fought and won a national election on a provincial rights platform that maintained the right of Manitoba as a province to take the action that she had. The French and Catholic element in the province nevertheless survived. It did not lose either its language or its faith. St. Boniface, in spite of its propinquity to the booming metropolis of Winnipeg, retained its distinctively and recognizably French flavor. What Laurier had won was actually an administrative compromise that permitted the minority to maintain its identity, even though it lost its legal safeguards. To have maintained these safeguards would have infuriated English-speaking Protestants, not only in Manitoba but in Canada at large. To have forced the French Catholics of Manitoba into the same mould as her English Protestants would have offended Quebec beyond endurance. Manitoba was not to be a new Quebec, but within her borders French-speaking Catholics could preserve, with some qualification, much of their cultural heritage. This may well mark the acceptance of a Canadian national policy that, whatever its uncertainties, did not equate assimilation with homogenization.

Meanwhile other elements had been added to the Manitoba mosaic. The first party of Icelanders arrived in 1875 and established themselves in what to others might have seemed the unpromising lands west of Lake Winnipeg. This region, however, bore some resemblance to their homeland—and they had come, after all, to establish a New Iceland. They had every intention of founding an exclusively Icelandic colony; misgivings which this may have aroused at Ottawa were stilled by Lord Dufferin, the governor-general.[1] When he visited the colony in 1877, Dufferin expressed a singularly unassimilationist point of view:

> ... I trust you will continue to cherish, for all time, the heart-stirring literature of your nation, and that from generation to generation your little ones will continue to learn in your ancient sagas that industry, energy, fortitude, perseverance and stubborn endurance have ever been the characteristics of the noble Icelandic race.[2]

Dufferin was an Irishman and the representative of the Crown. Two of his ministers, Mills and Pelletier, visited the Icelanders three days later and were most favorably impressed; they did nothing, therefore, to contradict Dufferin's advocacy of Icelandic cultural survival.[3] Tacit assent to such doctrine by the ministers for the Interior and for Immigration—both directly concerned with western settlement, one English, the other French-speaking, one a representative of Ontario in the cabinet, the other of Quebec—supported the view that those responsible for federal policies were not likely to adopt a vigorously assimilationist position, with all its possible consequences for French-English relations. It is worth noting that Mills and Pelletier had heard bitter criticism of the Icelanders in Winnipeg.

Even before the Icelanders arrived, the more numerous Mennonite settlers had by an order-in-council of March 4, 1873 received assurance that the umbrella was in good working order. This order-in-council deserves special attention. The Mennonites were not interested merely in good farm land; they indeed chose to settle in Manitoba rather than on superior land available in the United States because the Canadian government was prepared to give more satisfactory guarantees for the preservation of their peculiar culture, especially in so far as this involved religion, language, education, and exemption from the obligation of military service. Though the order provided a convenient exit in the saving clause "so far as the law allowed," the Mennonites certainly intended to preserve their cultural identity; and the Macdonald government not only raised no difficulties but also gave positive encouragement.

Its assurances were an embarrassment when the Manitoba majority decided to use education as a means of creating a culturally homogeneous society and when Canada found herself involved in a world conflict, but the Mennonite communities developed under the shelter of these assurances a position of strength that did not readily melt away under the pressures of an alien and different society. The Mennonites changed, but they changed much less rapidly than they might have done without the bulwark provided by federal policy. Today the descendants of the Mennonite settlers may appear at first sight to differ little from their fellow Canadians, but it does not take much probing to discover a cultural deposit all the more important because it lies in such sensitive areas of human rights as religion, education, and the obligation or lack of it to assent to the taking of human life.

The highly permissive attitude of the Conservative administrations of Canada's first three decades arose, of course, from a variety of factors other than the need of accommodation to the realities of the French-English presence. The empty lands had to be filled if the national objective was to be achieved, and Icelanders and Mennonites seemed promising as settlers. My argument is that there was opposition in the west to the policy of encouraging them and that this opposition was met with bland indifference at the federal level. In view of the necessity of preserving some working arrangement between English and French, a policy of assimilation would have been, if not impossible, of such complexity that its administration, and perhaps even its conception, would have been rather beyond the modest resources commanded by the politicians and civil servants of post-Confederation Canada. Local opposition to the preservation of cultural identity by immigrant groups did develop, but at worst only provincial action could be taken and this, as in the case of the Manitoba schools, only in the teeth of a federal desire to avoid arousing racial and religious antagonisms on a national scale.

Conspicuous among the group settlements in the Canadian

West is that of the Mormons. Though adherents of the Church of Jesus Christ of the Latter Day Saints are widely dispersed throughout Canada, the extreme southwestern corner of Alberta is still recognizably "the Mormon country." The Mormon identity differs from that of the Icelanders or the Mennonite in that ethnic origin and language do not enter into it. Mormon identity is conferred by religion, a religion that involves a very clearly formulated social and cultural organization. It may be noted that Mormons are overwhelmingly of northwest European origin and that the English language enjoys an unchallenged predominance. The Mormons came in part as refugees from persecution for religion's sake, in part as seekers after new land. Some were fugitives from the law of a neighboring country, but the Canadian government put no obstacles in their way though Sir John A. Macdonald's accustomed permissiveness did not extend to official approval of the practice of polygamy.[4]

Many of the earliest Mormon settlers had been substantial citizens in Utah; they had the full support of the Mormon Church; and they brought with them a knowledge of the techniques of irrigation likely to be particularly useful, given the physiographical circumstances of their chosen land. The Mormons had little difficulty in making a satisfactory economic adjustment, and their colony prospered, unhampered by difficulties over language or other outward appearances of peculiarity. The Mormon nevertheless retained an identity. Cultural ties with Salt Lake City remained very close, in spite of the fact that some of the early arrivals were from the British Isles. The Mormon pattern in the Canadian West is identifiably American; this in no way prevents Mormons from entering fully into western Canadian life, but the links with the United States remain unbroken. Thus it is by no means surprising to western Canadians when a prominent Alberta politician, widely regarded as a potential provincial prime minister, returns to Salt Lake City as apostle of the Church. It would be much more surprising if a western Canadian bishop, Roman Catholic or Anglican, were to be elected Pope or even Archbishop of Canterbury.

The Mormon newly arrived in Southern Alberta could not easily be distinguished from the immigrant from Ontario or North Dakota or Nottingham. Much more conspicuous in the railway stations and the shops of Winnipeg and Edmonton were the Ukrainians, one of the most important elements in the ethnic mosaic of the prairie west. Eastern European, speaking a Slavic language, using the Cyrillic alphabet, adhering to the Russian Orthodox or Greek Catholic churches, drawn largely (though by no means entirely) from peasant stock, the Ukrainians had no national base but possessed nevertheless a strongly held sense of national identity. They settled mainly in the park lands opened in the early years of the present century by the building of two new Canadian transcontinental railways, the Canadian Northern and the Grand Trunk Pacific, which were later fused into the Canadian National. Although Ukrainians arrived in Manitoba as early as 1891, their main migration followed the change in government of 1896 when Laurier and the Liberals replaced the tired Conservative administrations that held office following the death of John A. Macdonald.

Laurier's Minister of the Interior, Clifford Sifton, was a white Anglo-Saxon Protestant, a product of the wave of emigration from Ontario that had transformed the character of Manitoba. A lawyer and newspaper owner, founder of one of the notable Canadian fortunes, Sifton had played a part in the destruction of the bi-cultural basis of Manitoba society. He was to break with Laurier mainly over the question of separate schools in the newly emergent provinces of Saskatchewan and Alberta, though there were other strains in their relationship. A vigorous promoter of immigration at a time when conditions were ripe for a fuller settlement of the prairie west, Sifton, in spite of his background and his strongly held convictions, was an enthusiastic advocate of the East European immigration of which the Ukrainians formed so substantial a part. To quote again his much-quoted utterance:

> I think a stalwart peasant in a sheep-skin coat, born on the soil, whose forefathers have been farmers for ten generations, with a stout wife and a half-dozen children, is good quality.[5]

Many prairie Canadians disagreed with Sifton's immigration policies. Election results suggest, however, that these critics were by no means a majority, hotly though they denounced "Sifton's pets" as "the scum of Europe."[6] Others, accepting the view that the development of the prairie west would require a not too discriminating immigration policy, demanded that it be complemented by a vigorous program of assimilation. Opinion varied, of course, as to the pattern to which the new arrival was to conform. Even such a sympathetic and knowledgeable observer as Robert England took it for granted that the teaching of English was of paramount importance,[7] and it was on the use of English as the language of instruction in predominantly or almost exclusively Ukrainian communities that much of the controversy over methods of assimilation centered. Alberta adopted a vigorous program aimed at obtaining maximum results in a minimum time. There was strong and dogged resistance. Once again, as had so often happened in the educational systems of the prairie west, the policy was not pressed to its conclusion. The Liberal *régime* that controlled provincial politics in Alberta until 1921 had substantial support in areas where the French were a decisive influence, and they did well in ridings where non-English-speaking ethnic group settlements predominated. The Ukrainian group, like many others, was able to maintain itself. It was to some extent consolidated by its sense of isolation and of the danger of cultural aggression from outside. Simultaneously it was protected by the general reluctance of politicians and public servants to create a crisis over language, race, or religion.

So far attention has been directed only to the experience of groups which are easily recognizable in one way or another as substantially non-conformist in relation to the norms of either Ontario or Quebec. It should also be helpful to consider the fate under the umbrella of bi-culturalism of the settler from the United Kingdom, whether Irish, Scottish, Welsh, or English. Was he more likely to retain his cultural identity under the circumstances of the prairie west than he would have in a less permissive environment? Contact between the United Kingdom and what was to be Canada's prairie west was as old as the fur trade, and group settlement began with the arrival of Lord Selkirk's Kildonan Scots on the Red River in 1814. Certainly the Kildonan Scots were highly successful in retaining their cultural identity, as both the Hudson's Bay Company and the Church of England missionaries were from time to time made painfully aware. Immigrants from the British Isles continued to arrive, at a much accelerated pace after 1871 and in a positive flood during the great period of immigration to the Canadian West between 1896 and 1914.

Arrivals from the United Kingdom made up the most substantial portion of the body of newcomers to Canada in this period. Naturally they did not think of themselves as aliens, though employment signs saying "No Englishman need apply" may occasionally have aroused misgivings. As British subjects they enjoyed a preferred political position; there was no period of waiting to enjoy the privileges of citizenship. Language presented no serious problem. The society in which they found themselves was very different from that of the United Kingdom, but the maintenance of a political link and a strong predilection for various aspects of the British cultural tradition, not only in the west but also in Eastern Canada, eased the passage of the newcomer from "the Old Country"—a term very generally used in the west. Economic factors also operated; Britain was a natural market for prairie products, and the prairies could reciprocate by purchasing British manufactures. The Hudson's Bay Company had supplied its posts with British staples; account books of posts like Edmonton, when white settlement was beginning there, evidence the sale in the prairie west of commodities that today might be regarded as exotic luxuries. The Hudson's Bay department stores in western cities carried on the tradition, and their grocery divisions remained the first resort of those in search of such comestibles as Gentleman's Relish or superior China tea. The interaction between the cultural habits of the settler and the economic life of the prairies has not been closely studied, but it might well be a rewarding area of research.

Kildonan was the first, but by no means the last, attempt at group settlement by those of British origin. Lady Cathcart's crofters; the East London Artisans' Colony, in which that ubiquitous philanthropist Angela Burdett-Coutts was interested; Cannington Manor, an attempt to transport the life of the English shires to the prairies of Saskatchewan; and, best known and most ambitious of all, the Barr or Britannia Colony at Lloydminster, were not all as successful in retaining their identity as the Mennonites of Manitoba or the Mormons of southern Alberta. They did not, however, disintegrate under any pressure to conform to local patterns of behaviour but rather as a result of the unreality of their economic bases.

It was more usual for the United Kingdom settlers to merge, as individuals or as families, into the general trend of development. Many established themselves in cities and towns, often playing a prominent part in the business and professional life of those communities. Still larger numbers established themselves in agriculture. In some areas—the foothills of southern Alberta, for example—they came in such numbers from 1885 to 1914 as to give a definite and pervasive flavor to the manners and customs of the region. Their pastimes, their ways of building and furnishing their houses, their cultural interests, and their political and social attitudes were to persist beyond the first generation. The foothills region was particularly favorable to the small-scale ranching which provided a congenial livelihood to those who liked an outdoor life and had brought with them sufficient capital to moderate the rigors of pioneering. Even such a society, well adapted to its physical environment though it was, might not so readily have survived in a region less culturally permissive than Canada's prairie west. It was permitted to continue to enjoy an easy confidence in its own superiority long enough to become part of the accepted cultural myth of the prairie west.

It would be to go far beyond the limits of reality to suggest that cultural patterns as diverse as those of the Scottish crofters of Benbecula, the foothills ranchers, or the Welsh miners (who made up such a substantial portion of the work force of Alberta's collieries) survived unmodified in the prairie air. Groups and individuals alike were profoundly changed by their new environment, an environment which to many must have seemed strange indeed. Not all were as fortunate as the Icelanders on the lands west of Lake Winnipeg, or the Ukrainians who found the parklands agreeably reminiscent of their old homes in the Carpathian foothills. To the town-dwelling, working-class Englishman, the dense bush and muskeg of the lands along the Grand Trunk Pacific and the Canadian Northern west of Edmonton were less attractive than might be the cozy valleys and rolling grasslands of the foothills to the younger son of a Leicestershire squire or rector. But however challenging the physical environment to those struggling for economic survival in a way of life that was always partly and sometimes totally unfamiliar, the human environment was less hostile than it would have been in a society dedicated to a single and clearly defined ideal.

Certainly for the immigrants generally, pressure to conform was not wholly absent. In the matter of language there were obvious strains: the majority used English, and the majority of the majority was inclined to view other tongues and those who spoke them with some suspicion. Few communities were sufficiently sophisticated to see skill in the use of a variety of languages as a positive advantage, though there were plenty of individuals who echoed the views Lord Dufferin had so eloquently expressed to the Icelanders. The teaching of French and German, not to mention Latin and Greek, was entrenched in the curricula of all the prairie provinces, and the semi-legendary command of languages by early settlers in many western communities enjoys a place in the cultural myth second only to the gaiety and style of their entertainments. Though the daily use of languages other than English yielded inevitably to the demands of convenience, the pressure to abandon the culture which they symbolized was less intense in a society where many, especially those in positions of influence, were aware that the conflict over language could develop into a national tug-of-war. In these circumstances a program of really vigorous suppression of linguistic variety was unthinkable and, though there were moves in this direction, they were tempered by official discretion which was sometimes difficult to distinguish from official inertia.

Religious diversity in the prairie west was even more marked than linguistic, for many of the ethnic groups were themselves sharply divided in matters of theology. Gone were the old simplicities that allowed Sir George Simpson to equate English with Protestant and French with Roman Catholic, though even in his day such an equation was questionable. Indeed by 1880 devout Anglicans could be found who resented the suggestion that they were Protestants; and the Church of England, in spite of the sound and safe evangelicalism of its early missionaries, was spending a good deal of its energies in internal controversies. The Presbyterian and Methodist churches commanded a larger allegiance among the English-speaking settlers, but had no great success elsewhere. The Ukrainian community was sharply split between the Orthodox and Greek Catholic churches and, perhaps more than any other ethnic group, found religion as much a divisive as a cohesive force. The substantial German element was also divided; Lutheran congregations tended to be organized on traditional lines, and cooperation between them developed slowly. The Roman Catholic church was of more universal appeal; it was the church of the French-speaking, but it numbered among its members representatives of a great variety of ethnic groups and social backgrounds.

On the surface the prairie west appeared to be Protestant, and it was in Protestant circles that assimilationist programs had their greatest popularity. Such programs were intended to produce a uniformly English-speaking and Protestant society, British in its political allegiance but soundly American in its social attitudes. "American" is used here in the sense the word was understood in Protestant Ontario: suspicious of hierarchy in social as in ecclesiastical organization, but recognizing that Providence rewards the virtuous and the diligent. No more vigorous representative of this view existed than George Exton Lloyd, an Anglican bishop who had no doubt at all that he was a Protestant and who led a vigorous campaign for the exclusion of non-Anglo-Saxon immigrants and the speedy assimilation to his exacting standards of those who had unfortunately already found Canadian homes. Extremism of this stamp aroused no widespread enthusiasm and met the chilling indifference of governments schooled in the conviction that religious controversy was as dangerous to the national fabric as strife over language or race. The fate in 1934 of the short-lived Saskatchewan government of the ultra-Protestant J. T. M. Anderson suggests that the majority of voters in the province shared this view.

There are more subtle ways of promoting assimilation than by compelling people to speak a particular language or to attend a particular church. The desire to belong to the group—to share its life and to win its approval—seems to be a common human aspiration; and to wish to share with others the cultural heritage which one enjoys is scarcely an ignoble impulse. Assimilation in this sense is a kind of growing together that may be seen as the foundation of any healthy society. The road to this kind of assimilation does not lead through conformity, though conformity may appear to be an easy means to it. If conformity were always to the highest, it might be defensible—but the society produced would also lack variety. Even if the majority invariably chooses the best, and this seems on the whole unlikely, the determination of what is best has defeated philosophers more subtle than most members of the electorate. Conformity is more probably the road to mediocrity, to a comfortable but unexciting sameness that would give human existence a rather less than vegetable quality. No doubt for many, perhaps even for the majority who live in the present state of even a relatively affluent society such as that of the Canadian prairies, this would be an improvement. It is not, however, an inspiring ideal.

My argument has been that the Canadian West has been able to escape the extremes of pressure for conformity because it is a part of a country that, by the happy accident of a bi-cultural presence in its dominant region, has been obliged, in order to maintain its viability, to avoid policies productive of cultural conflict. Under the shelter of the bi-cultural umbrella, the mosaic of prairie settlement has retained much of its color and richness. Its pattern is abstract, still very much in the eye of its beholder; and, like most abstracts, its interpretation is not a matter of certainty but depends on the values of the interpreter. The prairie Canadian, I suggest, is in an excellent position to cultivate values that will enable him to appreciate the excellencies of his possession. Not only must he cherish and preserve his own inheritance, as Lord Dufferin so wisely counselled the Icelanders to do, but he must be alert to appreciate the inheritance of others. This goes far beyond tolerance. It is not enough that he simply accept difference in others; he must learn actively to enjoy it. He may thus experience the richness and variety of his cultural as well as his physical environment. The extremes of levelling out have luckily been avoided, and enough remains to provide ample opportunity to take a positive leap in the opposite direction.

The Canadian prairie west has been a melting-pot, but the necessities of Canadian politics have damped down the fires beneath it. No gale of nationalism has fanned those flames. The region has been spared the consequences of official intolerance of cultural difference. The values that in these circumstances can be developed have more than a regional significance. Canada's national situation suggests that if there is to be a norm of Canadianism it must involve an acceptance of difference within the Canadian culture and indeed a cultivation of a consciousness of the positive value of difference. A Canadian nationalism so oriented could have a usefulness beyond Canada's national boundaries. To preserve and develop this kind of Canadianism is not visionary and impractical. It is indeed highly practical, for it is a condition of the continuance of human development not in Canada only but in the planet at large.

Notes

1. W. Kristjanson, *The Icelandic People in Manitoba: A Manitoba Saga* (Winnipeg, 1965), 26.
2. Ibid., 75.
3. Ibid., 76–77.
4. Sir Joseph Pope (ed.), *Correspondence of Sir John Macdonald* (Toronto, 1921), 463.
5. John W. Dafoe, *Clifford Sifton in Relation to His Times* (Toronto, 1931), 142.
6. Ibid.
7. See especially his *The Central European Immigrant in Canada* (Toronto, 1929).

FOUR THE SHIRES TRANSPLANTED —MILLARVILLE

The essays which constitute this chapter and the one that follows concern the spiritual heartland of L. G. Thomas's Alberta—Millarville and Okotoks, where he spent his formative years. The essays were not conceived, though, as celebrations of his boyhood; rather, they were written in response to urban historians' preoccupation with large metropolitan centres. While acknowledging the value of the new schools of urban history and the importance of centres like Winnipeg, Professor Thomas nevertheless thought that urban historians had neglected some crucial areas in their study of demography and historical geography in the West. Indeed, it was his belief that small, sophisticated communities like Okotoks and Millarville, which developed under the umbrella described in the preceding chapter, were vital components in the Western Canadian mosaic.

By focussing on these two distinctive, yet representative, ranching communities the author also sought to re-examine the privileged settlers who resided in and around them. In doing so, he demonstrated that these small ranching communities were not just marketing centres or trading posts. They were cultural clusters, communities of like minds. They were in fact tangible examples of social contiguity, that concept which allowed a privileged minority in Alberta to assert and maintain a particular set of values long after it was engulfed by the immigrant tide from the United States and Central Europe.

FOUR The Shires Transplanted —Millarville

MILLARVILLE is a community lying some thirty to forty miles southwest of Calgary. It is not, and never has been, a town, a village, or even a hamlet. The name has been attached to a post office, a general store, a police post, an Anglican church, a race track, tennis and cricket clubs and a polo ground but these lie scattered along the northern side of the north fork of Sheep Creek westward from a point about ten miles west of Okotoks. This latter is the nearest small town if one excepts the urban cluster that has grown up around the Turner Valley oilfield that dominates the south fork of the Sheep. Millarville is still essentially a rural community though today it is increasingly becoming a dormitory for Calgary, whose affluent southwestern suburbs press steadily closer to its northern limits. . . .

Millarville's beginnings as a community reach back to the coming of the Canadian Pacific to a southern Alberta that in the early eighties was dominated by the ranching companies. These companies, financed by eastern Canadian and British capital, saw in the Alberta grazing lands an opportunity to reproduce north of the forty-ninth parallel the spectacular profits of the American range country. Millarville was to have a close and harmonious relationship with the ranching society but its first landholders were not ranching companies but highly individualistic stockmen, much more interested in horses than in cattle. Almost without exception the earlier arrivals on the north fork of Sheep Creek were

83

from the United Kingdom. Later arrivals came from eastern Canada, a few from the United States and rather more, taken as a group, from France, Belgium, Germany, Italy and Switzerland. Almost all came from the middle and upper levels of their native societies and all shared an interest in horseflesh and horsemanship.

The first arrivals were two brothers, sons of a Cumberland yeoman, who had some experience of farming in Ontario. They spent two winters in a stone-lined dug-out near the banks of Fisher Creek, the tributary of the North Fork which bears their name, and, satisfied as to the possibilities of the area, took up homesteads in 1886. Three other settlers arrived very soon afterwards, all of whom had seen service in the second Riel rising; Malcolm Millar, whose name the district was to bear, an ex-Mounted Policeman who was the son of a Scottish doctor, Joseph Deane-Freeman, an Irishman of family who had spent some time at sea and in Australia and Peter Welsh, an Englishman of Quaker antecedents who had some means and some training as a surveyor. In due course the two latter married sisters, Irishwomen named Le Bagge-Bagge, and thus laid the foundations for an intricate network of family relationships not only in the district but widely scattered throughout Alberta and British Columbia.

The valley of Sheep Creek has a peculiar quality among the valleys of the streams that flow out of the Rockies and through the foothills into the prairies to form the South Saskatchewan. Its scale is much smaller than that of its larger neighbours to the north and south, the Bow and the Highwood, and though it offers the same striking prospects of the soaring peaks to the west, it offers them from a setting that is relatively domesticated and intimate. On the north side of the valley open flats, treed only near the water's edge, give an impression of meadow succeeding meadow. The bench lands rise above the valley of the creek on either side, but much more gently than the heights of land that define the Highwood and the Bow. The proportion of wooded land seems higher and increases rapidly as one ascends the valley, leading the eye by one subtle variation after another to the splendour of the ever present mountains. The contrast between the valley's gentle undulations and the fierceness of the mountains caught and held the imagination of the early settlers for it offered at once a reminiscence of older scenes and a reminder of the west

Malcolm Millar's house. Malcolm Millar gave his name to Millarville and was its first postmaster. The photograph was taken ca. 1890-5 and there were a good many later additions. Glenbow Archives NC-12-26.

at its most spectacular. They sited their houses to indulge their taste for landscape, sometimes with little attention to the realities of stock-raising or to ease of access to the outside world.

Others of a congenial disposition soon joined the four originals, who by the early nineties had all established their families in log houses close to the creeks. Their houses were originally exceedingly modest but could be easily extended, and these additions tripled or even quadrupled their size. These were pioneers accustomed to the amenities of an older society. Though housekeeping to the standards of late Victorian English gentility presented a considerable challenge under the primitive conditions of Sheep Creek in the 1880s, the relative proximity of the railway and the possession of means somewhat above the average eased its difficulties. By the mid-nineties a fair standard of rough comfort had been achieved, a blend of frontier makeshift and the domestic sophistication of a well remembered past. Though the contrast could scarcely have been more marked between the houses where the settlers had been born and these new homes whose names often commemorated past splendours, this was not a particularly rigorous pioneering experience nor was it seen in this light. For one thing the rich self-curing grass, the relatively mild winters, the availability of winter shelter and plentiful water made stock-raising less onerous than the clearing, breaking and cultivation of the land for cereal crops on the open prairie to the east or in the parkland further north. The early settlers were almost without exception young men and women, in full vigour and disposed to see such essential activities as haymaking and the roundup as elements in the outdoor life that had attracted them from a more constricted and urbanized society. The most serious deprivation was easy access to medical attention but even this was not hopelessly remote. Above all, a little money went a long way and few of the group who gave Millarville its essential flavour were entirely without funds other than the immediate returns from their stock-raising activities. A steady though small infusion of capital from external sources was a notable ameliorative to the hardships of frontier living.

Millarville shared in the quickening of the pace of western settlement in the mid-nineties and, by the time Alberta became a province in 1905, the land near the creeks had all been taken up by homestead, preemption, or purchase from the Canadian Pacific or the Hudson's Bay Company. The Quorn and Quirk leases lying to the south and west were opened to settlement and on the other side of Sheep Creek and on its south fork homesteaders appeared with a rather different cultural background and a rather different outlook upon land use from those of the genteel horsemen who dominated the north fork. But by the end of the century Millarville's tradition was sufficiently well established to survive and the boom if anything intensified its vigour for among the immigrants from the United Kingdom who flooded into the Canadian West between 1895 and 1914 were plenty of young men and women who had a taste for the way of life that Millarville had developed and often the means to gratify it. They were ready recruits for the tennis, cricket, polo and hockey games, for the race meetings, for the dances at the Ranchers' Hall and for the services at Millarville church.

The Millarville Polo Team that played Montreal in 1909. A Millarville polo team survived until the War of 1939. Glenbow Archives NA-639-6.

The Millarville Races, 1920. The first recorded meet was on June 23, 1905 and the event is still held on or about July 1. Glenbow Archives NA-1742-2.

No account of Millarville would be complete that did not pay due deference to the rôle played in its society by the horse, and especially by the light horse. Though cattle provided the stockmen's most important cash crop and some obdurate Scotsmen raised Clydesdales, it was to horses that could trace at least a line of descent to a thoroughbred stallion that Millarville's people, man, woman and child alike, tendered their deepest reverence. In the golden years before 1914 cars were still a novelty; for its first three decades Millarville rode or drove horses not only in the daily routines of ranch life but also to all its social occasions. Trips of forty miles or more to Calgary, to Okotoks or to ranches near High River or Cochrane were lightly undertaken; one has an impression of boundless leisure and even more boundless hospitality. The horse was also the central figure in the sports of the community; polo games, race meetings, gymkhanas, horse shows, marked the peaks of its social activity. Conversation often revolved around the horse; men and women of otherwise unremarkable intellectual equipment could demonstrate fantastic powers of memory in their recall of pedigrees and prize winners. Sheep Creek grass was believed to be especially suited to the equine appetite, and certainly many admirable animals were nourished by it. Millarville people liked dogs very much, some liked cats, some must have been birdwatchers, but the horse was the divinity of a special cult. Perhaps the fact that the majority of the settlers were English or Anglo-Irish, drawn largely from the classes that had the closest contact with the rural life of the British Isles, affords some explanation but the mystique cut across the sharply defined class boundaries that Millarville covertly accepted and was fully shared by the Scots, the Germans, the French and even the Americans who found their way to Sheep Creek, in most cases attracted by the way of life of which the light horse was at once the symbol and the centre.

As an integrating force in the Millarville community the church was second in importance only to the horse. Soon after he arrived at Calgary to establish Anglican work there the Reverend E. Paske-Smith was delighted to report to the Venerable Society for the Propagation of the Gospel in Foreign Parts his discovery on Sheep Creek of a group of well-to-do ranchers, most of them from the Old Country, who appeared eager for regular ministrations.

For some years services were held in the ranchers' houses but in 1894 a young English clergyman, the Reverend Murray Webb-Peploe, took up land in the district in the hope that the high altitude and clear dry air of the foothills would benefit his indifferent health. With the assistance of his fellow ranchers a log church was built on land he gave and to his design. He had spent some time in Switzerland and Christ Church, like his ranch house nearby, was built of logs set vertically rather than horizontally. In spite of the headshakings of more conventional builders, the church, completed in 1896, proved not only a structural but an aesthetic success. It remains today as perhaps the most attractive of the pioneer churches of the foothill country and of all the surviving early structures in Millarville the one most evocative of the community's history.

The tradition established at Millarville church was distinctly Low, as was to be expected in a parish established by a son of Prebendary H. W. Webb-Peploe, a prominent nineteenth century Evangelical. The two sisters, Mrs. Deane-Freeman and Mrs. Welch, were both devout daughters of the Church of Ireland. Indeed the new church was almost called St. Patrick's; this proposal was lost but there were enough Anglo-Irish in the congregation to frustrate any tendency to undue ritualism. Though the majority of the Millarville settlers were Anglican the church had many nonconformists among its supporters, including a number who were more regular church-goers than their nominally Anglican neighbours, and too rigorous a position might have affronted them. As their children were often baptized and might in due course be confirmed as Anglicans there was from the missionary point of view some obvious advantages in the avoidance of extremes of churchmanship.

The church seems to have been built by subscription, with the congregation contributing labour as well as money. The records, which are more than ordinarily extensive, show as the only expenditures payments to a supervising builder and to a carpenter for, presumably, some of the finishing. The communion table, the lectern and other chancel furnishings were made of small logs with the bark left on; they have a delightfully rustic air. The handsome altar frontal and the kneelers at the communion rail were early gifts from England; the church is today full of memorials. There is

Christ Church, Millarville, which was completed in 1896. Glenbow Archives NA-882-1.

An interior view of Christ Church, Millarville. Glenbow Archives NA-2520-41.

no doubt of the generosity of the parishioners insofar as the building, furnishing and maintenance of their church was concerned. One man, for example, undertook singlehanded to provide stabling to accommodate the congregation's horses and the substantial structure survived until quite recently.

They were rather less generous when it came to the remuneration of the clergy. The parish was supported by a grant from the most adamantly Protestant of the Anglican missionary organization, the Colonial and Continental Church Society. In 1900 Prebendary Webb-Peploe, preaching an anniversary sermon before the society, referred, perhaps rather tactlessly, to his son's "hut" and the "huts" of his neighbours, "ladies and gentlemen by birth, but now having come down to the condition of hardworking farmers, with no attendants or servants of any kind." [Col. and Cont. Ch. Soc. R.R. 1900, Anniversary Sermon] It was a vision of themselves that might have startled his son's parishioners, but perhaps they would have appreciated the fact that the sermon was designed to raise money for missionary work. The younger Webb-Peploe presumably had some private means; the only record of payment of anything in the nature of a stipend is of two purses, of $210.00 and about $300.00 respectively, presented to him in 1897, when his health obliged him to take an extended rest in Switzerland, and in 1902, when he returned to England, where he died in 1904. Later lists of annual subscriptions dating from the prosperous, and indeed booming, decade between 1902 and 1912 throw an interesting light on Anglican church finances. One of the two largest subscribers, at $20.00 for the year, was certainly a man of substance and possibly the most devoted layman of the congregation, the other was a clergyman's son and, with his wife, reputed to be not merely well-off but exceedingly wealthy. The latter lady was indeed an exception to Prebendary Webb-Peploe's generalization about the servantless condition of his son's parishioners, at least if we may accept the evidence of her frequent registrations at Braemar Lodge, Calgary's most exclusive hotel, where she was invariably accompanied by her personal maid. One of the larger subscriptions came from a ranch far to the west of the church which was owned by a German lady whose affluent Munich background was Roman Catholic, though she con-

The Ranchers' Hall, Millarville. The early log building, dating to about 1890, was moved to Heritage Park, Calgary and restored, but was destroyed by fire. Glenbow Archives NA-1158-1.

sidered herself an agnostic. Most of the donations were for five or ten dollars and the total fell far short of the modest sum required by the diocese as a minimum contribution by the parish to its own expenses.

These were the contributions of men and women who were by the standards of the rural west before 1914 conspicuously well-off, and who had a completed, well furnished and relatively well attended church. Even so and in spite of the apparent parsimony of its people Millarville was a centre of missionary activity; Webb-Peploe conducted some of the earliest services at Okotoks, twelve miles to the east and the nearest railway station to Millarville. Later services were also conducted at the Ranchers' Hall, about ten miles to the west, and more accessible to the homesteaders who in the 1900s were moving optimistically into the more remote parts of the foothill country. The incumbent of Millarville was also after 1904 intermittently responsible for services at Priddis, where another and more or less self-contained community had grown up to the northwest. By that time Millarville had built a vicarage to the east of the church, an expense that was met with some difficulty. The War of 1914–18 brought a serious shortage of clergy and Millarville ceased to have a resident priest. None of his successors had as long an incumbency or quite the same impact on his parishioners as Webb-Peploe but the foundations he laid were firm enough to ensure continuing service for the church he built, a fate shared by few of the Anglican churches of rural Alberta.

The War of 1914–18 dealt a hard blow to Millarville's style of living. Most of its men were still of military age, many were single, most of them were British born; many of them were sons of families with a tradition of military or naval service. The proportion of enlistments was exceedingly high. Many never returned. Among those who were killed was Leonard Alfred Welch, the eldest surviving son of Peter Welch. Educated at Trinity College School in Port Hope and the Royal Military College he went overseas as a lieutenant with the Strathcona Horse but finding there was no opportunity for service at the front with the cavalry he reluctantly transferred to the infantry. He always kept, quite against regulations, a diary. He served in France with the 75th Canadian Infantry Battalion and on December 29, 1917 learned that he had received the Military Cross. He was then returned to the Strathconas and remained at the front. The last entry in his diary is for Sunday, October 6, 1918. It seems to me worth quoting. "Went to Holy Communion at 8 a.m. in the Y.M.C.A. tent. [The horses] grazed for an hour this morning and again this afternoon. Saddle cleaning and rifle inspection. A cold raw day; rained a little tonight. Fritz was over bombing last night but dropped none near us." It is a characteristic entry; he had fulfilled his religious obligations, he had attended to his horses, he had seen to the welfare of his men, he had noted the weather condition. He was killed in action four days later near Troisvilles. The war ended only a month later.

With no son left capable of carrying on, and himself in declining health, Peter Welch sold his land and, after nearly thirty-three years at Millarville, retired with his family to Vancouver Island. The Welches had played a central part in the life of the community particularly in the church but in other ways as well. As Justice of the Peace he had not tried many cases but he had arbitrated many disputes between his less eventempered neighbours and, in his capacity of Commissioner of Oaths, he had, if local tradition can be trusted, dispensed much wise advice to those with less experience of and less capacity in the world of business. Ardmore, as their place was named after the ancestral home of the Le Bagge-Bagges in County Waterford, preserved, perhaps more than any other in the district, the domestic refinements of a lively past. The second Mrs. Welch was a near championship tennis player; the informed eye can still discern the Millarville tennis courts not far from their house. The effects of the departure of a family like this are difficult to measure but they typify the sort of social dislocation that the War of 1914–18 brought to many western communities. Millarville was not numerically a large community; perhaps 150 families identified themselves with it before 1914; but even by the end of 1917 more than seventy men had enlisted. The war memorial in Millarville churchyard bears the twenty-one names of those who were killed.

Of those who did return many were unable to settle back in what remained of the prewar way of life. Much did remain for the years between the wars, but, as the district aged, its distinctiveness diminished. Millarville had a polo team even into the depression of the thirties; Calgary's social élite still made a point of attending the annual Millarville races. But one after another families moved away, many of them to the easier climates of Vancouver Island and the interior valleys of British Columbia. New families moved in who found less time for tennis, for exchanging flower seeds, for regular attendance at church. The new generation that grew up between the wars found opportunities elsewhere. Among those who remained the fondness for horses did not diminish but, especially during the depression of the thirties, raising horses did not offer much opportunity for earning a living.

Six more years of war between 1939 and 1945 brought further changes; another generation of young men and women left and again only a few returned. Rising agricultural prices brought a more mechanized and rather less casual approach to land use and with the postwar growth of Calgary, demand for land nearby forced land prices steadily upward. Calgary too had had a long love affair with the horse and, apart from the attraction of land in the foothills nearby as a long term investment with distinct tax advantages, nothing was more fashionable than to set up as a country squire on a few acres of land with an agreeable view of the mountains. By the beginning of the 1970s land values were so high that older styles of land use had ceased to be economic. Under these pressures the old Millarville still rallies for funerals at Christ Church and for the annual Agricultural Show but the last of the lawn tennis courts has long since gone, the old polo ground has vanished, most of the old log ranch houses have given place to ranch style bungalows and though the Millarville Races survive as a highly successful meeting, no one today is likely to be deceived into thinking himself at an English point-to-point.

You may well wonder what all this is about, why I should take up your time with a description of a community so inconspicuous on the map of Canada and so remote from the experience of most Canadians that it does not fit comfortably even into the mythology of the west. Millarville is only one in a long succession of efforts to transplant and nurture on Canadian soil a way of life developed elsewhere. Cannington Manor in Saskatchewan was a much more conscious attempt in the same direction; it has virtually disappeared. Vancouver Island, where so many Millarville people found a congenial haven, is losing its individual flavour under the impact of prairie settlement, but retains enough of it to be worth exploiting as a resource for the flourishing industry of tourism.

Millarville, unselfconscious though it was, might be interesting in any examination of the utopian strand in the history of immigration. It might also be viewed in terms of ethnic settlement, though as most of its settlers belong to one of the charter groups it cannot expect to enjoy the patronage of the office of the Secretary of State. In any case it would never occur to Millarville people to think of themselves as "ethnics."

I see it, apart from the intrinsic interest that it has for someone like myself who is looking at his roots, as not without significance for the student of the way in which a structure of controls, social, political and economic, developed in the Canadian west, controls that were coherent with those earlier established in older settled regions of Canada. In the settlement of southern Alberta, a region particularly attractive to the cattle rancher, violent confrontations between the cattlemen and the settler like those which occurred on the range land of the United States are conspicuously absent. There is however incontrovertible evidence that similar strains between the two groups did exist and ultimately the rancher retreated and modified his methods before the onset of the plough and the barbed wire fence. Yet these strains were contained.

I tried to make the point earlier that the Millarville settlers, though they called themselves ranchers, were not really ranchers at all. They were small stockmen, precisely as were the squatters who elsewhere so annoyed the great ranching companies and pressed them into actions which elsewhere would have provoked violence. But in the history of Millarville no such tensions appear even in the late 90s and early 1900s, when the pressure of the homesteaders upon the available land became intense. Indeed there was an established and cordial social exchange between Millarville and the Quorn, the great horse-ranch owned by Leicestershire interests whose lease spread southward from the south side of Sheep Creek. The Quorn's occasional harshness in its treatment of squatters evoked no hostile reaction on the north side of the river. The early ranching companies were dominated, as far as capital and management were concerned, by United Kingdom and eastern Canadian interests, the latter intimately involved with the Conservative establishment of the time. I suggest that the social contiguity, if I may use that phrase, between the ranching compact and the Millarville stockmen, explains the lack of hostility between them, though their economic interests were far from coincidental. You did not burn down the shack or cut the fences, or burn the hay-lands or maim the bulls, of a man who might be your host at the Millarville Bachelors' Ball at the Ranchers' Hall, be your opponent at poker or your partner at bridge at the Ranchmen's Club, your neighbour at a meeting of the Synod of the Diocese of Calgary or whose wife might be exchanging pleasantries with yours in the dining room of Braemar Lodge.

Admittedly Millarville's evidence cannot be conclusive; it was on the fringe of the ranching country and its social mix may have been uniquely homogeneous. Nevertheless I think its experience is suggestive enough to make it worthwhile to examine other foothills districts and their social relationship to the ranching interest, and to take this further and examine the small towns from Okotoks to Pincher Creek that were on the edge of the foothill country. A recent study has delineated the way in which, politically and economically, the cattle compact is related to the broader policies for western development of the Conservative administrations prior to 1896.[1] This study throws light on what I have called the "social contiguity" of the cattle compact and the dominant groups in eastern Canada and I hope its author will explore much further the fascinating vistas that he has only had time and space to indicate. Another study of the Mounted Police demonstrates how neatly the force fitted into the pattern and how completely its members shared the values not only of Millarville, where from an early date the members of the detachment were valued members of the community, but also of the ranchers further south whose economic interests the Mounted Police so staunchly and effectively defended.[2] A further area of exploration, unhappily still neglected, would be the history of the churches in southern Alberta, and particularly of the Church of England. It was surely not for purely theological reasons that soon after the arrival of the force Colonel Macleod wrote to the bishop of Saskatchewan imploring him to send an Anglican missionary to defend his men, not against Indians or American traders, but against the far greater perils of vice and non-conformity.

Notes

1. David H. Breen, "The Canadian West and the Ranching Frontier, 1875–1927," unpublished Ph.D. dissertation (University of Alberta, 1972).
2. R. C. Macleod, *The North-West Mounted Police and Law Enforcement, 1873–1905* (Toronto: University of Toronto Press, 1975).

FIVE A RANCHERS' COMMUNITY—OKOTOKS

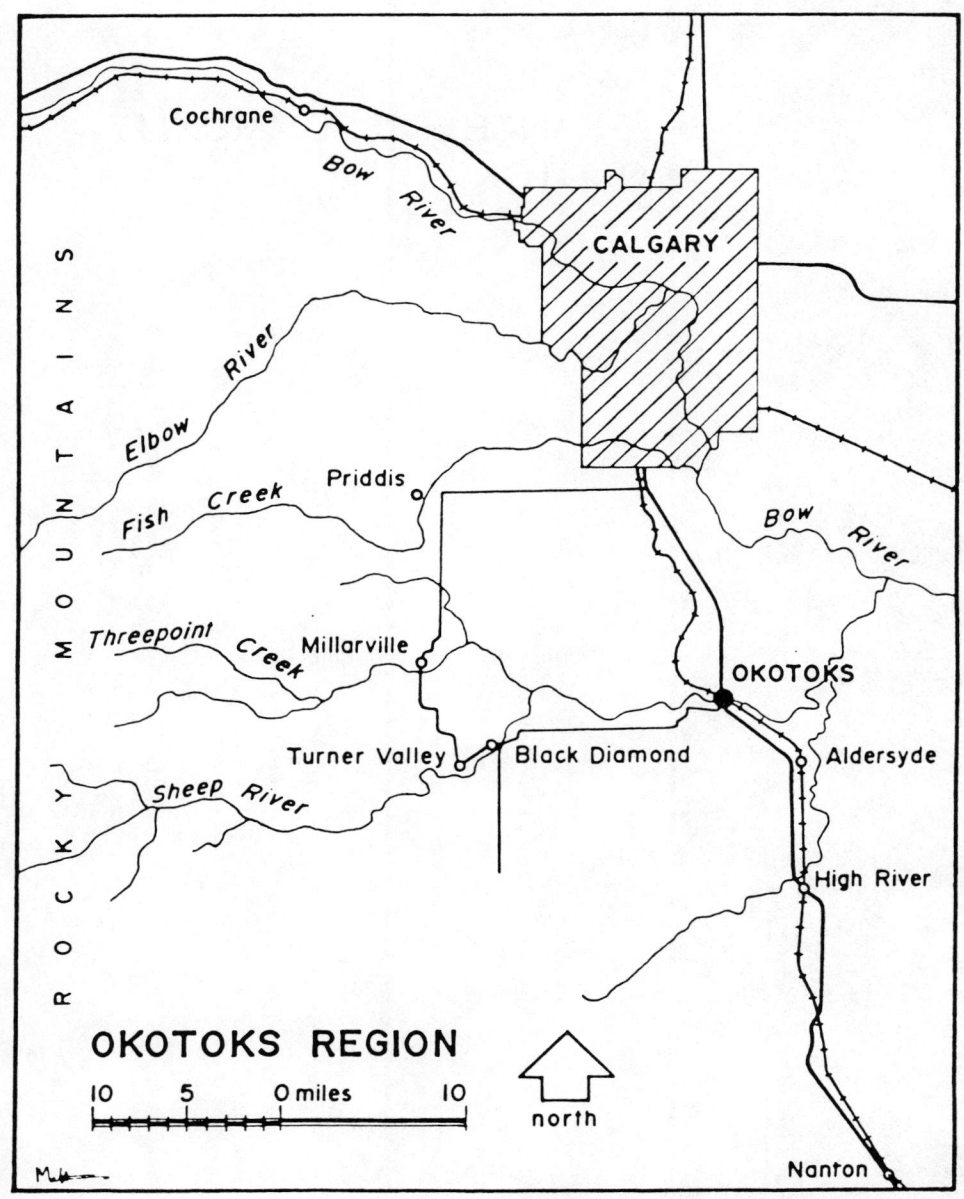

The Okotoks Region. Map prepared by Lillian Wonders.

FIVE A Ranchers' Community—Okotoks

OKOTOKS lies about 27 miles southwest of the centre of the city of Calgary (see Map 1). I use the word "centre" advisedly, for since the war of 1939–45 Calgary's rapid expansion is pushing its southern limit so steadily forward that Okotoks and much of its rural hinterland are today engulfed by its exurban sprawl. This experience is a significant aspect of the town's contemporary history but I shall make few allusions to it. It should, however, be borne in mind that Okotoks and its environs are part of the Calgary conurbation.

Okotoks is situated on Sheep Creek or, as the geographers insist on calling it, the Sheep River, a designation that seems to a native tiresomely pretentious when applied to this charming but essentially modest flow of water. Sheep Creek is one of the smaller of the many streams that flow out of the Rockies and their foothills to come together to form the South Saskatchewan and ultimately to drain much of the water of southern Alberta into Hudson's Bay. Sheep Creek's forks lie about ten miles west of the town and the river shapes the landscape of much of its western hinterland. This is a landscape on a much smaller scale than the formidable hills that roll back from sister streams like the Bow and the Highwood, a landscape more domestic than dramatic. The southern bank of Sheep Creek rises precipitously; the "cutbank" that is so familiar a part of the prairie scene. Okotoks lies largely to the north of the river; indeed, the rise of the land to the south is so steep that there is barely room for a park through which passes the sole road that gives access to the country lying to the south. On the north side the banks rise only a few feet above the normal level of the stream and the older part of the town lies on a river flat, not much more than 300 yards wide, between the river and the bench that shelters the valley from the north. Both the steep south bank and much of the flat to the north were well wooded, with some spruce on the northern slope and on both sides cottonwoods of a size sufficient to impress an eye accustomed to the prairie landscape. In this fertile, sheltered and well watered valley, enjoying the higher rainfall and milder winters of the foothills, gardeners soon discovered that domesticated flowers and shrubs grew quite as well as native plants and trees. Even the flats of the valley offered glimpses of the Rockies some fifty miles to the west; from the bench lands north of the town the prospects were superb. Given this combination of the cosy domesticity of its setting and the formidable splendours on its horizon, Okotoks could, more justly than many of its prairie sisters, be described as a "pretty" town.

It is difficult to believe that Okotoks owed its setting to any aesthetic appeal that it made to the engineers who chose the route for the branch of the Calgary and Edmonton Railway that was built south to Fort Macleod between 1890 and 1892. The terrain south of Calgary suggests that a line slightly further to the east would have been cheaper and easier to build and operate; its track would have avoided the stretch of river valley that has always been vulnerable to flooding when early summer rains transform the innocent and sparkling waters of Sheep Creek into a treacherous torrent. There had been a nucleus of settlement at this point long before 1890; indeed, local tradition maintains that a whiskey trader from Fort Benton, then the metropolis of Montana, had, as early as the 1860s, a post east of what became the townsite. The evidence for this early cultural penetration from the United States is flimsy but there is more reason to believe that the crossing at this point was much used by the Indians. The name "Okotoks" was long held to be a Blackfoot word meaning "stony crossing." "Stony" the crossing was but recent researches establish pretty conclusively that "Okotoks" is really much closer to the Blackfoot for "near the big rock," a reference to the enormous glacial erratic not far to the southeast. The latter, incidentally, was recently

A Ranchers' Community—Okotoks 103

View of Okotoks, 1912. John Lineham's house is in the left foreground. The large brick house in the right hand corner was Josiah Pugh's, a pioneer of the oil industry. Glenbow Archives NA-1230-4.

saved for posterity by local indignation. This secured the official intervention that frustrated the plans of an enterprising contractor who saw in "the big rock" a promising source of inexpensive road material.

In the early 1880s, even before the completion of the Canadian Pacific in 1885, most of the land in the vicinity of Sheep Creek was leased to ranching interests. The region was however much too close to Calgary, an important point of takeoff for settlement, not to be attractive to the squatters, intending homesteaders who were not content to accept the ranchers' monopoly. Though Sheep Creek was important enough to the ranchers to have a Mounted Police detachment, it was inevitable that land in the vicinity would be opened to homestead. Indeed, as early as 1884 the cattle compact suggested, to a federal government very much under its thumb, that Sheep Creek should be the northern boundary of the area from which sheep should be excluded. From the point of view of the settler who wanted to become a small stock raiser the land along Sheep Creek was exceedingly attractive, quite apart from its relative accessibility, and well before 1890 much of it had been taken up.

In 1886 the little settlement on Sheep Creek had about 20 houses; the Sheep Creek post office was named "Okotoks" in 1891. When the railway line was built south from Calgary to Macleod, Okotoks owed most of its importance to the saw mill established by John Lineham in 1890 to exploit his timber leases much further to the west on the South Fork of the river. Though Sheep Creek was a small stream its floodwaters could carry logs and its flow was sufficient to power what was to prove a highly successful operation. The presence of the Lineham mill may explain why Okotoks did not suffer the fate of many early settlements; the railway ran through it and it did not have to choose between sudden death and a move to a railway-owned townsite. This probably also explains why Okotoks, almost alone among the towns along the Calgary and Edmonton Railway, does not have streets consecrated to those tutelary spirits of land speculation, Osler, Hammond and Nanton. Through the 1890s it remained the largest settlement between Calgary and Macleod.

Its pace of growth accelerated during the later nineties as western Canada passed into the period of boom that lasted almost until the outbreak of war in 1914, the period which spawned prophecies far wilder than Wilfrid Laurier's, the period when it seemed not only probable but inevitable that as the nineteenth century had been the century of the United States so the twentieth would be the century of Canada. More and more land went under the plough as farmers turned from cattle and horses to wheat as the quickest way of grasping their share in the anticipated bonanza. Okotoks, with its stock-raising western hinterland, remained less dependent on wheat than towns further east in Alberta or in Saskatchewan and Manitoba. The gentlemanly settlers to the west turned more and more to raising horses; they were still gratifying this passion for horseflesh in the 1920s and even into the 1930s in spite of the painful indications that they were waging a losing fight against the realities of the marketplace. Also west of the town but to the south of the river the huge lease of the Quorn Ranch, the most ambitious horse-raising venture of all, still maintained into the 1900s a bastion against the plough. To the east of Okotoks mixed farming was general, though grain provided a larger part of the farmers' income than cattle or horses. But all contributed to the rising prosperity and mounting ambitions of the "Biggest Little City in the West."

In the pre-war years, when the car was still a luxurious novelty, when teamsters had not yielded to truckers, and when the railway journey of an hour or more was still the fastest and most convenient way of reaching the neighbouring city, Okotoks was far enough from Calgary to provide a great variety of services. To a large extent its growing population lived by taking in one another's washing, even though it was sustained by a comparatively prosperous hinterland and fed by continuing infusions of immigrants into a country that had suddenly become not only the promised land of Europe but also the last best west of North America. The town had an exceedingly vulnerable economic infrastructure. Its industries, its lumber mill, the flourishing brickworks at Sandstone, a few miles along the railway to the west, the quarries that supplied sandstone foundations for its more substantial buildings—all depended upon a buoyant construction industry. There were plenty of plots and plans for attracting other industries but none of these, except that for a flour mill, was carried to successful fruition.

Nevertheless, the town provided a complex network of services that made it a highly attractive focus for the life of a large rural area and provided for its inhabitants a pattern of living that offered more than most farms in the way of material comfort, neighbourly interchange and social diversion. The ranchers, happy with their horses and often sustained by nourishing remittances from distant families, might sniff at this society of shopkeepers, but they did not disdain to make use of its amenities, and were frequent guests at its three hotels and even more frequent celebrants in their well supplied bars. The farmers, though generally more conservative spenders, were equally dependent on the services provided in the town and if anything rather more disposed to involve themselves in its social patterns. This established lines of communication that involved much more than a pure buyer-seller relationship.

The dominant interest of both town and country during the boom period was in real estate. The comparatively early close settlement of the area, the high quality of its land, and its accessibility to the railway operated to push up land prices. The first decade of the twentieth century in the west was essentially an era of speculation, speculation sustained by buoyant markets and a steady rise in the price of real estate, urban as well as rural. The first settlers in the vicinity of Okotoks, those who came in the eighties and the early nineties, were overwhelmingly from the United Kingdom or from English-speaking eastern Canada. Those who survived the hardships of the pioneer period had by 1900 established themselves as the owners of valuable properties. For many of them the conditions of rural living could only be compared unfavourably with the amenities offered by the new communities growing up along the railways. The educational advantages were among the most apparent, but there were many others. At the same time the towns offered opportunities for investment and for entry into the highly attractive speculative activity that preoccupied the prospering westerner from the midnineties on. Towns like Okotoks thus became the base for those pioneers who had had enough of the rigours of life on the land, who had, as it were, made a stake, and were seeking new fields to conquer. There were also those who, having tried farming and failed, sought a new opportunity in less uncongenial surroundings.

The towns of Alberta generally may thus have provided a base from which the first wave of settlers, overwhelmingly English-speaking, Protestant and British in their background and attitudes, continued to assert a predominance which was threatened by the flood of immigrants not only from Europe but from the United States. Certainly Okotoks saw itself as a stronghold of British tradition, though often these traditions were expressed in terms of an Ontario or Maritime inheritance. To a greater extent than in the case of many other Alberta towns, the hinterland shared its prejudices, but this only fed and reinforced the determination of the townspeople to recreate and maintain a society that conformed to the norms established "back east" or, for the United Kingdom immigrants, "in the old country."

By 1912 the peak of the boom had been reached. The town, which optimistically claimed a population of more than 1,000, though the census of 1911 placed the number at 516, had filled the rather constricted area between the railway and the bench that formed the northern limit of the valley. There were really only two streets, Elma Street and Main or Elizabeth Street, both named in honour of John Lineham's daughters, and most of the lots had houses, a few of them substantial brick structures that reflected at once the affluence and the aspirations of their builders. In the centre of the town several brick business blocks testified to the resources of its leading citizens. The four room school in the east end had proved inadequate; a new and more commodious school had been built on the bench immediately to the north. Then in 1912 the town slipped slowly and painfully into the recession that preceded the war. The Great War completed the devastation begun by the collapse of the boom; as in other areas with a preponderance of British-oriented young men of military age, enlistments and casualty rates were equally high. The price in social dislocation paid by the youthful communities of the west in the aftermath of 1914 has seldom been accurately calculated or even adequately described.[1]

Certainly the Okotoks of 1920 was a shadow of the optimistic and bustling town of the first decade. The substantial houses were still there, though many had changed hands and the largest of all had been unceremoniously divided to house two families. On some of the relatively few vacant lots abandoned excavations gave mute evidence of the sudden disappearance of the housing shortage. On Main Street larger cellar holes spoke of the casualties of fires, an ever present risk in a town that had not provided itself with an adequate water-supply, and cannily depended on the fact that almost anywhere in the valley a shallow well would provide excellent water which the gravel beds on which the town stood protected from contamination by the ubiquitous earth-closets. The lumber mill had closed, the brickworks at Sandstone was falling into decay. No one worked the quarries. The flour mill survived for a time, but it was not rebuilt after its destruction by fire. There was one doctor where there had been three; the lawyers now came occasionally from High River or Calgary to see their clients. Many of the stores had closed, especially those that had attempted a specialized trade. The skating rink, the most ambitious civic enterprise of the pre-war years, still stood but even its roof soon collapsed under the weight of an exceptionally heavy snow storm.

Gradually Okotoks limped forward into a semblance of prosperity that lasted until the onset of the depression of the thirties. The first of the two decades between the wars is usually represented as one of comparative prosperity for Canada; it is doubtful if this was wholly true for the prairie west, where a painful process of adjustment to postwar realities was complicated by the infirm foundations jerry-built in the boom years. Okotoks' recovery to something like normality was assisted by the development of the oil and gas industry in neighbouring Turner Valley, the first significant producing field in Alberta. Nevertheless, although this was good for business in the town and provided employment for its young men, and husbands for some of its young women, it offered nothing like the stimulus provided to Alberta as a whole following the Leduc discoveries of 1947. But as the 1920s wore on older houses were being repainted, a few new houses were built, business premises were refurbished and new ones opened, often to replace those destroyed by the frequent fires. Cement pavements replaced the old wooden sidewalks, the streets were regraded and regraveled and trees planted along the boulevards. Natural gas superseded wood and coal as a source of domestic heat and the supply of electric power came to be more than sporadically available during the hours of darkness. The provision of watermains and sewers continued to be a matter of debate. The rink was, by a major effort, rebuilt and remained the winter focus of the town's athletic life.

The population declined to 448 in 1921; it rose gradually during the 1920s to 760 in 1931; in the last half of the decade the town was growing faster than the province. It was still overwhelmingly Protestant, overwhelmingly Anglo-Saxon in origin (see Table I). There were few Americans, even fewer than before the war. There was almost no one who could be described as "foreign." There was one French Canadian, a former Mounted Policeman who had moved into the Alberta Provincial Police and thence into the management of the new hotel that was built after the repeal of prohibition and named, characteristically, in honour of the then Governor-General. There were no Indians. There were two Chinese business establishments, a restaurant and a laundry. Their proprietors played no part in the social life of the town, though it must be said that when two Chinese boys appeared at the local school there was no overt sign of racism. There were no

Jews in Okotoks, though two brothers farmed west of the town. Anti-semitism was so lacking in expression that, until I found myself in a Calgary boarding school, I had no idea that being a Jew was in any way different from being a Baptist. They were simply two groups who happened not to be Anglicans.

If there was little evidence of outspoken racism, there were plenty of indications of a rigid, stratified and complex class structure. Not that anyone ever talked about class; it was even then one of the great Canadian unmentionables. A decent reticence was universally preserved but the implications are clear enough in the retrospect of memory. Nowhere was this structure more clearly exemplified than in the local churches (see Table II). In its

TABLE I   Ethnic Origins of Population of Sub-district of Okotoks, 1901, and Town of Okotoks, 1911—1931

Year	British	French	German	Dutch	Others	Totals
1901	583	6	30	40	12	671
1911	452	14	18	4	28	516
1921	407	6	11	14	10	448
1931	599	22	34	12	93	760

SOURCE: *Censuses of Canada, 1901—1931.*

TABLE II   Religious Affiliation of Population of Sub-district of Okotoks, 1901, and Town of Okotoks, 1911—1931

Year	Roman Catholic	Anglican	Presbyterian	Methodist	United Church	Baptist	Others	Totals
1901	36	114	281	87	—	91	62	671
1911	27	132	145	111	—	62	39	516
1921	8	140	176	47	—	58	19	448
1931	33	174	24	—	429	36	64	760

SOURCE: *Censuses of Canada, 1901—1931.*

heyday, Okotoks had no less than six congregations: Presbyterian, Anglican, Methodist, Baptist, Roman Catholic and the Disciples of Christ. By 1921 the latter had disappeared altogether, the congregation of St. James' Roman Catholic Church was almost entirely drawn from the country adjacent to the town and dependent upon the ministrations of an itinerant priest, the Baptist Church was closed and the Presbyterians, in the pre-war years much the most numerous group, had, long before the formal emergence of the United Church of Canada, joined in a union with the Methodists, who had a larger and more impressive church building. St. Luke's Presbyterian Church, for a time sporadically used by the Anglicans as a parish hall, in due course became a chopping mill. The United Church congregation was in the 1920s by far the largest but that of St. Peter's Anglican Church was still able to support, not in great luxury, a resident priest, though he, unfortunate man, also served a number of points in the predominantly Anglican foothills region to the west.

Because it is the congregation most familiar to me I shall attempt a description of St. Peter's in the 1920s. I shall say little about its clergymen; they succeeded one another with some rapidity. The immediate postwar period was not a happy one for the Anglican Church in the west; until a new and exceptionally able and vigorous bishop appeared on the scene the Diocese of Calgary attracted few priests who could be described as outstanding. The incumbents of St. Peter's were scarcely among those few. The congregation had, however, a life of its own and somehow struggled on, fulfilling its part in defining the values and standards of the community it served.

One family played a unique part in its leadership, as indeed they did in the life of the town as a whole. The nearest thing to a squire that Okotoks had was Colonel Alfred Wyndham, a well-connected Englishman who came to the west to serve in the suppression of the Riel Rebellion of 1885 and remained to ranch, retiring to Okotoks in 1910 and dying there in 1914. His wife, Caroline, whose Family Compact connections were as impeccable as those of her husband with the English and Irish nobility, lived on until 1933. Their numerous progeny and their grandchildren in turn passed in and out of the Wyndham house but the permanent residents in the 1920s were Mrs. Wyndham, her bachelor

Mrs. Alfred Wyndham (née Caroline Stuart), ca. 1930, in her Okotoks home. Taken by J. Vanderpant, who practiced photography in Okotoks only briefly but remained a friend of the Wyndhams. Glenbow Archives NA-84-5.

son, retired from the Mounted Police, her cousin and contemporary Jane Seymour and her spinster daughter, who ran this rather extraordinary establishment. The Wyndhams' style of life was quite unlike that of the town at large. To begin with, none of them had by the 1920s gainful employment. What was even more distinctive, the Wyndhams dined regularly at seven; the rest of the town took its main meal in the middle of the day and was sitting down to its supper not long after the tea things had been removed from Miss Seymour's sitting-room. The latter was the nearest thing to a *salon* that Okotoks could boast. For a good part of the decade "Cousin Janie," then in her eighties, was in effect confined to her *chaise longue*. She had tripped over a large and affectionate Labrador called "Tory," and the broken hip that had resulted never mended. Her intellectual vigour was, however, unimpaired, as was her appetite for bridge, backgammon, books and conversation.

Across the street at St. Peter's (which everyone in the 1920s still called "the English church") the Wyndhams were regularly in the two front pews on the epistle side, the ladies of the family in one, the gentlemen in another, with Miss Seymour in her wheelchair at the chancel steps. In churchmanship the Wyndhams were distinctly High; both Mrs. Wyndham and Miss Seymour had been baptized by Bishop Strachan. He had indeed called Jane Seymour

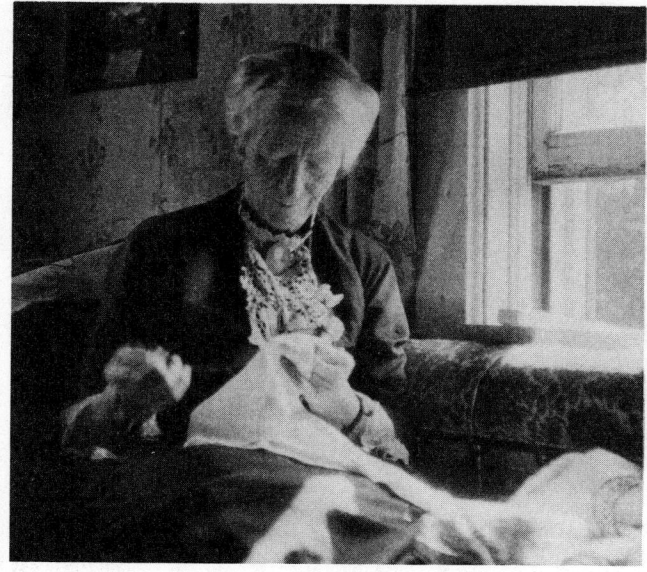

Miss Jane Seymour, ca. 1930, in her sitting room in the Wyndham's Okotoks house. Born in Nevis or St. Kitt's, Miss Seymour came to her Toronto connections and was employed, through the intervention of Sir John A. Macdonald, in Ottawa. On retirement she came to live with her cousin and contemporary, Caroline Wyndham. Glenbow Archives NA-3715-2.

"his little Jacobite," some indication of the elevation of her political views. Yet as parsons came and went, some High, some Low, some Broad, some merely confused, no word of criticism of the incumbent ever passed the family's collective lips. Miss Wyndham somehow kept a Sunday School in being, maintained the altar linen in good order, polished the altar vessels and arranged whatever flowers came to hand. Her brother Alec was a perpetual Rector's Warden; he dealt with the recalcitrant furnace and rang the bell for every service. And at every service, no matter what the liturgical posture of the current rector, he marched stiffly up to the altar, paid it his reverence and lit the altar candles. There was, in the duck of his head and the precision of his about-turn as he made his way back to his pew, something that said to even the most evangelically inclined that this much at least of Catholic faith and practice would be maintained at St. Peter's.

The congregation was a cross-section not only of the town but of the surrounding countryside. It included the doctor, the editor of the newspaper and an Englishman, of genteel antecedents and some substance, who carried an increasing responsibility for the direction of the affairs of the town on the basis of sheer character and his conviction of the individual's responsibility for the welfare of his fellow men. Some of the merchants also attended, bank employees and teachers came and went, but in the church and its organizations many of the most faithful supporters were drawn from less prestigious occupations. The parish also drew heavily both for its congregation and for its financial support upon the farms nearby. Its people in the 1920s were predominantly of United Kingdom birth or their children. There was, however, a strong minority with an eastern Canadian, and particularly an Ontario, background. The High Church sympathizers were drawn largely from those of the English whose religious attitudes had been formed in Anglo-Catholic parishes "at home"; the exception was one of the merchants, a Baptist by upbringing, an agnostic by conviction, an Anglican by marriage and a ritualist by preference. The Wyndhams, who gave the High Church wing much of its effective force, represented both eastern Canadian and "Old Country" traditions. In matters of church policy they could work very effectively with allies drawn from other layers of the town's social structure. In spite of divisions of class and churchmanship the congregation formed a tightly knit and cohesive group, sustained by mutual loyalties and a mutual respect that cut sharply across the alignments of social class or cultural background.

Though the Anglican population of Okotoks was proportionately rather larger than in other small southern Alberta towns, it was still apt to see itself as a beleaguered minority in relation to the much more numerous congregation of the United Church. It was indeed declining in numerical terms (from 31 per cent in 1921 to 23 per cent in 1931) but scarcely in its sense of identity. The division between the Anglicans and the United Church was very sharp indeed; the two congregations watched each other carefully and there was some consternation when an Anglican soprano yielded to the allurements of the much superior United Church choir or a well-off Presbyterian from the country appeared with suspicious frequency at St. Peter's. This division did not however effectively isolate the two groups from one another. In the town's organizations, less numerous than in the pre-war years but still very active, they worked together without much evidence of interdenominational bickering. The gradual liberalization of Protestant attitudes to such matters as card-playing, dancing, smoking and drinking made itself evident in this period. Anglicans, whose views on these matters had been rather less rigid, accommodated themselves with ease to this change in the social climate. One could, I suggest, make a case for a taste for auction bridge as a social indicator in a small Alberta town of this period. An analysis of the membership of the two women's bridge clubs of the time, for which my sources are regrettably incomplete, would, I think, result in a pretty even balance between the two persuasions. If one assumes that these two clubs approximately represent the *élite,* and I think they really thought they did, the conclusion would be that membership in that *élite* was not dependent on adherence to a particular religious position, though an Anglican's chance of being included within it was slightly better.

Much the same group dominated the Colonel Wyndham Chapter of the Imperial Order of the Daughters of the Empire, though few of its members belonged to the Women's Christian Temperance Union. Prohibition was in the 1920s a declining cause though in the 1900s the issue had divided the town. When the provincial government of the United Farmers of Alberta proposed to replace prohibition by government control, the issue was debated in the Okotoks High School. Significantly the affirmative team was Anglican; the negative United Church. Though drinking ceased to be illegal it remained for the most part a domestic practice. Certainly few if any respectable women entered the local beer parlour. Nor did women smoke in public places in Okotoks, and few even indulged in private, though United Kingdom example was gradually breaking down this taboo.

There was a close contact between the town and its rural hinterland, a contact that went beyond the relationships imposed by the service function of the town and which was based on a degree of social congeniality. The churches particularly, and the schools to some extent, fostered close affinities between country and town families who shared a common background. Sports activities, particularly curling, brought town and country people together. The annual Okotoks Agricultural Show was another meeting ground, with representatives of both town and country on its Board of Directors. Many Okotoks people, especially those who in retrospect constituted the town's *élite,* attended the Millarville Races, a classic country race meeting that was the high point in the social life of the horsemen whose properties lay to the west.

Political action also involved close cooperation. Okotoks and its hinterland was before 1921 predominantly Conservative. John Lineham, whose lumber interests had fed its prosperity in the 1890s, represented it in the territorial legislature. He may be taken as a representative of the Eastern Canadian strain in the dominant group in the region, where his numerous relatives remained after his death in 1914. His place as the leading Conservative was taken by George Hoadley, a Yorkshire born rancher and horseman, whom Okotoks in 1909 returned to the legislature as one of three Conservatives elected to that predominantly Liberal body. When in 1921 the U.F.A. dislodged the Liberals from office, he ran as a U.F.A. candidate and succeeded in carrying his constituents with him. An able and effective cabinet minister, he represented Okotoks until the Social Credit sweep of 1935. His personal prestige and popularity and his Conservative antecedents combined to bring elements in both the town and the country into the U.F.A. fold that elsewhere would almost certainly have been comfortable enough in the traditional parties. Though his support was somewhat stronger in the country than in the town, his uninterrupted electoral success reflected the way in which the older strains in the settlement of the province managed to maintain their influence against the American and continental European strains that were numerically increasingly predominant.

Okotoks and its environs formed a society that was horizontally as well as vertically stratified. The horizontal lines are not easy to discern, for they are drawn through a community that was, in Alberta terms, more than ordinarily homogenous in ethnic origin and religious affiliation. They had relatively little to do with economic status, at least in the immediate sense of relative income. They had a great deal to do with the quality of life which individuals enjoyed or to which they aspired. Perhaps the most rigorous line of all was that which divided the clean from the dirty. Certainly the horizontal stratification was largely determined by social congeniality, itself very much a matter of common values. Yet in spite of its horizontal fragmentation this was a closely knit society. Whatever the private discriminations, the town's institutions, and particularly the churches, cut across the strata and held the population together in mutual respect and esteem. This was by no means a one way relationship, from the top down. From time to time Miss Wyndham, among her many roles a member of the school board, would trudge sturdily up the hill to conduct a personal investigation of the school. The school janitor knew that, if his work was well done, he could rely upon her substantial support against any uncooperative trustee, teacher or pupil. The hierarchy of the structure, and the hierarchy of values upon which it was based, largely derived from older societies in eastern Canada and the United Kingdom, were both in the 1920s beginning to break down. What I would suggest is that a further and closer examination of the small towns of Alberta, and perhaps of western Canada, might reveal that these were the bases from which the settlers before 1895, and those later settlers who shared their attitudes and convictions, maintained their values, not to mention their prejudices, well into the twentieth century. I would further suggest that this may be a neglected area of investigation that is relevant, not only to the establishment of the western identity, but also to the Canadian experience.

Notes

1. John H. Thompson, *The Harvests of War: The Prairie West, 1914–1918* (Toronto: McClelland and Stewart, 1977). This book is a luminous exception.

SIX   RANCH HOUSES OF THE ALBERTA FOOTHILLS

In the early 1970s, the federal government considered purchasing a ranch in Alberta, with a view to developing it as a national historic site. Lewis's son, Greg Thomas, himself a student of the cattle industry in Western Canada[1], was asked by the National Historic Sites Board to carry out preliminary research and to prepare a report on existing literature pertaining to pioneer ranch houses in the West. But as Greg Thomas soon discovered, virtually nothing had been published on the subject. Even more distressing, he found that very few structures had survived from the "Golden Age of Ranching." These facts prompted Lewis Thomas to take a close look at his own boyhood home, reputed to be the earliest ranch house in the Sheep Creek area; having done so, and to compensate for the dearth of secondary literature, he agreed to write a descriptive essay on "Cottonwoods" and several neighbouring ranch houses for the Historic Sites Board.

As it happened, the federal government did not proceed with its plans to establish an historic ranch site.[2] Professor Thomas's essay, however, was published by the Board as one of its Occasional Papers in Archaeology and History. It remains one of the few essays available on ranchers' domiciles and as such is a valuable reference work

117

for historians of the ranching industry, as well as for those interested in heritage conservation and the built environment. Besides providing a detailed record of building styles and interior decor, "Ranch Houses of the Alberta Foothills" is a warm, personal memoir offering an intimate and engaging view of some of the province's privileged settlers in the early decades of the century.

Notes

1. Gregory E. G. Thomas, an historian with Parks Canada, wrote his M.A. thesis on "The British Columbia Ranching Frontier, 1858–1896." Completed at the University of British Columbia in 1976, the work was supervised by Lewis G. Thomas's former student, Dr. David H. Breen. Greg Thomas's unpublished dissertation is the most authoritative history of the B.C. cattle industry yet written.
2. Although Parks Canada did not establish an historic ranch site in Alberta, the idea was taken up by the provincial government's Historic Sites Service, which undertook the restoration of the Cochrane Ranch, north-west of Calgary.

SIX Ranch Houses of the Alberta Foothills

An increasing interest in the social history of the Canadian West gives a significance to the domesticities of the region's early settlers that might a generation earlier have been dismissed by the scholar as totally irrelevant or at most merely amusing or picturesque. In spite of diligent collecting by institutions, groups and individuals, the number of adequately authenticated artifacts is comparatively small. There has been little written on their provenance or their relationship to one another in their daily use, and farm and ranch houses, even some built as late as the early 1920s, have in many cases perished or, more often, fallen into ruin or disuse. Even where there has been an intelligent and careful attempt to recreate the setting of a pioneer room, the product often seems to the observing eye, no matter how sympathetic or perceptive, sadly unconvincing as a means of transmitting historical knowledge to the beholder. It may be that the weakness of the exhibit arises not from the use of the wrong materials, but from an absence of information about the social history of the period and locality portrayed. The contriver of the exhibit is certainly not to be blamed if his tableau fails to come alive; the onus rests on the historian who has failed to record and even more to interpret the past in a way that conveys to his audience the kind of sensitivity to the implications of a piece of china or the hang of a curtain that converts an object into a visual, emotional and intellectual excursion into the past.

Recent studies have begun to illuminate and indeed to reinterpret the past of the ranching community in southern Alberta. They view it as an experience that, although related to large-scale stock raising in North America and indeed in the world at large, was at the same time uniquely Canadian, significant not only for the locality but also for the region and for the nation. The uniqueness of the ranching community in terms of its economic and governmental relationships has been convincingly demonstrated; the impact of these relationships upon the social development of southern Alberta has been less fully explored. In such an exploration, the houses in which the ranchers lived, the way they were equipped and the way they functioned in relation to the ranch buildings and to the world outside are all relevant.

This paper, the reader should be warned, is very much the product of the personal experience of the writer. He grew up in the Alberta foothills in the years between the wars, in a district that lay on the northern fringe of the ranching country not very far, even by team or on horseback, from the urban influences of Calgary, which were felt in this area as early as the 1880s. The nearest town was Okotoks (previously known as Sheep Creek and, briefly, as Dewdney) on the north side of Sheep Creek. Most of the families who settled along the north side of the valley of Sheep Creek before 1914 called themselves ranchers though they were really small stockmen. The overwhelming majority were of United Kingdom origin though a few well-connected families from continental Europe contributed a cosmopolitan note and fitted easily and creatively into the life of the valley. An even more overwhelming majority shared a passionate addiction to horses, and polo, racing and the gymkhana lingered even after the war of 1914–18 dealt its shattering blow to the polite society of the Alberta foothills, if such a society ever existed. The majority of the prewar arrivals had at least a sentimental attachment to the Millarville church. Christ Church, uniquely built of vertical logs, survives as the most important architectural relic of the community's past.

Cottonwoods, the house in which the author was born, was built in the early 1890s by the Austins, one of the relatively few Eastern Canadian families to settle as early as this and as far west of Okotoks. George Frederick Austin, a retired surveyor, probably from the Ottawa valley, came to homestead in 1885, accompanied

Cottonwoods from the southeast, ca. 1919. L. G. Thomas quips that this picture was taken "before the lawn mower."

by his much younger wife, the intensely musical daughter of a clergyman, and his son, Edmund. The house they built is reputed to be the earliest frame house, as distinct from a log house, to be built in this part of the foothills. The site of the original log house, slightly to the west of the existing frame house, may still be distinguished. It was burned about 1910 as a sanitary precaution: it was infested by bedbugs. The site successfully resisted the archaeological fumblings of a young boy inspired by the exploits of Dr. Schliemann of Troy.

The frame house, originally consisting of two ground-floor rooms each about 16 feet square, with bedrooms above, is T-shaped and each part has a steeply sloping roof. It is believed to have been built in two stages, with the kitchen that forms the stem of the T added to the original living room, now the dining room of the house. The stairs rise steeply from the latter room, and the locations of the outside entrance to the cellar and of a trap door, long unused, in the dining room floor suggest that this room and the bedrooms above formed the dwelling unit for the family at least for a short time. The difference in interior finishing of the two bedrooms above the dining room and the two above the kitchen also suggests that the house was built in two stages as the latter (and presumably later) are almost entirely finished in conventional lath and plaster and milled lumber like the two downstairs rooms, while the inside walls of the former and the doors into them are of wide plank. The two bedrooms over the kitchen (though not the door to the fairly large linen closet that, except for a landing or corridor, occupies the rest of this floor-space) have conventional doors and locks rather than latches. The doors on the ground floor differ in style and though some of these have been moved from their position of 1910 when the house passed from the possession of the original owners to that of the writer's family, this seems to confirm that the house was built in stages.

The chimney, most of its original brick still intact, is of a yellowish-brown brick, quite unlike the red brick made not far away at Sandstone, just west of Okotoks. (It reminds the writer of the brick of old houses in Calgary and indeed, subject to confirmation, of the brick used by W. R. Hull to build the substantial ranch house on Fish Creek, east of Midnapore, which later passed into the possession of Patrick Burns and was more recently extended and restored by the latter's great-nephew, Richard Burns.) The chimney runs up the south wall of the kitchen, the common wall between the two original rooms. If the kitchen were built later than the dining room, the chimney, if built as part of the first unit, must have been on an outside wall. This may seem unlikely as the chimney is not brick-built to ground level, but rests on a timber frame. The latter opens to the kitchen and, with a shelf half-way up and just behind the kitchen stove, still forms a convenient airing-cupboard. A door out of the kitchen into a small pantry under the stairs presents a puzzle as it is of the same plank construction as doors in the bedrooms above the dining room. In 1910 the cellar steps were reached by a trap door in the middle of the kitchen floor. They were moved to the pantry in the interests of safety. If the door to the pantry were put in while the first section was in use as a dwelling, it would have served little purpose and caused a draught formidable even to hardier and more youthful pioneers than the original owners of Cottonwoods.

The T-shaped floor plan, steeply pitched roof and frame construction are common on the prairies not only of western Canada but also of the United States and, for the late 19th and early 20th centuries, might almost be called "typical." The house is also evocative of those built in the later 19th century in the Ottawa valley, with which the Austin family had associations. Its outlines are perhaps less grimly Gothic and more comfortably Georgian than is characteristic of the style, but this impression may be due to the setting in what has become a grove of tall trees, most of them Russian poplar planted about 1930. Certainly the earliest snapshots suggest a bleaker line.

The impression may also owe something to the later additions. These, a sitting room (the term commonly used by most of the Sheep Creek settlers, "drawing room" being too pretentious and "lounge" not having achieved its later vogue in the United Kingdom), an adjoining sun porch, an entrance porch, a verandah, at first open but later screened, and a "toy house," now used for storage, on the north, were added to provide additional amenities. Most of these assumed their present form as the result of alterations in 1928–29 when the sitting room and sun porch were added though the "toy house" and the porches at the front (south) and back (east) doors were built in 1910 when the property changed hands. Though the porches also served as cloakrooms and as storage space for indoor and outdoor tools and for the tennis net and racquets, their primary function was to protect the inner door and those who used them against the weather. The small verandah was added about 1912 to provide a protected outdoor play-space.

The effect of these alterations and additions was to give Cottonwoods a distinctive character. This arises, in the writer's view, from the way in which the roof lines of the additions echo the line of the roofs of the original T and the shed roof of the sun porch and sitting room. This was, I am confident, a fortuitous rather than a contrived effect. The basic pressure for the additions came from my mother who knew what she wanted and undoubtedly, if the success of her room arrangements is a criterion, had an eye for the relationship of shapes as well as for colour and texture. Though she sketched in pen and pencil and painted a little in watercolours and in oils, it would not have occurred to her that her talents would extend to producing builders' drawings. The work was executed wholly by my father and his bachelor partner, both with some training in civil engineering in England. The partner was much more interested in carpentry than my father, who was essentially a horseman. Whatever the source of the design, it may be properly designated as vernacular architecture. Indeed it would be difficult to think of any foothills buildings of this period that owe much to formal training in architectural theory or practice though many were enriched by skilled craftsmanship. This is not to say that the buildings, however simple in construction and primitive in material, owed nothing to architectural tradition or to eyes insensibly trained by looking at the architectural heritage of older societies.

The original house and the additions were all built not on stone or concrete foundations, but on wooden sills resting on the rocks and boulders plentiful so near a creekbed. The house, after as much as 80 years, still appears to be sound and is easily heated; it has long enjoyed the reputation of being warm in winter and cool in summer. Electric power and propane central heating were installed recently without major alteration to the structure and the two original cellar-holes are still in use for storage. On the hill behind the house, excavations, presumably for root cellars, may still be seen, but these have not existed within present memory though quite commonly used elsewhere in the district and throughout the ranching country of the foothills.

Water supply has never been a problem as, apart from Sheep Creek, there are flowing springs in the vicinity and water is reached in the gravel of the valley by digging a few feet from the surface. The gravel also provides excellent drainage. Water has never been piped in for domestic use, but for a time a pump in the kitchen provided water for the sinks and for the washbasin and tub in the adjacent bathroom, made in 1928 by partitioning off part of the kitchen. The water from the well this pump served was slightly sulphurous to the taste, a not uncommon phenomenon in a location so close to the pioneer oil field at Turner Valley, and sweeter water is now pumped from a well outside the kitchen door, not more than ten yards away. An earth-closet, not the original, is still in service.

Little of the original siding has been replaced and a number of the original window frames and four-paned sashes survive where least exposed to the action of the weather and the fumes from Turner Valley. It is said that the soundness and durability of the structure owed much to the fact that the Austins had the materials on hand for at least a year before they began construction and the wood was thus thoroughly seasoned. The wood probably came from Okotoks, eight miles by road to the east, where the Lineham lumbermill was the major pioneer enterprise. The Linehams came to southern Alberta from Ontario and the milled lumber, used to trim doors and windows, the balustrade that protects the upper landing from the stair opening and the older hardware have in their modest ornament a late Victorian flavour that perhaps lingered longer in the colonial atmosphere of central Canada than in the more sophisticated metropolis. Whatever the Austins' taste, and Mrs. Austin's few surviving letters do not suggest an easy fit into the stereotype of the pioneer woman, people building a house on Sheep Creek in the early nineties would have little choice to exercise in terms of the niceties of design unless a great deal of money was to be spent. By the late twenties a broader choice was available, but in a household of limited means was still restricted.

The same restrictions of variety and cost affected the interior furnishings. Little can be said of the appearance of the rooms at Cottonwoods before 1910 except that Mrs. Austin had both a piano and an organ and it would be surprising if the rooms were not strewn with books and magazines and sheet music. Apart from a taste for music, the Austins were great readers; the attic when they left was filled with old numbers of periodicals like *Blackwood*'s and *Etudes*. Some of their furniture remained in the house after they departed and an elm double-drop-leaf kitchen table with turned legs and at least two chairs with moulded backs and shaped seats, made of an extremely tough wood also probably elm, painted black and exceedingly comfortable, are almost certainly of Ontario workmanship. They are of a design still popular as late as 1870. Whatever their virtue for today's admirer of Canadiana, these pieces were not highly regarded as objects of beauty by my parents and probably not particularly cherished by the previous owners who, after all, left them behind.

The furnishings of the house after 1910 can be described in more precise detail. The heavier pieces were generally of Canadian manufacture and some were homemade, including a huge cupboard in the kitchen, one of whose doors later became part of a built-in corner cupboard which was among the many products of my mother's inventiveness and my father's partner's addiction to joinery. Also in the kitchen was something called "the bamboo cupboard," certainly not homemade though it stood on a homemade stand that concealed behind a discreet green curtain my father's boots except for his best riding boots which, because of the height of their wooden trees, were allowed a place in my mother's wardrobe upstairs. "The bamboo cupboard" was perhaps not fully appreciated as the elegant expression that it was of the first fruits of the revolt against the overwrought elaboration of Victorian domestic furnishings. Only its frame and those of the doors were decorated with bamboo; its top, sides and doors were covered with carefully wrought cane. It had a long career: for a time it served, on a more carefully carpentered stand, as the sideboard in the dining room of the small house in Okotoks which we occupied during the weekdays of the school term, my parents having lost confidence in the one-room school nearly three miles from Cottonwoods which my sisters had briefly attended.

Where "the bamboo cupboard" came from I do not know, but it may have been from the same source as the chairs in the dining room which until 1928 was simply the eastern half of the sitting room. These chairs, a set of six including two armchairs, had been purchased on a visit to "the old country" at an auction sale of the effects of an invalid lady. She must have furnished her house in North Wales under the influence of William Morris for the chairs, of light oak with woven rush seats, had the simple and slender lines of the movement he inspired. The dining table, which could be extended to seat a crowded 12, was by contrast dark and heavy, presumably made in eastern Canada. The finish was probably described by the original vendor as "walnut." When not in use it was covered by a fringed greenish-brown chenille cloth. The sideboard was unashamed fumed oak, solid and simple in design and extremely well-made. The date would be approximately 1910 as I believe it was purchased new at a respectable Calgary furniture shop. It has—it is still in the same room—a mirrored back and a plate rail which displays some of the plates of a dessert service, certainly purchased at a North Wales auction, I believe for half a crown for its 16 pieces, and perhaps from the same invalid lady as her simple green and white Foley (or Shelley) china was for a long time part of our daily life.

The dessert service, lavishly decorated in black, gold and deep autumnal shades and with a curious crackled surface that suggests earthenware rather than fine china, has never been identified as to maker or period. Self-styled connoisseurs have both praised it as of exceptional beauty and antiquity and dismissed it as the worst sort of Art Nouveau, but no one has been able to interpret its obscure and scarcely visible markings. Along with other odds and ends, the service had been packed for export as "settlers effects" in a tin hipbath, formerly the property of my Flintshire great-grandmother. So skilfully was it packed that it survived the passage, all except the two-tiered centre comport which broke at the join between the two parts. My mother placed it in the rubbish bin where it was shortly observed by her Scottish neighbour, a lady noted for her business acumen and her plain-speaking, who did not hesitate to reprove this reckless discard of a valuable object that could be easily and inconspicuously mended. Perhaps tired by her exertions in putting her house in order and possibly resenting this Scottish aspersion on her own West-Country industry, thrift and appreciation of fine things, my mother rather crisply offered the comport to its admirer. The gift was carried off; what became of it was never revealed though I was a frequent and, I think, observant visitor at the recipient's house. The episode, trivial though it may be, indicates how casually household objects were often treated even though their merits were appreciated. My mother was on another occasion scolded by a male caller for using an oriental rug as a hearth-mat. It had been a family relic, but had been tied across great-grandmother's hipbath and the projecting handles had rubbed holes in it. My mother mended it carefully, but stuck to her guns and the rug ended its career at the back door.

The sitting room chairs included a gold-oak armchair with wide

The sitting room at Cottonwoods, about 1912, with L. G. Thomas's sisters, Dorothy and Gwynydd.

wooden arms and an adjustable back, dedicated to the comfort of my father's partner. Its two loose cushions were upholstered in a hideous but durable velour, a kind of plaid in reddish-brown and black that recalled Queen Victoria's worst excesses at Balmoral and Osborne. Such chairs are commonly illustrated in Canadian newspaper advertisements and catalogues from the 1890s to the 1920s; they are sometimes characterized as "mission." A sturdy table stood beside this chair to support a lamp that must have been the most commanding object in the room. The operative part of the lamp was of glass, but this was set in a bowl supported on an elaborately decorated column on claw feet, all silver-plated. This formidable base was surmounted by an equally elaborate silk shade. Where it came from I do not know; perhaps it was a wedding present, perhaps a trophy of the auction room. When it was new it must have been most expensive and I am quite sure my parents would not have thought of such an extravagance. It may have been Edwardian, but I am inclined to think of it as high Victorian at its most robust. As a lamp it was an early casualty of children's play—the table on which it stood had, like the dining table, a cover that reached almost to the floor and served once too often as a safe refuge in a game of hide-and-seek—but as a stand for many years it held a plant—wandering Jew or Irish moss—until at last the silver-plate yielded to the many cleanings dictated by the sulphur-laden air that was carried eastward from the oil field across the creek at Turner Valley.

The other furnishings were less substantial. My father occupied a wicker armchair that had the same light and elegant lines as the invalid lady's dining chairs; my mother, a tub-shaped chair with legs and back trimmed with cane or rattan and upholstered in green. The latter chair had, at first only on occasions when guests were invited, a slipcover made of a heavy cretonne or chintz closely patterned in blue and white which matched the slipcover my mother tailored to fit the Winnipeg couch, called "the sofa," whose rather drab green-covered mattress with its pendant frill did not greatly please her eye. There were a number of cushions on "the sofa," whose covers changed with the years. One, very much her "best," was a floral chintz, predominantly rose, with a corded edge. I can remember removing it from under the feet of a visitor in 1920; I noticed it not long ago still doing duty as part of the bed of a much-cherished cat. An upright piano and stool were not part of the original furniture but were added about 1918. The only other piece of furniture I recall was a small fumed oak desk with two bookshelves below; the lid dropped forward to form a writing-surface and though it was really intended as a lady's desk, it was in its pigeonholes that my father kept his papers and there he wrote his letters, including his weekly letter to his mother. The desk, very simple in its lines and extremely well-made, was probably purchased in North Wales in 1910 as it was a gift from my father's sister and seems to me to reflect her advanced and somewhat austere taste.

The carpet was an Axminster of bold design, richly floral and predominantly red. It covered most of the sitting room side; the floor of the dining room part had a brown linoleum intended to imitate parquet and requiring at least as frequent waxing and polishing. The illusion of wood was scarcely sustained by the brass tape that covered the joins. The kitchen linoleum, a green "inlaid," was prone to lose bits of its inlay not by any inherent defect or for any lack of care, but because of the roughness of the wooden floor beneath.

The curtains of the four windows did not match. In the sitting room the two windows had delicate lace curtains, net with a pattern appliquéd over it in a heavier thread. They were floor length and tied back to allow the view to be seen. There were no side drapes, though a heavy red one was pulled over the outside door to minimize draughts. Instead, cream-coloured blinds on rollers with a spring action gave protection against the sun and were pulled down in the evening more for cosiness than for privacy which was adequately assured by the mile of uncertain trail that led to the nearest public road. For the two dining room windows my mother made simple straight curtains, of cream-coloured casement cloth, whose brass rings pulled back and forth on thin brass rods. At a later date the faithful carpenter made window boxes that held houseplants and which, on the coldest nights, could be conveniently removed to a place of safety.

This room, like all other rooms in the house, was calcimined annually. Pink and green were the common colours, but my mother was quick to take advantage of other shades when these became available. She was also soon experimenting with wallpaper and became adept at hanging it with the assistance of anyone tall enough to be useful. The doors, the wooden trim around them and the windows, and the skirting-boards were varnished though it was not far into the twenties when the possibilities of light-coloured paint were discovered and one by one the rooms transformed.

There were many ornaments, though fewer than was perhaps the general fashion. Two of my English uncles had a taste for carving and fretwork and contributed a clock-case, a rather unstable plant table, whose lower shelf displayed a Japanese bowl in the Imari style, and a small hanging corner cupboard which had a lock and key and served as a medicine chest. All three were painstakingly carved and stained black. A large oak tray, left in its natural colour, was carved in a representation of the arms of the City of Gloucester. Bits of china which varied from a Chelsea piece, badly chipped but of some rarity, to souvenir plates of the coronation of George V, small silver boxes and mugs, a small brass dinner gong on a stand, vases of flowers when flowers were available and framed photographs all found a place somewhere. The pictures on the walls were a heterogeneous lot reflecting, among other things, my father's interest in horses and my mother's hobbies of painting in oils and watercolours and of photography. The only picture of more than sentimental value was a sketch in oils of an old man's head and shoulders by George Morland, one of the many he is said to have done to pay for a drink. It had caught my father's eye at an auction and he had bought it for the proverbial half-crown. The large photograph of race horses belonging to King Edward VII, showing the owner as well as the trainer and jockey, did duty for the portraits of royalty so widely popular throughout the empire. Several colour prints of the works of the cowboy artist, C. M. Russell, recalled my father's early experience in South Dakota and Montana.

The room was heated by a stove, the only source of heat, except for the kitchen range, for the whole house. Its stovepipe disappeared through the ceiling and reappeared in my parents' bedroom, whence it crossed the upstairs landing to the single chimney which also served the kitchen stove. Perhaps the earlier occupants, ageing central Canadians that they were, had a stove upstairs. There was space for one on the landing and an opening for another stovepipe, but there was never a stove there after 1910. Instead the space was enclosed to accommodate a chemical toilet which could be served by the convenient vent.

The first sitting room stove that I recall was a gigantic "base-burner" which could, with suitable attention, be kept going for 24 hours. Its place was taken, when the chimney and stovepipes were cleaned in the spring, by a small air-tight stove. Then the briquets which fed the voracious appetite of the base-burner ceased to be available or perhaps became too expensive and it was relegated to the granary and replaced by a Quebec heater, splendidly black and much ornamented by gleaming steel, an excellent and economical source of heat but incapable of maintaining a fire through the winter night. Cutting wood for the two stoves was a time-consuming task especially as it was all done by hand using axe and saw. Willow was plentiful on Sheep Creek and its quick and intense heat made it the wood preferred for cooking.

The four bedrooms allowed even more scope for improvisation than the downstairs rooms. The beds had enamelled iron frames, some with ornamental brass rods, and were severely practical. There was one feather mattress but it was regarded with some suspicion as possibly unhealthy and its contents were gradually transferred to make pillows, cushions and the quilted "eiderdowns" that supplemented a supply of blankets that never seemed quite adequate. Each bedroom had its washstand, all but one made of packing cases of one size or another, suitably padded, lined and draped. Dressing tables and bedside tables were similarly contrived. Only two rooms had a chest of drawers; these were of eastern Canadian manufacture as was my mother's dressing table. The narrow boards of the walls in two bedrooms were later painted or papered over, but for a time those in the room my sisters shared were covered with pictures cut from every available source and pasted to the boards.

I cannot begin to describe in equal detail the other Sheep Creek houses that I knew well in the years between the wars and can offer little more than impressions. Out of the composite of those impressions emerges a sense that they had more than a little in common, yet they were of great variety and individuality and all reflected the backgrounds and characters of their owners. It is sad that so few have survived, as Cottonwoods has survived, as crystallizations of nearly a century of foothills living.

Many of them were of log, of great variety in size and design, and almost without exception built in successive stages. One of particular interest, the Gate Ranch house, lay far to the west with a long view up the meadows of the north fork through the foothills' ridges to the splendour of the Rockies. Like many of the earliest houses, it seemed to have been sited with regard to the outlook and its dependent buildings and corrals were, as was generally the case, so placed that they did not obstruct the prospect from the main rooms of the house. From the first the house was seen not merely as an adjunct to the work of the ranch, but as the foundation of the owner's private life and the setting for his social life.

Log house built at Kew, Alberta, ca. 1932 by Mr. and Mrs. Joseph Fisher. Jane Fisher (née Johanna Freiin von Rummel-Waldau) grew up at and greatly loved The Gate Ranch.

The first dwelling here proved to be too close to the creek and this may explain why the first unit of the house that developed was more carefully constructed than many of its contemporaries. The builder and owner, Joseph T. Waite, had a knowledge of carpentry acquired in northern England and in the oldest part of the house the logs were squared and the corners painstakingly dovetailed. This part of the house, the bar to the future T, was almost square, divided into two rooms, one much wider than the other, and with a steep stairs between to an attic which was high enough to provide sleeping quarters. The second stage, the stem of the T, was much more ambitious and reflected the tastes of a new owner, a former British officer. It consisted of two very large rooms, a sitting room and a kitchen-dining room. These rooms were both lined with narrow tongue-and-groove which darkened with age. The two two-paned sashes of the windows were set to move horizontally rather than vertically; these were called "lazy windows" and their effect was to heighten the impact of the view and to emphasize the horizontal lines of the house as a whole. The logs of this and other parts of the house and of the outbuildings were left in the round with the saddle-back corners characteristic of much foothills log building. At right angles to the kitchen was the bunkhouse, itself a building of considerable size. The roof of the bunkhouse projected to join that of the kitchen and thus gave a sheltered passage which had a door at its north end and at once gave communication between and separated the bunkhouse and the kitchen. The passage at its south end was open to the verandah that stretched along the east wall of the sitting room and, in the years between the wars, looked over a flower garden which was thus well-protected on the north and west from wind and frost. Another range of buildings was destroyed by a fire from which the house narrowly escaped and the working buildings and the corrals were, when I knew the place best, all to the northeast of the house. They were admirably maintained and kept meticulously tidy. Some of the outbuildings, all of log, were stained or allowed to weather to a silvery grey, but the roofs, like that of the house, were painted red. The logs of the house were regularly whitewashed and the trim painted black. The house was banked with earth; it had banked so often that by 1930 the grass grew almost at the level of the windows and the whole house appeared to grow out of its surroundings. It no longer exists but I am sure that the scene of which it was the focus was for many others, as it was for me, the epitome of the log house of the southern Alberta foothills.

Like the other houses of Sheep Creek, the furnishings of this house were a miscellany gathered over the years, some passed down from earlier occupants, many improvised, and some made by a handy craftsman who could easily manage a shelf, a bench or a cupboard even though he certainly would not have considered himself a cabinetmaker. One of the things that distinguished this house in the years between the wars was the bold use of colour, in paint and in materials, in a way that recalled the vernacular decorative arts of south Germany. The family then occupying it were indeed from Munich though with connections reaching into almost every European country. The house was full of books; though well-filled bookshelves were no rarity in the Sheep Creek houses, one did not often find a library in four languages, German, French and Italian as well as English. Nowhere was the syn-

Viewfield Ranch, ca. 1919, with Miss Cathie Sinclair-Smith in the foreground. Viewfield was one of the few stone ranch houses on Sheep Creek. It was built by a well-off Englishman and is remarkable for the refinement of its interior finishing. The kindness of the present owner, Stuart Sinclair-Smith, Esq., is gratefully acknowledged for permission to use this picture.

thesis of the exotic and the local more gracefully and unselfconciously accomplished. It never for a moment seemed odd that at one end of the sitting room there should hang a portrait painted by one of Europe's most fashionable artists while in the corral nearby the subject demonstrated her notable ability to shoe a horse.

Though sandstone was locally available and much used in southern Alberta prior to 1914, Sheep Creek had only one house, the Viewfield Ranch house wholly of this material, though another nearby, now derelict, had a basement and ground floor of stone and a charming adjoining garden walled on two sides with blocks from the same quarry. The Viewfield Ranch house, which like many others commanded a handsome prospect of the valley and the mountains, was built by a well-off Englishman. It was of a very simple design: a long, low rectangle with a wooden verandah placed asymmetrically to shelter the front door. The huge attic, lit by a dormer window, was not used. The plan was very English. The front door opened into a square sitting room, almost a hall in the English sense. It had a brick open fireplace in one corner; the chimney served the stove in the adjoining dining room, a somewhat larger room to the left, and the range in the kitchen behind the dining room. What seemed a long passage led off to the bedrooms to the right of the sitting room. The upper sashes of the windows had a number of small panes; the thickness of the stone walls gave the windows very deep ledges. The house must have been expensive to build; apart from the skilled craftsmanship needed to work with the local stone, the plasterwork of the walls and ceilings and the tiled bathroom were exceptional in this period and this setting. The date when the house was built is not known; the other house where stone was used was built about 1906, perhaps a little earlier. Both had furnaces, though these were not notably efficient, and one had "waterworks" and, by about 1920, a somewhat temperamental electric lighting system.

Everyone had a kitchen garden and almost everyone a flower garden though the latter were not always as faithfully maintained or as ambitious as that at Cottonwoods. Again the gardens reflected the transatlantic heritage of most of the gardeners. They were not elaborate; few attempted more than the cottage garden of England. Plants and seeds were exchanged and the hardiest flourished. Scarlet lychnis or Maltese Cross, perhaps one of the first "exotics" attempted on Sheep Creek, flourished everywhere, notably at the Millarville church. The humble hop and the annual cucumber vine were popular creepers; Virginia creeper was not considered hardy enough to withstand the late and early frost of the foothills. Though the cottonwoods attained a respectable height along the creek, other than native trees grew slowly though gardeners were soon planting Russian poplar, Manitoba maple and caragana to give shelter not only from the wind but also from unseasonable frosts. The gardens and indeed the whole landscape of Sheep Creek by 1930 gave a feeling of sheltered lushness very unlike the stereotype of the prairie, but photographs dating from the eighties and nineties suggest a much more open and less wooded view and indeed these were the years when prairie fires were still a menace. The present garden at Cottonwoods dates only from 1910 and it was much enlarged to accommodate the sheltering trees at the end of the twenties. Dating the gardens is even more difficult than dating the houses and their furnishings, but I am inclined to think that Cottonwoods was exceptional in the absence of a garden in its early years. I am inclined to think that by 1890, and more certainly by 1895, almost all the early settlers had attempted something like an ornamental garden, however modest.

An extraordinary number of Sheep Creek houses had tennis courts; I can think of at least 16. They were grass courts though it is possible that the tennis club courts, near Ardmore, were clay courts, as the second Mrs. Welsh was a player of near championship quality. The vogue for lawn tennis seems to have spread to Sheep Creek almost as soon as the game was invented in North Wales and its popularity survived the war of 1914–18 though by the end of the thirties few of the courts were still maintained. "Maintained" is a relative word for the courts reflected the same talent for improvisation as the furnishing of the houses. The one at Cottonwoods was largely my mother's work. There was a piece of more or less level turf directly south of the garden and approximately the size laid down by *Pears' Encyclopaedia,* a much-thumbed work of reference. The lines, determined by the same authority, were laid out with lime and an old broom. The net had to be taken down between times as stock roamed at large; indeed to make the court my mother cut turf to fill a cow path that bisected diagonally her chosen site. The court ran east and west, which gave a certain advantage to the players with the sun at their backs. There were no backstops and balls had frequently to be retrieved from the little creek that in wet seasons ran only a few feet beyond the court's southerly limit. Our equipment was modest: balls were used year after year, surviving frequent total immersion, and one of the racquets was of such antiquity that, judging from its curiously unbalanced shape, it must have been made before any nonsense about standardization.

The Sheep Creek houses that I remember had great individuality yet they reflected certain common concerns that grew out of a diversity of backgrounds. Their mood was to a degree nostalgic, a harking back to a past that was remembered with affection, if not always, or even often, with regret. Their mistresses showed remarkable adaptability and in the interest of comfort and convenience they did not hesitate to compromise. Thus they drew their furnishings from a variety of sources. In one house a fine pair of early Wedgewood vases might sit on a carpenter-made cupboard or a Chippendale dressing-mirror on a golden-oak chest of drawers from Lindsay, Ontario. Family portraits from the 18th century might hang side by side with a carefully tanned coyote-skin. No one furnished a house with antiques, but if they had cherished possessions from another age and another way of life they used them and enjoyed them. On these extraordinary juxtapositions the patina of a generation's living imposed a congruity of their own.

SEVEN ASSOCIATIONS AND COMMUNICATIONS

In 1972 Lewis G. Thomas was elected president of the Canadian Historical Association (CHA), a fitting honour and tribute to his many contributions to historical scholarship in Canada. The Association was then celebrating its fiftieth anniversary. The following year, in his presidential address delivered in Kingston, Ontario, Professor Thomas considered the early years of the CHA: he accounted for its founding in Ottawa in 1922 and its relations with the Public Archives, the Champlain Society, and kindred institutions which comprised the "national historical establishment" in Canada between the wars. But the subject of his address was not so much the CHA as it was the "communications networks" that had existed in Canada prior to the Second World War. In particular, he was interested in the networks that had linked the prairie west and Central Canada. Communications being the basis of understanding, he was concerned that channels of communication between the regions were breaking down. His principal theme, therefore, concerned the importance of maintaining the national entity, a topical theme in view of Western alienation and the separatist sentiments which were then being expressed in some quarters.

Professor Thomas suggested that in its early

years the CHA was a model of the internal communications networks which once existed between people who were in responsible positions across the country. The scholars who were members of the CHA, he said, comprised

> a very tight and cosy society, a society where everyone knew each other. Though they did not necessarily like one another, they knew how each fitted into the structure, the peculiar interests that each had and to whom to go when something had to be done. Ottawa was a small city, Canada was a country with a small population. The number of people of sufficient means, education and position to give leadership was exceedingly limited and communication between them was, because they could know each other so well, very easy. The ramifications of this society extended into every Canadian city of any size, and a net of relationships existed, based on family ties, school and university friendships, and a community of manners and interests. . . .

"A community of manners and interests:" here Lewis Thomas was touching on his theme of social contiguity—a theme which, as we have seen, runs like a unifying strand throughout so much of his work. He developed this theme at length in his presidential address and used, by way of illustration, the experiences of the privileged ranchers in southern Alberta. This portion of his address is reprinted in the chapter that follows.

Professor Thomas concluded his address by considering the social, political, and economic "pressures" that altered the communications networks which he had described. Such pressures, he said, were "exceedingly subtle." He suggested, however, that the process of change could best be observed by the "close study of quite small communities, rural as well as urban." The validity of his suggestion is evident in his work on communities like Okotoks and Millarville.

SEVEN Associations and Communications

It is difficult to escape an uneasy feeling that we have found no adequate substitute for the informal network for communication that existed before 1939 but which had conclusively broken down even before Canadians intent on crossing the nation took to the airplane and abandoned the club cars of the transcontinental railways, those superb vehicles for the leisurely exchange of trans-Canada gossip.

This system of internal communication depended heavily upon what for convenience may be called social contiguity. This was more than a cluster of attitudes, values or convictions held in common. These had to be supported by opportunities for more or less frequent meetings for the exchange of information, for encounters that were essentially informal and often accidental. It depended upon some degree of education, the possession of some means and, much more important, some leisure. It was a system that worked efficiently in the small Canadian cities of our earlier history. The vast distances of Canada presented obvious difficulties in extending such an establishment to national proportions and in terms of the west these difficulties might well have seemed insurmountable. But even in the prairie west it proved possible to reproduce the same kinds of intimate contact between those in a position to forward development that eased for men like [George M.] Wrong and [Lawrence J.] Burpee the establishment of organizations like the Canadian Historical Association.

We may find the roots of this success in the fur-trading past. Though the officers of the Hudson's Bay Company and the missionaries were not always on the most amicable of terms they could at least communicate with one another. Both groups accepted the idea of an orderly society, though they might differ as to the means by which such a society could be brought into being. They might deplore the impact of settlement upon the fur trade or the threat of civilization to their Indian converts but they did not seriously question the values of the society which John A. Macdonald and his colleagues planned to extend from sea to sea. Though the process of submergence by a tide of newcomers was never wholly palatable the peculiar society that had developed among the English-speaking people of Red River put up no concerted resistance. Their leaders were indeed as committed to the virtues of growth as any twentieth century politician. The French-speaking there were in no stronger position. Their clergy were ambivalent and the handful of new pioneers from Quebec were as much developers as their associates from the Eastern Townships, the Maritimes, Ontario, the United Kingdom or the United States. As far as there was an established order in the prairie west it submitted to the new without more than a grumble and many found comfortable places in it. A Red River inheritance was to prove no handicap in a growing centre like Calgary, where the Anglican bishop, the magistrate, a prominent lawyer and the most enterprising leader of business all had this affiliation. The society planned for the new West was not one which the Indian and the *metis* could easily find congenial or even acceptable but mixed blood in itself did not constitute a barrier to successful adaptation to it. The values of the missionary and the fur trader were sufficiently those of nineteenth century Britain to ease their passage and that of their children into an order that substantially accepted those values.

What Canadian governments, and what may be roughly described as the informed Canadian public, envisaged for the west was as far as it could possibly be from an unplanned and chaotic movement of the frontier of Ontario. The plan was essentially for an orderly development based on a body of information about the territory involved. This was the plan: what happened in its execution was something rather different as the first Riel rising quickly demonstrated. That at least proved not only that potentialities for serious disturbance existed but that these could drastically affect the balance of relations between French and English speaking Canadians. The North West Mounted Police was created to maintain domestic order as a preliminary to settlement. It succeeded in realizing the intentions of its founders by functioning not merely as a police force but as the arm of the federal administration. Its members were not only policemen; they were the prairie west's first civil servants and social workers.

It was apparent that a large movement of population into the prairie west could be supported only by agricultural development but it is doubtful whether the promotion of settlement on a large scale was the primary concern of the post-Confederation administrations. Their attention was directed not so much to the peopling of the region as to the orderly and profitable exploitation of its resources, its mines, forests and grass as much as its arable lands. Thus the quality of the immigrants was even more important than the quantity. The possibilities for grazing cattle, horses and sheep in vast numbers were early recognized and ranching developed in southern Alberta well before the building of the Canadian Pacific, for the needs of the Indian provided a local market. Yet even the kind of development envisaged for the west in the 1870s required improved communications and, in the circumstances of the latter part of the nineteenth century, the preoccupation of the Macdonald governments with railway building is wholly understandable. The expansion and prosperity of ranching, as much as that of mining or lumbering, depended ultimately upon the provision of markets beyond the possible limits of the cattle drive, markets that only a railway could open.

The development of a grazing industry in the west fitted admirably into the central government's conception of the part the region was to play in the national development. Ranching provided a means of utilizing land which was regarded as unsuitable for tillage; it accorded with the less optimistic of those estimates of the west's agricultural potential available to government. The development of ranching on the southwestern prairies of Canada proceeded more or less contemporaneously with the development of ranching in the western United States, but, as a recent study has made clear,[1] ranching north of the 49th parallel was not simply an extension of the American industry; it had a distinct character of its own. Capital came from eastern Canada and the United Kingdom; good connections with the Conservative party were useful in obtaining leases, though there are indications that Macdonald put development before patronage and even his tolerance was strained by the greed of his partisans. Management was, with few exceptions, in the hands of eastern Canadians or Britons. American cowboys appeared but their skills were soon acquired by men of Canadian or British birth. The ranchers and their wives, accustomed as they were to the amenities of life available to the well-off in eastern Canada or Britain, quickly developed a way of living and a system of social contacts that bore little resemblance to the stereotype of the frontier.

The ranchers found no difficulty in cooperating with the Mounted Police, drawn as the latter were from much the same sort of social background. They had a close relationship with Calgary, which soon replaced Fort Macleod as the capital of the ranching kingdom, and this was a social as well as a business relationship, extending into such institutions as the Anglican church, of which many of the ranchers were adherents. The ranchers also maintained a close connection with the federal government while it was in Conservative hands and even managed to retain some degree of influence at Ottawa in the Laurier period, though they found this hard to sustain after their sworn enemy Frank Oliver, the dedicated friend of the farmer-settler, became Minister of the Interior.

Much of western Canada, and not only the ranchers' paradise in the foothills of southwestern Alberta, was well adapted to the raising of beef on the large scale that the rancher's command of capital made possible. As drought and depression made painfully evident, especially during the 1930s, the breaking of much of the prairie sod was a disaster. It was a disaster foreseen by a few agriculturalists and by a few government servants who, like William Pearce, had some perception of the consequences of the climatic cycle which in successive years of drought would erode the fertile soil that in an occasional wet year could provide such a bountiful crop. Pearce espoused the cause of irrigation, viewing it as a valuable support for the grazing which was the most obvious use of much of the land. The ranchers saw him as an ally and gave him substantial evidence of their appreciation of his support. But the pattern of land use visualized by Pearce and the ranchers was one of large holdings linked to and supported by the hard work of producing crops on irrigated land. Such an economy could be the basis of an hierarchically organized society of large land holders and agricultural workers, a kind of society which held no horrors for those who were ready, and indeed eager, to idealize the social order of agricultural England. But while a society so conceived might appeal to Anglican missionaries, Mounted Police officers, well-to-do ranchers and prosperous professional and business men in the towns, and seem quite reasonable to civil servants in Ottawa or Calgary, it was a conception singularly out of touch with the public mind of Canada in the 1890s and the 1900s, obsessed as it was by the conviction that the small family farm was the only sure foundation for the economic, social and political health of individual and nation alike. Nor were the vast majority of potential settlers in the United States or across the Atlantic in the British Isles or on the continent of Europe likely to be attracted to a country which openly espoused ideas that they could only see as hopelessly reactionary. Certainly the politician could not swim against such a tide and he hastened to identify himself with policies that would put a working farmer and his family on every quarter section in the prairie west.

Though this ideal was mercifully left unrealized, settlement flowed into the west in the two decades prior to the war of 1914–18 at a rate that, given the fact that no rational pattern of land use was enforced, was far beyond its absorptive capacity. The complaints of the western farmer about his exploitation by eastern business stem ultimately from the hard fact that he was attempting what was next to impossible even on the best of western farm land and under the most favourable of prairie climatic conditions. None but the most exceptionally fortunate and the most exceptionally provident could make the quarter section family farm a continuing financial success; the unit was too small to begin with and it could not generate sufficient additional capital to permit its enlargement to an economic size by consolidation with adjacent small properties. The farmer's grievances against the grain trade, the elevator companies, the railways, the banks and the federal government that maintained what was to him an iniquitous tariff structure were real grievances, but behind them lay the fact that he had been permitted and indeed encouraged to place himself in an impossible situation.

Western alienation is rooted in this colossal national blunder. The settler himself entered all too willingly into what he saw as the road to new opportunities for himself and his family. The politicians failed to find a means of shaping policies that would have given the pressure for development more creative direction. Those in positions of authority, though like William Pearce often not wholly unaware of the dangers inherent in indiscriminate settlement, failed to make an effective case for restraint either to the politicians or to the public. The network of internal communications, though it worked well enough in such matters as placing the ranchers' case before the government, could not function effectively when it came to dealing with a matter so highly charged emotionally as settlement.

The case of the rancher seems particularly instructive. The use for grazing of enormous quantities of allegedly arable land, thus withholding it from development as intensively cultivated family farms, was in the circumstances of the 1890s something it would have been impossible to justify. Even in southern Alberta, where the ranchers were well established, where they could count on support among influential townspeople and where they were admirably placed to exert influence, the cause of rational land use was hopelessly handicapped. They fought a skilful rearguard action, making astute use of the terrain and withdrawing to the foothills and to areas whose aridity was so obvious that, if they did not repel the homesteader, he was at least quickly discouraged. The cattle industry survived but the network of communications, and especially its social component, was drastically impaired. The cattleman could no longer see himself as an essential part of the force behind Canadian development with an important rôle in the creation and maintenance in the Canadian west of a society consonant with his traditional values. He was instead beleaguered by a new order that stigmatized him, not as a conservative in the best sense of the word, but as the blackest of reactionaries. Deprived of any sense of playing a truly Canadian part it is not surprising that, in one generation or another, he comforted himself with the toys of the ranching stereotype of the United

States frontier or escaped to a gentlemanly retirement on Vancouver Island.

The rancher was an important part of the network of influence that appeared in the west in the 1870s and 1880s. By 1914 he had been isolated from it and his isolation was confirmed in the decades between the wars. His case may represent an extreme but it may also shed light on what happened between east and west after 1895. The word "élite" is one which a Canadian uses with some hesitation, preferring circumlocutions like "those in positions of authority," but there are times when it becomes indispensable. The Canadian élite had adjusted comfortably to the west before 1896, barring such minor unpleasantnesses as the two Riel risings, and had indeed laid out a pattern for its development. The pattern had been followed for more than a generation, proceeding with reasonable decorum if not with particularly spectacular results. The acceleration in the settlement process that began in the mid-nineties produced a new west and indeed, by the stimulus to development it provided, a new Canada. More than a generation of settlement almost everywhere on the prairies had by this time produced in the prairie west an élite of its own, with a sense of its national as well as its regional rôle. It was not only in southern Alberta that the settlers before the mid-nineties were drawn largely from eastern Canada and from the United Kingdom. After 1895 the newcomers to all parts of the West were increasingly from the United States and from continental Europe.

The new west with its new pattern of close settlement was thus in its ethnic and social mix not entirely to the taste of the earlier generation and certainly not to that of the established élite. The old guard was in no way discouraged by the new situation. They plunged enthusiastically into the exploitation of the opportunities it offered even while resenting the pressures exerted by the massive presence of newcomers with different values. Many of them had by the beginning of the new century built up a substantial stake in the west and the rising property values in what was essentially a gigantic real estate boom gave them the capital for new ventures. My suggestions here are tentative, based on very limited investigation, but my impression is that at least in Alberta they used the growing towns and cities as a base for their operations. Thus as the countryside became increasingly the preserve of

American and European settlers, the urban centres remained much more under the dominance of elements with strongly British and eastern Canadian affiliations, especially as the towns and cities tended to attract many of the new arrivals from eastern Canada and the United Kingdom. The old élite was thus, if my conclusions are correct, able to make a new stand for old values, at once maintaining contact with eastern Canada and the United Kingdom but at the cost of some alienation from their own hinterland.

An element in the established national system of internal communication was thus preserved but it was no longer an element that could speak with authority for its region as an entity. Its weight in the formation of opinion was thus seriously attenuated. It could present a case but it could not deliver the votes. At the same time, dependent on a hinterland that did not share its attitudes, it was under some pressure to modify its position in a way that would compromise such authority as remained to it in speaking to the élites of other regions. It would be easy in this connection to overlook the effect of the substantial number of immigrants who came to the prairie west from the United Kingdom in the two decades preceding 1914. Though many of them came to farm, they were highly susceptible to the allurements of life both in the western cities and in the smaller towns. Though the effect of their drift in the urban direction was to reinforce the predominance there of English-speaking, Protestant and British oriented elements, their recent departure from the British Isles gave a particular flavour to their contribution. Irritating though the newcomers from the British Isles might be they moved easily into positions of influence, major as well as minor, free as they were from the handicaps of alien language or citizenship. With no previous Canadian experience they might quickly become westerners but they were less likely to accept the view of Canadian nationhood that was developing in central Canada. From their point of view it was better to be a second-class Englishman than a third-rate American.

In spite of the hardships involved in indiscriminate and uncontrolled settlement, the prairie west was thoroughly convinced of the reality of its own myth as a land of boundless opportunity. The three provinces experienced a remarkable development. They elaborated an institutional framework in terms of public and private services comparable with that which older societies had taken generations to build. The war of 1914–18 shook their immature society to its foundations and much of the energy of the west in the 1920s was spent in repairing a structure which, complex and expensive though it was, had been too rapidly improvised to be entirely sound. The prairie west somehow continued to see itself as a land of opportunity but that illusion was to die in the depression. The ability of what remained of its élite to speak for the prairie west was still further impaired and politically it had become an irrelevance. It might still register and implement decisions made in central Canada, but it had no weight to put behind its desire to be heard in the making of those decisions. When war broke out again in 1939 the prairie west was almost completely disenchanted not only about its own future but also about any prospect of rescue by the central region from the despair into which it had fallen.

Notes

[1.] David H. Breen, 'The Canadian West and the Ranching Frontier, 1875–1922." Ph.D. thesis, University of Alberta, 1972.

EIGHT PRIVILEGED SETTLERS

In his introduction to the new edition of A. S. Morton's *History of the Canadian West,* Professor Thomas said of Morton: "[He] was no Turnerian .... His sharpest insights ... indicate an attitude of mind remote from that of the apostle of the frontier."[1] The same might be said of L. G. Thomas. He was never very comfortable with Frederick Jackson Turner's "Frontier thesis," which depicted the frontier as the great social leveller and the nursemaid of democracy. Nor did he subscribe to the environmentalists' school, which held that physical environment was primarily responsible for a region's historical development. Both theories were based on traditions emanating from the American—rather than the British North American—frontier; both involved stereotypes which inevitably consigned individuals and events into artificial categories. "The acceptance of stereotypes," he cautioned in this regard, "impoverishes our perception, as surely as a recognition and appreciation of differences enriches it."

In the essay that follows, Professor Thomas deals with some of the pioneers who did not fit into the Turnerian scenario—the privileged settlers who constituted Alberta's "influential minority." Elaborating upon his earlier theme of social contiguity, the author discusses the close relationships that existed between genteel settlers of diverse backgrounds. A good example of this kind of interaction is provided by the Maurice Destrubé family, who settled in the Rife district, north-east of Edmonton, in the early 1900s. With strong family ties to France as well as England, the Destrubés subscribed to many of the social values associated with the influential British ranchers of southern Alberta.

"Privileged Settlers" originally appeared as the introduction to *The Maurice Destrubé Story,* published in 1981 by the Historical Society of Alberta.[2] This essay complements the author's introductory essay to the journals of Marcel Durieux, another French-speaking, Roman Catholic pioneer who moved easily among the province's predominantly English-speaking, Protestant elite.[3] Both Destrubé and Durieux were a part of what Professor Thomas calls "a community of manners" which extended "across religious and linguistic barriers" in the Canadian prairie west.

Notes

1. A. S. Morton, *History of the Canadian West to 1870–71,* 2nd ed. (Toronto: University of Toronto Press, 1973), p. xxvii.
2. James E. Hendrickson, ed., *Pioneering in Alberta: Maurice Destrubé's Story* (Calgary: Historical Society of Alberta/Alberta Records Publication Board, 1981), pp. ix–xxii.
3. See Roger Motut and Maurice Legris, eds., *Ordinary Heroes. The Journal of a French Pioneer in Alberta by Marcel Durieux.* Introduction by L. G. Thomas (Edmonton: The University of Alberta Press, 1980).

EIGHT Privileged Settlers

In the public mind the settlement of the Canadian prairie west is firmly linked to the image of the homesteader. He may be the son of an impoverished backwoods farmer from the central or eastern provinces, he may be a fugitive from the industrial slums of the United Kingdom or from the high land prices of the established farming areas of the United States, he may be an oppressed peasant from eastern Europe. His only resources are willing hands and a strong back and perhaps, especially if he comes from eastern Europe, a working wife and plenty of children. He is essentially a man without privilege, even what in educational circles might be called a "disadvantaged" person. His only aspiration is to establish himself on the land and to lead on his farm of one hundred and sixty acres the good and wholesome rural life that has been part of the mythology of the western European tradition since the Greeks and the Romans, not to mention the Hebrews.

One does not need a very high level of intellectual sophistication to recognize this image as a stereotype. If one is a Canadian one will quickly perceive it to be a stereotype that owes much to the experience of our neighbours in the United States and the way they have perceived their experience. The student of Canadian history will immediately link it to the view of the North American experience developed by Frederick Jackson Turner and his followers and critics in the frontier school. Though Turnerian theory

The Gate Ranch, Kew, Alberta, painted, ca. 1913, by Roberto Basilici, an Italian artist, Elsa Hirth's third husband. Used with the kind permission of the late Elisabet von Rummel. The photograph of the oil painting was taken by Aileen Harmon, a long-time resident of Banff, Alberta.

never fully naturalized itself in Canada, Turner's work had some influence on Canadian historiography. Certainly a strong vein of environmentalism runs through much of the writing on Canadian history, though not necessarily expressed in terms of the Turnerian hypothesis.

The essence of the environmentalist view of history seems to me to be that, no matter what human ingredients you put into the environmental pudding bowl, they will emerge, given the passage of generations, homogenized into a particular type. May I quote Turner?

> The result is that to the frontier the American intellect owes its striking characteristics. That coarseness and strength combined with acuteness and inquisitiveness, that practical, inventive turn of mind, quick to find expedients; that masterful grasp of material things, lacking in the artistic but powerful to effect great ends; that restless, nervous energy; that dominant indivi-

dualism ... that buoyancy and exuberance which comes with freedom.... [1]

No reputable Canadian scholar, I believe, has gone as far as this in denominating the characteristics of the Canadian intellect. Nevertheless a pervading environmentalism has made us perhaps too casual in our consideration of the human materials in our concentration upon the collective response to the Canadian situation. Thus stereotypes creep into our thinking and insufficient allowance is made for the infinite variety of the human condition. To generalize is often to oversimplify, and this is a step towards homogenization, something which it is the essence of Canadianism to resist. The acceptance of stereotypes impoverishes our perception as surely as a recognition and appreciation of difference enriches it.

Like most stereotypes that of the Canadian prairie homesteader has in it elements of reality. Indeed it is possible that the majority, perhaps a substantial majority, of the settlers fit into it. This is, however, by no means established, even though it is often taken for granted, and the trend of research suggests that other elements, numerically less impressive, had a powerful effect on the shaping of western society.

The process of settlement in the four western provinces was virtually complete by 1921. This does not mean, of course, that the movement of people into the west ceased after that date, or that the redistribution of the western population, so marked a feature of the last quarter century, was not a continuous process. What it does mean is that after 1921 no movement of people from outside Canada into the region had a radical effect upon the composition and distribution of its population. Movement within the area did of course radically affect the nature of western society. Groups like the displaced persons of central and eastern Europe who arrived after 1945 had an important effect on a city like Edmonton but they acted as modifiers, not as determinants. It is perhaps premature to suggest that this group, despite the misery of the situation from which they came, could be described as "privileged" settlers.

Who should be classified as a "privileged" settler? Anyone, I suggest, who had access to financial resources beyond the bare minimum necessary to bring him to his destination. A small capi-

Elisabet Hirth, 1879-1986, m. (1) Freiherr Gustav von Rummel-Waldau auf und zu Pifflass (2) Dr. Fritz Weinmann (3) Roberto Basilici, who in 1911 accompanied her to Canada with her three daughters by her first marriage, Elisabet, Johanna and Eugénie. Glenbow Archives NA-3917-11.

tal, or even the prospect of acquiring capital, by gift or by inheritance, was a potential advantage, and could greatly ease the process of establishment on raw land and enhance the prospect of success in remaining there. It could also open the way to successful entry into many of the opportunities, professional and commercial, in a pioneer society that addressed itself from the first to the speediest possible provision of the amenities of civilization.

Another criterion of privilege is a superior level of education, whether in the sense of liberal education or of professional training. This brings into the ranks of the privileged all the members of the professions, law, medicine, the officers of the armed services and the police, the civil servants, often the journalist and the teacher, and the clergy of the churches of denominations emphasizing educational qualifications for admission to their orders.

A third criterion was inherited social position, closely linked to education and money, both important determinants of status in the older societies from which the settlers came. No matter how egalitarian the professions of the frontier society of the prairie west might be, the genteel reached out to the genteel, even across religious and linguistic barriers, seeking in a community of manners the same human warmth, comfort and support that the ethnic groups are said to have found in block settlement.

Privilege in terms of material resources, education and position has not always been viewed as an asset. The highly negative image of the remittance man, who was generally supposed to possess all three, suggests that these were an almost fatal handicap to a successful and permanent economic and social adaptation. There is some evidence, however, that the popular judgment of the remittance man has become harsher and less shaded as the lapse of time permits its assimilation to a stereotype developed in the United States mythology of the frontier. The acceptance of privilege as an asset, though it was certainly seen in this way by the instigators of much early propaganda addressed to potential settlers, ran counter to the much publicized egalitarianism of the frontier. Possibly it is the materialism of the present western society that leads, in some of the numerous local histories now appearing, to claims to ancestral splendours that it would be difficult to support. Yet even that tutelary deity of the prairie west, Louis Riel, laid claim to descent from the Kings of France. At the same time many of these local histories reflect a disposition to homogenize the image of the pioneer into conformity with the stereotype of the frontiersman to which I have already referred.

Whatever the west today has come to think of privilege as an asset to the settler, the privileged settler of the 19th and early 20th centuries fitted nicely into the plans of those who, in central Canada, were designing a new society in the newly acquired hinterland. John A. Macdonald and his contemporaries in the élite of Central Canada were thinking in terms of a colony, duly subordinated to the federal government, whose resources would fuel the expansion of Canada into its magnificent but vulnerable heritage as a new nation state. These resources were viewed as primarily agricultural but the grazing lands, the minerals and the forests were by no means overlooked. The model of the new society was Ontario, though there were gestures towards Quebec in the constitution finally granted Manitoba and rather more substantial understandings with the business community of Montreal and the wealthy agricultural interests of the Eastern Townships. If the model was Ontario, the ideal owed something to rural England. Though the ordered society of rural England was moving, if not into obsolescence, at least into a time of troubles, dreams of its splendours still exerted a compelling fascination on the élite of Canada, and on those who aspired to that status.

At the same time a horrible example of what not to do in an empty hinterland existed near at hand. The expansion of European settlement into the western United States had been accompanied by disorder and tumult that was everything that adherents of the British tradition most deplored. American frontier violence might easily spill over the forty-ninth parallel into the vacuum to the north, and place an insupportable and fatal burden on the new Canadian polity. That vacuum must therefore be filled, and filled as quickly as possible, by a peaceful and orderly society, basically agricultural but at the same time sufficiently controlled from the centre to permit a rational and profitable development of its resources by Canadian enterprise, if necessary with capital assistance from outside, preferably from Britain. In critical areas, like the essential trans-continental railway, American influence should be rigorously excluded.

In such a colony the settler with capital or access to it, with some degree of education or with some professional skill, could play a vitally important part. Even if he had nothing more than inherited social position, this should guarantee an attachment to the values that buttressed a hierarchical structure. Aspirations to the way of life that was seen as characterizing the English countryside, at a time when to establish oneself in that order in England itself was crushingly expensive, could be a compelling motive for emigration. The well publicized opportunities of the colonies, and the assurance that life there would not involve deracination but rather a contribution to the salutary Britannicization of the new worlds of Canada, New Zealand and Australia, combined to influence young men and women, not only from the ranks of the privileged in the United Kingdom but also from the élite of Canada's older components. Emigration to the colonies, or a movement westward, could be not merely a potentially profitable investment but conjointly a contribution to the realization of the imperial destiny.

A paper at the Edmonton meeting of the Canadian Historical Association in 1975 drew attention to the importance of the frontier literature circulating in the United Kingdom in the late 19th and early 20th centuries and directed particularly at the children's market, for example, *The Boy's Own Paper*.[2] These, aimed at a largely middle class readership, portrayed an idealized version not only of middle class life in the British Isles but also of life in the colonies, where middle class British values could be reinforced and developed in a land of opportunity. Periodicals and books like this circulated in the colonies as well as in the metropolis and were parentally acceptable reading for children in the homes of settlers from both the eastern provinces and the United Kingdom. As their readers were largely the children of those who could be classified as privileged settlers, the congruity of their propaganda thrust with the cultural objectives of the central Canadian colonizer is a factor in the shaping of western society worth consideration.

Viewed from central Canada in 1870 the great resource of the prairie west was its agricultural land and the great challenge to government was the encouragement of the exploitation and settlement of that land. Land policies as they were developed under the aegis of Ottawa were fully cognizant of the part that might be played by the privileged settler. Though the small family farm and the quarter section homestead were accepted as the basic unit, provisions were made for the acquisition of larger holdings that envisioned the establishment of an order of gentleman farmers in Manitoba. This had some foundation in Red River tradition, where retired officers of the fur trade used their substantial resources to acquire larger than average holdings, notably in the fashionable parish of St. Andrew's in the vicinity of Lower Fort Garry. Further west the best known gesture towards the tradition of the shires was the English settlement of Cannington Manor, with its grand houses, well appointed church and steeple chase course. At Indian Head Lord Brassey collaborated with Bishop Burn to establish, in a somewhat more promising environment,

W. H. King's Galloway Ranch at Millarville, 1915. King was the only child of Chief Trader William Cornwallis King. Glenbow Archives NA-2333-3.

something recalling the traditional cooperation between rector and squire. It was, however, even further west, in southern Alberta, that the privileged settler found his most congenial and fruitful opportunity. There, where the environment was ideal for the cattle rancher who had already done very well on the interior plains of the United States, grazing leases were made available to those who had influence to secure them and capital to stock them. These leases could be princely in extent, they were reserved to British subjects with the explicit intention of excluding American stockmen, and they offered some degree of protection from the plough and fence of the intending homesteader, who had already pushed the rancher off much of the choicest range land further south.

The cattle companies of southern Alberta enjoyed their golden age in the 1880s and the 1890s. Their capital came from the United Kingdom and from the eastern provinces, where the interest of Tory partisans in western possibilities for investment shocked even John A. Macdonald. A pioneer in the industry, and a leading figure in what a recent writer[3] has aptly dubbed "The Cattle Compact," was Senator M. H. Cochrane, an experienced stock-raiser from the Eastern Townships of Quebec, the region that also contributed to Alberta the Galt family, and their entrepreneurial adventures in mining, railway building and irrigation. The Galt interest centered on Lethbridge, only a few miles west of Fort Macleod. The early headquarters of the Mounted Police,

Macleod was the first focal point of the ranching interest. It soon lost its predominance to Calgary, but not before it had, from retired members of the force, provided the cattle interest with some of its leading figures.

Though the élites of most eastern Canadian centres—Halifax and St. John did not ignore the opportunity—were represented in the ranching compact, the leading entrepreneurs did not often follow their capital as settlers, though they did make stately progresses through their domains, occasionally leaving rather mixed feelings in the minds of the humbler elements with whom they came in contact. A classic account of such a progress is that of Alexander Staveley-Hill, *From Home to Home,* which provoked a sharp rejoinder from Staveley-Hill's sometime manager at the Oxley Ranch, John Craig, the crusty Scot who was the author of *Ranching with Lords and Commons.*

Though the major entrepreneurs did not often settle in the west they drew their managerial staffs from their own group, and to a considerable degree, their work force. For technical expertise, especially in the earliest years, there was some dependence on the American industry, and the most conspicuous folk-hero of southern Alberta is John Ware, the black cowboy. But young men attracted to the west by the prospect of an outdoor life soon learned the techniques of an industry where horsemanship was an indispensable qualification. Many of them were able, often with financial assistance from their families, to establish themselves as ranchers, generally on quite a small scale. Once established their way of life assimilated itself to that of the larger ranches, modelled on that of the worlds from which they came, or to which they aspired. To them and to their wives it seemed a simple, even an austere life, but judged by traditional frontier patterns of living it had elements in it of comfort, sophistication and refinement. It was not a way of life that could be maintained without a struggle, and, where its manifestations survive in Alberta mythology, it is usually seen as an aspect of the indomitable pioneer's battle against a hostile environment. Earl Pomeroy long ago warned the student of the frontier against the danger of underestimating the significance of the cultural baggage brought by the pioneer. For many of the southern Alberta settlers of the ranchers' golden age it was privilege that packed their bags.

Though the cattle compact's free enjoyment of the open range was often challenged, and their virtual monopoly was to be broken by the flood of settlers that was flowing westward by the turn of the century, the ranching interest remained a powerful force, able to keep open the channels that gave it access to those who determined federal and provincial policy. Squatters, acting in the tradition of the American frontier, did have the temerity to attempt to break the hold of the cattle companies on their leases. They received little sympathy from government, and the Mounted Police, the effective arm of government in southern Alberta, took action against them. Admittedly the police sometimes expressed their distaste, on humanitarian grounds, for such action, but they were not disposed to question it in principle.

The attitude of the smaller stockman has been less fully explored. There is little evidence of active hostility to the companies. In the rather full records of one small community of small stockmen, who called themselves ranchers and demonstrably assimilated themselves to the general tradition of the larger ranchers, there is no evidence of hostility to the company whose huge lease was immediately contiguous to their holdings and which blocked their expansion southward. Instead there is a great deal of evidence of an easy and intimate relationship. It is true that this company was the largest of the few that raised horses rather than cattle, and much of the contact involved a common devotion to the cult of the horse, but company employees also subscribed to the support of the stockmen's church. In the absence of evidence to the contrary, it seems reasonable to suggest that the presence of the privileged settler, and the identity of his cultural climate with that of the cattle compact, tended to damp down any hostility between the large operators and the smaller stockmen.

Though southern Alberta appears to offer a peculiarly fruitful field for the exploration of the role of the privileged settler in the rural areas of the prairie west, evidence exists in the published literature as well as in the available primary sources that he played a more influential part than most of the popular literature, especially contemporary popular literature, would suggest. Indeed much of the older scholarly literature also reflects what seems to me a monolithic view of the prairie settler. Much of what we depend upon for our view of the history of the west is the work, not of historians, but of social scientists. Yet even an historian of the quality of Arthur Silver Morton discounts the working of privilege in this sense in his pioneer *History of Prairie Settlement* as much as he takes it for granted in his *History of the Canadian West to 1870–71*. Exception must be made of the authors of two distinguished western provincial histories, Margaret Ormsby and W. L. Morton. In their histories of British Columbia and Manitoba, the operations of privilege are given due weight and the privileged settler is given his place, though perhaps more explicitly in Dr. Ormsby's work. But for the student of the west in general, the privileged settler is a shadowy, even a dimly disreputable, figure. The present trend of research, happily, appears likely to give him, whatever his deserts, a much clearer outline.

The increasing scholarly interest in Canadian social, urban and business history is likely to clarify considerably our picture of western settlement and to throw a particularly clear light on the privileged settler's relationship with the western urban centre. A study of the smaller, as well as the larger, centres should be rewarding. Though I can claim no breadth or depth of research in this area my impression is that it was in the towns that the privileged settler consolidated his influence. For the professionally trained, the doctor, the lawyer, the clergyman, the town had an obvious attraction and, with the business man, and sometimes the teacher and journalist, these constituted a natural élite. Bankers and senior railway employees, like teachers and clergymen, were apt to be transient and their influence, though substantial, was qualified by a lack of permanent commitment. They might be pioneers of the region but they were not usually "settlers" in the full sense in the smaller centres. They sometimes were in cities like Calgary and Edmonton, where promotion did not necessarily mean movement. Thus a smaller town could have no equivalent of William Pearce, who came to Calgary as a senior civil servant, remained in that capacity long enough to be denounced as Czar of the West, then entered the employ of the Canadian Pacific and ended his days as the recognized patriarch of Calgary's development.

A small town could, however, not only attract a nexus of privileged settlers but, by reason of the amenities it offered, it could also construct a network of relationships with privileged settlers in its rural hinterland. The latter were more likely to be able to afford such amenities and, what was perhaps more significant, were more likely, in the disposal of such resources as they had, to attach a higher value to amenities which were within their tradition. Their choices, though not always realistic in terms of economic survival, did establish and maintain a network of relationships, fundamentally social and cultural but also of economic and political significance. There also appears to have been, by the turn of the century, a movement into the towns of those who had, in the years of relative stagnation in the 1880s and the 1890s, sufficiently husbanded or consolidated their agricultural holdings to take advantage of the rising price of agricultural land during the boom years prior to the War of 1914–18. Not all of these, of course, were drawn from the ranks of what I have called "privileged" settlers. They were, however, often already assimilated to the local élites and provided a useful reinforcement at a time when settlement was proceeding at an accelerated rate throughout the west. If this is indeed the case, the towns and cities were in a position to be the bastions from which the privileged settler defended his values and his conception of what the western society should be.

He had good reason to look to his defences for by the turn of the century the national view of the west's rôle had changed, at least in its emphasis. The west was seen, not simply as a colonial hinterland but as the section whose rich resources and rapidly growing population would fuel the movement of Canada into the twentieth century. The west began to perceive itself as the dynamic force of confederation, rushing towards the fulfilment of the long deferred promise of prosperity. In this boom, not to say "booster," spirit the privileged settler participated and indeed, as I have already tried to indicate, hastened to take advantage of the new opportunities the unparalleled expansion offered. Though he was often deeply involved both in speculation and in more reasoned projects for development, he was not, in the public eye, a symbol of the new mood. The boom seemed to be built on the settlement of the lands that were opened by the new railways, the Canadian Northern, the Grand Trunk Pacific and, less realistically, the multitude of others in which governments, national, provincial and municipal, hastened to involve themselves with every encouragement from the Canadian public. To occupy the lands required settlers, and the homesteader replaced the frontiersman pioneer as the symbolic figure of the new west. In the optimistic mood of the period he would not be a pioneer for long; the fertile soil and beneficent climate of the prairies would quickly transform him into a prosperous yeoman farmer, the durable foundation upon which a healthy Canadian society would rest. The populist tradition within the dominant Liberal party at once embraced and propagated this attractive myth. Western ministers like Clifford Sifton and Frank Oliver had no hesitation, unlike some of their Conservative predecessors, in embracing the common man. The farmers of this period, especially in southern Saskatchewan, began to organize for action against those they saw as their oppressors, especially the Winnipeg grain trade. But in the boom years they were on the whole content to work through the Liberal party. They made a convert of Laurier but not of central Canada and the election of 1911 was deeply disillusioning. As the recession deepened and the war approached the image of the homesteader as the archetypal prairie man remained, but the bloom was off and he looked less and less the prosperous yeoman and more and more the oppressed helot.

Though the prevailing temper of the west grew increasingly egalitarian, the privileged settler maintained his position. The ranchers of southern Alberta, for example, fell back before the plough to the areas that were least promising for wheat, to the foothills with their late and early frosts, to the arid lands of the southeast of the new province and to the remote interior valleys of British Columbia. They were nevertheless sufficiently influential to convince successive governments that some protection for their industry was in the public interest. The ranchers bided their time until natural and economic forces undid the work of the booster and they could reoccupy the lands from which the unhappy homesteader had retreated, the tragic victim of the triumph of an unthinking optimism over any rational approach to land use. Not all the cattlemen who survived were drawn from the ranks of the privileged but, of four of those recognized as particularly influential, A. E. Cross and William Roper Hull could certainly be so characterized, though Patrick Burns and George Lane were proudly self-made men.

The War of 1914–18 damaged the privileged settler much more

than the boom and recession of the preceding decade. It had, particularly perhaps in Alberta, the last province to be engulfed by the tide of settlement, a traumatic effect on the western institutional structure which the privileged settler had done much to create and which encapsulated the values to which he subscribed. It would be wrong to generalize from the experience of the one rural community on which I have the most information but its experience is at least suggestive. Its institutional structure relatively well in place by 1900, and largely the work of its high proportion of privileged settlers, its collective life was at its liveliest in the years between 1900 and 1914, reinforced by the arrival of a number of immigrants of the same character. Partly because of the predominance of younger men, and partly because of the climate generated by the community's values, or its prejudices, the number of enlistments, like the number of casualties, was high. During the 1920s, though the area shared in the modest prosperity of the latter part of the decade, its social and institutional life did not recover until, in curious contradiction to current representations of the depression years, the 1930s.

No examination of the role of the privileged settler should be confined to the English-speaking, or indeed to the charter groups. The privileged French-speaking settler was often not a French-Canadian. The best known in Alberta are the military settlers at Trochu, a cosmopolitan group but predominantly French. Their efforts to establish a community that would be economically as well as socially viable were frustrated by the outbreak of war. They are well documented but only a promising beginning has been made on a definitive scholarly examination. The Trochu settlers had links with French settlers elsewhere. A manuscript memoir written by another Frenchman reveals not only these links but also relationships with the French-Canadian community at Edmonton, which had moved into a position of leadership among their compatriots in central and northern Alberta. The link in this case was a leading Edmonton physician, later appointed to the Senate. In the maintenance of associations within this group the clergy were particularly important, for the European French were so scattered through Alberta that their spiritual guides were forced into what appears to have been virtually an itinerant ministry. The German ethnic group is of course a substantial one and examples of "the privileged settler" certainly exist. I have not come across any notice of a peculiar rôle played by these in relation to their fellow nationals. The one family at which I have been able to look closely certainly had a strong influence on their predominantly English speaking neighbours but their interest seems to lie in that relationship rather than that with their co-nationals. They provide an excellent example of the ease with which the educated, socially well placed and relatively affluent could establish themselves without a marked impairment of their cultural singularity. Other ethnic groups are receiving attention in an Alberta that is increasingly comfortable with multi-culturalism. There are at least signs that, if analysis becomes more sophisticated, there will be ample material for observation of the privileged settler.

The influence of the privileged settler in the prairie west was supported by his ability to relate to the dominant minority which established itself in positions of power and influence under the aegis of the central government, and which reflected the values of the dominant elements in central Canada. He could readily, as it were, "plug in" to the network of communications that connected the hinterland, by infinite gradations of social contiguity and material interest, to the metropolis. The members of the dominant minority saw themselves, not as colonials, but as colonizers. In that relationship there was no sense of inferiority, no insupportable grievances. The federal and the regional interest were mutually supportive, indeed identical. In the years of rapid expansion early in this century the sense of a shared and interdependent dynamism carried the western population, and not only the western élite, into a glowing acceptance of the national structure. Though time and the changing generations attenuated the personal relationships that gave cohesiveness to the Canadian beneficiaries of privilege, it must be remembered that definitive settlement of the west took place in an era of rapid and easy communication, of which the relatively well-off took full advantage. It could, I think, be argued that the lounge cars of Canadian transcontinental trails at once lubricated and cemented Canadian unity, and that their replacement by the jet has been a national deprivation. Even if personal links grew weaker the factor of interest remained, for many of the privileged westerners depended upon the prosperity of the national structure for economic survival.

In the harsher years after 1914 those in the west who benefitted from their place in the national structure came to be perceived by many less privileged westerners as the pawns of interests alien and hostile to the region. Thus Social Credit in its extremist days denounced eminent members of the Alberta élite as "bankers' toadies." Such asperities would be out of place in the prosperous Alberta of today, or indeed anywhere in a region that is conspicuously not the worst off in the country as a whole. Whether it is the result of an egalitarian dislike of the appearance of privilege or the result of a dislike of difference in a society that embraces homogenization as a positive good, the portrayal of the privileged settler in the popular version of western Canadian history current today seems singularly at variance with much of the available evidence, and indeed with the trend of scholarly research as far as it has gone. Whatever our assessment of his contribution may ultimately be, a more judicious appreciation of the part the privileged settler played is a necessary preliminary.

Notes

*Supplementary notes indicated by square brackets [].

1. Frederick Jackson Turner, *The Frontier in American History* (New York, 1920), p. 37.
[2.] Patrick A. Dunae, "The Popularisation of the Canadian West Among British Youth," subsequently published as " 'Making Good:' The Canadian West in British Boys' Literature, 1890–1914," *Prairie Forum*, 4 (1979): 165–181.
[3.] David H. Breen, *The Canadian Prairie West and the Ranching Frontier, 1874–1924* (Toronto: University of Toronto Press, 1983), pp. 61–69.

NINE HISTORY AND FICTION

It is generally assumed by students of Canadian literature that fiction reflects reality; or, in the case of regional literature, that the physical environment of the area, in conjunction with the experiences and traditions of the local populace, will inspire writing which in some way conveys regional realities. The assumption rests on the belief that those who live in an area, or who write about it, understand its history and character. At a conference on Western Canadian literature held in 1978, however, Lewis G. Thomas startled his audience by posing the question: "Do the discomforts of living in a society that suffers from a widespread delusion about its nature affect the way in which that society's denizens write about its experience?" He went on to suggest that the image of the Canadian West in popular fiction often bore little semblance to historical realities: in too many cases, he said, the images were based on the experiences and traditions of the United States.

In his address—part of which is reprinted in the chapter that follows—he emphasized the necessity of distinguishing between the "realities of Western [Canadian] society in the past and the way in which that past has come to be perceived." Fundamental to the process was an appreciation of the fact that the Canadian prairie west was not a lawless, unregulated frontier during the settlement phase. On the contrary, from the 1870s until the late 1920s, the West was intended to serve the interests of the more developed parts of the Dominion. It was to be a peaceful, orderly, subordinate region—a "colonial society"—in relation to central Canada.[1] Hence the encouragement given by the federal government to the wealthy ranchers and other privileged settlers from the United Kingdom during the period. "Such settlers, when they came from relatively privileged backgrounds in relatively structured societies, could be expected to support precisely the kind of society the central Canadian elite envisaged for the West." These settlers, Professor Thomas continued, did not often conform to the stereotypes of popular fiction; unquestionably, though, they played a considerable part in forming the character of Western Canadian society—a point which many popular writers of prairie history are apt to neglect.

Note

1. Ottawa's intentions and policies in the West are discussed at length in L. G. Thomas's introductory essay to *The Prairie West to 1905: A Canadian Sourcebook* [L. G. Thomas, ed.] (Toronto: Oxford University Press, 1975).

NINE History and Fiction

THE CANADIAN west's perception of itself today is much encumbered by stereotypes, not all of them of native origin, but most of them built upon some aspect of western experience. The acceptance of these stereotypes dims the realities of the Canadian past, blurs the outlines as much of Canadian as of western identities, and, in the headlong rush of the post-industrial world towards homogenization, diminishes us at once individually and collectively.

The critical years of western settlement seem to me to be the half century that lies between 1870 and 1920, the years between the Canadian takeover of western British North America and the end of the Great War of 1914–18. These were the years in which the political, institutional and economic structures of the prairie west were established and the relationship of the region to the central government was firmly maintained. That relationship was essentially that of a colony to its metropolis. The role of the prairie west was to serve as the means by which Canada was to enter into the transcontinental heritage so fortunately preserved by the continuing British presence in northern North America after the War of American Independence. Unless this task of creative expansion was accomplished quickly and effectively, the vacuum to the west would be filled by the aggressive and dynamic republic to the south and Canada's national dream would be ended forever.

The achievements of Canada in the west, in what was not much more than two generations, were substantial. The resistance of Riel and his Metis was overcome. Lieutenant-Governor Archibald made a promising beginning in the reconciliation of the other Europeanized inhabitants of the Red River colony to the new regime. The Mounted Police carried law and order to the foothills of the Rockies, and, as the chief arm of the Canadian government, performed services to the emerging territorial community far beyond the normal demands of police duties. The Indians were assigned to reserves and the task of assimilating them to a settled society was left, one might almost say abandoned, to the missionaries. Governmental institutions were established for Manitoba and the Territories, and in 1905 Manitoba's second class provincial status was extended to Saskatchewan and Alberta. By 1885 a Canadian transcontinental railway system was in operation. Two more transcontinental systems emerged in the decade preceding the outbreak of war in 1914 and a network of branch lines spread across and beyond the populated areas of the prairies.

Settlement proceeded as the federal government elaborated this impressive infrastructure. Government also provided a land survey and a system for the allocation of land derived largely from the free homestead system of the United States but with some significant departures based on central Canadian and British imperial experience. For a generation the pace of settlement was painfully and disappointingly slow. The more promising farm lands of southern Manitoba filled up and, in the territory of Assiniboia to the west, farm settlement spread out from the Canadian Pacific's main line. In southern Alberta the ranching companies enjoyed their golden age on their bountiful leases but the population of the most westerly of the territories remained thin even in the most agriculturally favourable areas. Though Winnipeg began to see itself as at once the gateway and the metropolis of the west, Regina and Calgary were little more than the bases from which the federal government and the Canadian Pacific, institutions that were virtually indistinguishable, could assert their control over central Canada's hinterland.

Somewhere about the middle of the nineties of the last century the pace of settlement accelerated. Settlers began to pour in not only from central and eastern Canada and the United Kingdom but also from the United States and central and eastern Europe.

The flood of immigrants, the provision of additional railway facilities and the end of the world depression of the latter part of the nineteenth century combined to produce for the prairie west not merely the promise of prosperity but an actual boom. The west, British Columbia as much as the prairies, could perceive itself, not as a neglected hinterland, but as the region that provided the dynamic base of a dynamic Canada, a Canada that, after a century of disappointments, could look forward to a century of expansion and progress comparable to that enjoyed by the United States. Those who had established themselves in favourable positions in the western polity could perceive themselves, not as a lonely and isolated garrison, but as the spear-head or the cutting edge of Canada's progress towards the final realization of her national dream.

The boom collapsed into recession in 1913 and the west went into the war years in a chastened, though still optimistic mood. The recovery of agricultural prices during the war was not sustained into the 1920s and the prairie west went into the long winter of discontent that was to last until the war of 1939–45 ushered in the period of comparative affluence that only in recent years has seemed to be more fragile than many Canadians believed. Three decades of relative prosperity have not wiped out the memories of the three decades of war and depression that followed the half century in which the process of prairie settlement was defined.

What was the nature of prairie society in this critical period of western settlement? In the first place it was a colonial society, living in a colonial polity, living with a colonial economy. Important decisions were made elsewhere. They were made by people who saw the development of the prairie west as a creative exercise of Canadian power in an empty hinterland, at its best in the interest of the people of Canada as a whole, at its worst in the interest of the business community of central Canada. Only secondarily, and generally very much secondarily, were the immediate interests of the people of the west given any recognition in major matters of national policy. It is, of course, only fair to say that generally government held that the decisions taken would be in the best long range interests of the western settler, an assertion which must have had a hollow ring for many of the members of the House of

Commons from the maritime provinces. The fact that Canada was a democracy, and that the central government was concerned to provide democratic and representative local governments in the west, was of little consequence. The weight of population was always with Ontario and Quebec and the sphere of local government was limited, and especially limited in the prairie region while control of lands and resources remained at the centre.

Even those in the prairie west who occupied places of influence were in a subordinate position. Political parties, the federal civil service and the Mounted Police, the railways, to a large extent the churches, the banks, the administration of justice, even businesses, were in a dependent relationship to the metropolis. Though influential westerners might and did, as individuals, form part of the network that pervaded the Canadian structure and made it work, and though they might be able to exert some influence on policy through their manifold associations, the decisions that they implemented were not in the last analysis theirs, or those that might have enjoyed the support of the majority of their fellow westerners. The decisions made in Ottawa at the instance of Montreal and Toronto were likely to be acceptable to them, but if they were not they had no option to giving them force. They could see themselves as colonizers, carrying the national dream to the hinterland, but as colonizers they served, and were expected to serve, the purposes of the centre. They were part of the national establishment, but their role was that of creative agents in the new society that establishment was bringing into being in the west. They were not expected to be policy makers.

That new society was to be formed in a mould acceptable to the elite of the central provinces. It found its ultimate inspiration in Britain, and particularly in an idealized version of the rural life of nineteenth-century England. To transplant the shires to Canada's prairie west, or even to the more promising climate of British Columbia, was a formidable and possibly an unrealistic undertaking. The life of a country squire was an elusive ideal, even in Ontario or the eastern townships of Quebec, but the dream still lives in the rural or semi-rural environs of Toronto and Calgary, and of Winnipeg and Edmonton.

The determination that the new society should be British was complemented by a still stronger and more forcibly expressed determination that the Canadian west should not go the way of the western parts of the United States. To exclude American influence from the Canadian hinterland was in the interest of the Canadian business community and this supported a resolve that the violence and brutality perceived as characterizing the American frontier should have no place in the peaceful and orderly society of the Canadian west. As the railway must precede settlement so law and established institutions should be in place not only to support the settler but to ensure that he accepted the social disciplines that lay beneath the British conception of freedom.

This emphasis on trans-Atlantic social ideals and this abhorrence of North American continentalism was, at the policy making level, most explicitly expressed during the long period of the Conservative party's dominance at Ottawa. After 1895 more was heard of another social ideal, that of a society resting, not upon an ordered hierarchy that included large land owners, but on the strong back of the yeoman farmer, with a sturdy settler and his family on every quarter section. Though more in tune with the populist attitudes of many who gave their support to Laurier and the Liberal party, subsequent experience was to show that policies related to this optimistic view of the agricultural potentialities of the west were even more productive of human misery than earlier attitudes that at least gave some scope for reasonable land use. The populist and more egalitarian ideal was indeed acceptable to the business community, whether in the counting houses of the east or in the Winnipeg grain trade, for it promised an enormous expansion at once of western production and the western market. Those in the west who were in positions of influence, if not caught up in the spirit of the great boom of the early 1900s, could console themselves with the reflection that they were at least comfortably in place, and with the hope that the institutional structures they had created could accommodate and control this unprecedented expansion. Until the outbreak of war in 1914 the influential minority in the west had little reason to suppose that the region would not remain peaceful, orderly and British.

What the influential minority did not sufficiently take into account was the fact that theirs was an immigrant society. Most societies can of course be so described, and certainly the older societies of Canada east of the Great Lakes. Immigration to the west, however, took place under peculiar circumstances. The definitive period of western Canadian settlement was relatively short. In fifty years the west passed from the appearance of an empty and barbarous wilderness to that of a settled society with the appurtenances of western European civilization. That the wilderness had not been quite empty and that the appurtenances were of a somewhat jerry-built nature were contradictions that the westerner of 1920 ignored without much reflection.

This hasty passage occurred in an era when rapid communication, the product of the railway, the steam-boat and the telegraph, had already revolutionized the world to which the west looked for its models. The western settler could maintain a contact with his homeland much more easily than the generations of North American settlers who had come before the early nineteenth-century revolution in communications. Indeed the very speed with which the west was settled was a function of the revolution. It was also a major factor in bringing into the realm of possibility the whole enterprise of building a new society in the west and in maintaining the control over it of the central authority. For no one in the west was this ability to communicate easily and quickly with his home base more significant than for the members of the influential minority.

The use of a term like "influential minority" suggests that the view of western society put forward here departs radically from the stereotype of western Canadian development that portrays it as wholly the work of the sturdy homesteader, drawn from the ranks of the needy and oppressed of the world, who created, by heroic toil and suffering, an egalitarian, classless and unstructured society. Such weaknesses as a society so envisaged might have resulted from restrictions placed upon it by forces external to it or from infections spreading out from less wholesome and self-sustaining structures on its periphery. This view of western society is at least as far removed from reality as the stereotype of western history that supports it. Though the latter gives some recognition to the colonial relationship of the west to central Canada it ignores the social objectives of the national government as completely as it does the attitudes of the creative minority who acted as that government's effective arm.

This stereotype also obscures the part played by what may be called the privileged settler. It in no way derogates from the accomplishments of the pioneer to say that some of the settlers of the formative years had advantages of birth, wealth and education that enabled them to make a distinctive contribution to the western polity. Certainly the policy makers of the first twenty-five years saw them as a valuable element in the kind of society they hoped would emerge. Such settlers, when they came from relatively privileged backgrounds in relatively structured societies, could be expected to support precisely the kind of society the central Canadian elite envisaged for the west. Even those whose advantages were comparatively modest might aspire to an improved position in their new homes.

The factor of aspiration, which is almost always recognized even in the crudest stereotypes of the immigrant, was certainly an important element in the motivation of the privileged. Their aspirations were linked to a highly romantic view of the west as a land of opportunity where the best of life in the British Isles or in eastern Canada could be realized without the restrictions imposed by the density of population and the scarcity and high cost of land. The vision of the west current among the advantaged was heavily oriented toward the outdoor life, and especially toward both work and pastimes closely related to horsemanship. The writings of the Irish poet Moira O'Neill, who was also, as Mrs. Walter Skrine, the wife of an early Alberta rancher, provide a sensitive response not only to the foothills landscape but also to the way of life of the golden age of what David Breen has called the Cattle Compact. Her view was one that could only be seen from the back of a horse and it is not surprising that, after the Skrines returned to Ireland and their house was set on fire during the Troubles, all that Mrs. Skrine thought to rescue was her side-saddle.

The love of equestrian pursuits did not preclude an attachment to other values the privileged minority might have in their baggage. The institutions of the new society were heavily influenced by their attitudes to the church, the school, the courts, the professions, the public service and the provision of cultural amenities. These attitudes they saw as British, whether they were imported directly from the British Isles or, at one remove, from the eastern provinces or other parts of the British Empire. The coincidence of their values and attitudes with the objectives of the policy makers and organizers of the western polity is a fact of considerable significance in the shaping of western Canadian society and for its relationship with the Canadian polity as a whole.

In the structured societies upon which the western societies were modelled, and from which most of the privileged settlers came, status was determined by considerations that were ultimately economic, but complicated over the generations by breeding and education. In dynamic and fluid societies like those of nineteenth century Britain and the eastern provinces of Canada, a high degree of social mobility existed and the definition of the limits of gentility was increasingly nebulous. The monopoly of influence by a single caste had indeed been broken but even in late Victorian and Edwardian Canada enough of a class structure survived to ensure that the genteel could and would reach out to the genteel to provide, as far as was possible, the same human support that arises out of policies promoting group settlements based on ethnic or religious affiliations.

This factor of social contiguity in promoting and reinforcing the values that the dominant element in central Canada sought to establish in its western hinterland deserves further exploration. Why, for example, was the confrontation endemic in the rancher-squatter relationship, and evident in southern Alberta from the earliest stages in the development of the Cattle Compact, so successfully contained? Was it because so many of the small stockmen who moved into the ranching country had a common background with the ranchers and shared their aspirations to a particular way of life and their ideal of a rural and structured society? The exploration of such a problem cuts across deeply entrenched stereotypes of western egalitarianism and the homogenizing effect of a harsh environment that erases every evidence of human distinctiveness. The very suggestion that some settlers in the west had privileges, privileges which proved an advantage rather than a handicap in making their adjustment to the western environment, provokes a hostile response on the assumption that such an assertion implies a defense of privilege by its beneficiaries.

These stereotypes are entrenched not only in the west's collective perception of itself, a concept perhaps too flimsy and evasive to be intellectually respectable, but in much popular writing about the west, including much of what passes as popular history. They have not been wholly absent from academic writing about the west, especially in the field called social science. The trend of academic historical research, however, seems to be towards their rejection and towards a representation of the west that is much more complex, much more shaded, and, to me, much more interesting.

In a structured society that has attained a degree of maturity the place of the individual in the hierarchy is relatively fixed. The characteristics of a member of the influential minority are recognizable in terms of economic and social position. Levels of education and manners in a broad sense imply an acceptance of a collective way of life, supported by the acceptance of a complex of values. In an immigrant society like that of the prairie west the structures did not exist, except in a rudimentary form in the Red River colony and in the fur trading society to which it was affiliated. To create structures similar to those existing in central Canada, and in an idealized Britain, was the primary task of the central government. It was apparent that such structures were not necessarily of compelling interest to many of the potential immigrants they hoped to attract. They turned therefore to those whose backgrounds would suggest that the structures assumed to be best would be congenial. The objectives of government thus gave an opportunity to the privileged settler to move into an influential position and to use that position to realize aspirations that were coherent with the purposes of government.

When the pace of settlement began to quicken in the late nineties a western elite was in place, well established in cities like Winnipeg and Calgary, not to mention Victoria and Vancouver, and with significant connections in the rural west and in smaller centres, centres that might be resource based, like Lethbridge with its coal, or agricultural marketing centres like the towns of Assiniboia and Manitoba. Though the privileged settler was very much in a minority among the new arrivals of the boom years he reinforced and helped to develop the patterns of life he found already established. As he usually came from the eastern provinces or the United Kingdom his model of the good life was not much altered from that of an earlier generation. Though he might not have attained the material success of the established minority, he was more likely to aspire to association with the influential element than to seek to break its control. Easy communication with eastern Canada and the United Kingdom continued to support relationships with his home base and to promote entry into the associations, political and economic as well as cultural, that bound Canada together.

In this period of optimism about the western and the Canadian future, the beneficiaries of these associations were not inclined to denounce them as evidence of western subservience to the metropolis. During the war of 1914–18 no element in the west supported the Canadian war effort more strongly than the privileged settler. Even for those of the western elite who did not have the special concerns of the recent arrival from the United Kingdom, the disposition to make no distinction between a Canadian and a British cause was overwhelming. For the west, with its high proportion of young men and of recent arrivals, the war was an especially shattering experience, not only in its high casualty rates among a vitally important element in its population but also for its disruptive and destructive impact upon its relatively immature institutional structure. Though the elite's associations with Britain remained in working order, in the inter-war years they were no longer sustained by the infusion of privileged immigrants from overseas that had been so marked in the pre-war period. Though the world of the influential minority in the west was still London-centred and Americans remained suspect, its associations with central Canada assumed an increasing importance. Immigration in the twenties and the thirties no longer radically affected the patterns of settlement. There was in this period no major internal movement of the people comparable with the urbanization and rural depopulation that characterized the years after the war of 1939–45, though the drought and depression of the thirties did push many desperate farmers out of the stricken areas of the south. The influential minority became increasingly city based, though still maintaining its small town and rural outposts. A few of its affiliates were to be found in the popular movements that dominated prairie politics between the wars but the western establishment generally preferred to co-opt and tame the populist leaders. When leaders with recognizable establishment connections like Duff Roblin and Peter Lougheed appeared, western society was notably different from what it had been in the post-immigration period between the wars.

The western elite, whether in 1890 or in 1930, was a small minority in the total population of the region. In an immigrant society like that of the west in the settlement period, its values and attitudes were shared by many of the newcomers. It recruited itself easily, especially from the ranks of the privileged settlers. For its way of life it continued to look for its models across the Atlantic, or to eastern elites that looked in the same direction. It was increasingly urban and, in the larger cities, was concentrated in distinctly upper-class neighbourhoods, though its older generation was slow to leave the houses they had built close to the city centres. It continued to maintain social procedures that might have aroused more animosity had they been more conspicuous. It did not abandon its rural connections and these were reinforced by its continuing orientation towards outdoor sports. Its addiction to horses survived the automobile, and horse-shows, race meetings, and even polo, qualified the increasing addiction of the larger public to the rodeo. The west between the wars was by no means affluent and even the comfortably circumstanced on the whole refrained from the conspicuous consumption that is said to breed social hostility. Indeed the elite might almost be said to have pretended that it did not even exist, that its members were completely assimilated into the classless society of North America.

The structures of western society as they emerged from the painful decades of consolidation between the wars still reflected the social ideals and attitudes of the social planners and social engineers of post-Confederation central Canada. Yet whatever the attitudes of the elite, the political history of the period amply demonstrated the dissatisfaction of the majority of the prairie population with the region's continuing colonial relationship to central Canada. This dissatisfaction has usually been explained in terms of economic injustice, of which all westerners are equally the victims, and of the environmental hazards to which all westerners are impartially exposed. Yet in the kind of structured society that the west was meant to be, and did indeed become, the discriminations and divisions implicit in the structure imposed social discomforts that were likely to affect the individual response of the westerner to his society. Though the general acceptance of the pretense that the west was an egalitarian society veiled these internal frictions, this was no more effective in reducing them than the belief in Canada's essential democracy was in eliminating the strains imposed on the west by its colonial relationship to central Canada.

The affluence of the three decades that followed the war of 1939–45 profoundly affected the west. So did the changes in the world power structure as Canada perceived it. The predominance of the United States and the relative decline of Britain and France removed substantial obstacles to the penetration of North American continentalism. Nowhere in the west was this more obvious than in Alberta. The new wealth from oil and gas gave a new mobility within a society structured on the assumption of an agricultural base with all the limitations that implied. No matter how sedulously the elite had maintained its Canadian and trans-Atlantic associations, these had suffered and continued to suffer the attrition of generational change. Second cousins twice removed do not experience or maintain the intimacies of parent and child, or of brother and sister. Now these associations felt new pressures from outside. Calgary, even in the thirties the most English of prairie cities, became the most American. Edmonton, except in the university community less exposed to the assault from the south, was transformed into something resembling a cosmopolitan city under the influence of the new emigration from Europe. The new immigrants came, not to farm in ethnic groups, but to use their talents and their training in an urban environment. The old models of the good life, though they did not wholly disintegrate, were considerably modified by North American consumerism and aspirations to a style that was in its inspiration more international than purely British.

The post-war years raised the general level of material well-being in the west. This blurred the distinctions between the levels in its social structure, distinctions that were in any case yielding to the homogenizing tendencies of post-industrial society in North America and much of western Europe. Individual voices were raised to protest against injustice to groups like the Indians which had not conspicuously benefitted from the pervasive prosperity, but the collective conscience of the west was not noticeably aroused. Official recognition that the west was now a multicultural society won a comfortable acceptance. Inequities within that society aroused far less interest than the region's continuing concern with its relationship to central Canada. The more conscious the west became of its comparative prosperity, the more it resented the retention of the power of decision by a more populous centre. This discrepancy in the location of political power and economic resources posed questions to the individual in the western society that were not wholly new but to which he had never before had to respond from anything resembling a position of strength.

TEN ALBERTA 1905–1980: THE UNEASY SOCIETY

The following essay is one of Professor Thomas's most probing and topical works. Originally delivered as a paper to the Western Studies Conference in 1980, it was written at a time when Ottawa and Edmonton were engaged in sometimes acrimonious debate over the question of sharing Alberta's petroleum resources. It was a time when many Albertans were expressing dissatisfaction with their role in Confederation, a time when the concept of Western separatism was being discussed approvingly in many circles.

In this essay the author seeks to explain the tensions which have characterized federal-provincial relations in recent years. Some of these tensions, he suggests, stem from the relationships which have developed between Alberta's elite and members of the Establishment in Central Canada. The relationships have altered over the past century.

In the 1880s, the elites of Western Canada owed much of their regional influence to their alliances with more powerful groups in London, Ottawa, and other metropolitan centres. Although the privileged settlers of Alberta recognized this fact, they did not resent their subordinate position. Most of them were recent immigrants who, as we have seen in earlier essays, retained strong ties to their parent societies. Many of the privileged settlers regarded themselves as colonizers: they took pride in their role as agents of what promised to be a dynamic national/imperial system.

The First World War undermined the position and the confidence of the regional elite. When immigration from the United Kingdom and the older Canadian provinces subsided, and as imperial enthusiasms declined, many of the ties which had bound the privileged settlers to outside centres of power were weakened. The Western elite then found itself isolated—culturally, politically, attitudinally; more and more, members of the elite felt estranged from what they perceived to be a distant and indifferent federal government. Particularly was this the case in the 1930s.

Prosperity returned to the West after the Second World War, by which time a new elite had emerged. Like the Victorian/Edwardian Establishment, the new elite was conservative in temperament, and so it has remained. Yet there were fundamental differences between the generations. The post-war elite was more affluent, more ostentatious: material success, rather than congeniality and a set of shared cultural values, was the passport into the upper echelons of Alberta society. Most important, Alberta's new elite had developed an acute sense of regional identity. Far from being agents of London or Ottawa, members of the elite had become militant defenders of regional economic autonomy.

The regionalism and materialism of the new Establishment is not surprising, given Alberta's experience over the last fifty years. But what is understandable is not necessarily desirable. In this essay, the author feels that the priorities and preoccupations of the new elite may have contributed to the "uneasiness" which he has detected in Alberta society. More worryingly, the estrangement of the federal and provincial elites in 1980 did not bode well for "the future of Canada as an undivided nation."

TEN Alberta 1905–1980: The Uneasy Society

SEVENTY-FIVE years ago, when Alberta became a province, her mood was optimistic, self-confident, even euphoric. She expressed few doubts about her role as part of a dynamic west that would fuel the development of Canada into a great British North American nation. Alberta today has achieved a material prosperity equalled only in the dreams of the boosters of 1905; a prosperity the more conspicuous because it is exceptional in the industrialized nations of the world and shared in Canada, and that only in part, by the neighbouring provinces to the east and west. Alberta in 1980 would appear at once to have realized the dreams of her pioneers and to have reached the goals of the nineteenth-century planners for Canadian greatness. In a world in which energy supplies are crucial, Alberta has the apparent capacity to keep Canada warm and prosperous in the obviously difficult future, and to maintain her own high level of prosperity far beyond the exhaustion of the easily accessible reserves of oil and gas upon which it has been based since the postwar discoveries.

In these circumstances Albertans might seem to have good reason to accept complacently and to play with enthusiasm a part in confederation even more vital to the action of the drama than that in which she was cast in the booming years of the early twentieth century. Yet obviously this is not the case. Though few Albertans would reject the part out of hand, there is certainly a widespread determination that Alberta should control the stage direction.

There is also a conviction, perhaps less general, that the part should be rewritten in concert with the views of other provinces who believe their parts unduly constrict their capacity for full self-expression.

These reservations about Alberta's role, and the way she should play it, reflect concern that Alberta will be done down by her colleagues, especially her larger and more populous colleagues, Ontario and Quebec. Uneasiness in this regard is rooted in Alberta's perceptions of her historical experience. In contemporary terms it is perhaps most sharply expressed in the resentment, very widely felt by Albertans, of the assumption that Alberta is a monolithic society, inward looking and wholly preoccupied with material rewards, and predictably oblivious of the main stream of human development outside her borders. Though this view from outside is given some credibility by Alberta's political behaviour, and the eagerness with which she embraces the symbols of affluence produced by technological change, even her dissident minorities find this external verdict decidedly unflattering, and probably unjust. If there is anything that unites contemporary Albertans, the most self-critical with the most complacent, it is their common dislike of the stereotype that proclaims that they have ceased to see themselves not only as Canadians but as members of the human race.

Albertan sensitivity to the opinions of their fellow Canadians contributes to their conviction that the mechanisms of the federal relationship are loaded against them, and indeed against all the less favoured regions and provinces, in favour of central Canada, that is, the provinces of Ontario and Quebec. As long as the central provinces retain the preponderance of population, they can control the decisions of the federal government. Alberta's control of her resources came to her by federal decision. That decision could be reversed within the bounds of legality, if not of reason. Such a frontal assault on the foundations of Alberta's prosperity could be expected to bring such a chorus of outrage from the provinces as to make it seem unthinkable. Not all Albertans, however, are wholly convinced of the impregnability of their position.

There are, in the uneasy world of 1980, other reasons than uncertainty about the federal relationship for Albertans to be nervous about the future. In common with the rest of the world Alberta has lived since 1945 in the shadow of nuclear war. In common with the rest of Canada Albertans have for two generations been growing up between two nuclear giants, giants whose posture towards one another has been consistently hostile. The world was very different for Albertans whose minds were formed before 1939, when the centre of the North American land mass seemed a comfortable place in which to be, especially while British naval power was a major factor in the equations of politics.

Another disturbing, though perhaps ultimately less intimidating, cause for uneasiness is the evidence that the economies of the western industrialized world are in serious difficulty. Though Alberta's current prosperity has an insulating effect, Canada, a nation that historically has lived by its exports, is deeply involved. Even the most optimistic or isolationist view can scarcely pretend that Alberta could remain a smug island of affluence in a world in economic chaos.

Concerns about Alberta's role in Canada, and about the impact on her fortunes of nuclear war and the disintegration of economic structures, are equally concerns about relationships. The achievement of a reasonably satisfactory relationship depends upon a balancing of interests. Self-interest demands a recognition of the interests of others. Such a recognition involves hard decisions. The current tussle between the organized oil-producing states and the industrialized powers throws into relief the failure of the latter to find a way of respecting the interests of countries who cannot combine to exploit their production of commodities less vital and more widely available than oil. That the ultimate self-interest of the industrialized countries demands that they recognize and help to cope with the problem is obvious. The difficulty is to find mechanisms. In this formidable task the society that is most likely to make a useful contribution is one that has made some progress towards solving its internal conflicts of interest and thus established at least a relatively easy and comfortable relationship between its own elements.

Whether any society has achieved this goal is highly questionable. It becomes very much a question of degree. A society so at ease with itself that all tensions, creative or otherwise, disappear completely is scarcely within the range of human probability. Even if it were, external threats would serve to keep it on its toes and alert to the danger of allowing its self-interest to preclude a creative response to the promotion of the interests of other groups in an inevitably interrelated world. The purpose of this paper is to examine Alberta at various stages in the last century of her development, paying particular attention to the possibility that a relationship exists between her role in the larger Canadian polity and the creation within the borders of the province established seventy-five years ago of a society that is, to a greater or lesser degree, at ease within itself. This involves some consideration of the relationship between the influential element in the society, if such an element exists, and other groups, whether within or without Alberta.

Two characteristics of Alberta's development as a self-conscious unit within the Canadian structure require special notice. The first is that Alberta was in 1905 an immigrant society and that she remains today a society profoundly influenced by the movements of population both within her boundaries and from outside her boundaries. The immigrant comes to a new home primarily to better his position. He brings with him a great variety of cultural baggage. He may look back to his former home as a model for the new society or as a prison from whose structures he was fortunate to escape. In these backward glances nostalgia may mingle with relief. He finds himself in an environment in which he is at once the creator of a new order and the material from which the new order is being created. As the new structures develop he may be their beneficiary or their victim or both. He may be at ease with those structures or alienated by them. Reaching an accommodation with a social environment that is itself in process of change may be a matter of generations. Old loyalties and old hostilities do not die easily, even under the touch of material prosperity.

Not only has Alberta been an immigrant society with a high degree of mobility in physical terms, but its development has taken place in a comparatively short time. She was the last of the provinces to feel the full impact of European settlement, with all this implied in terms of her European cultural inheritance. Alberta, seen in one generation as a virtually empty land, was a relatively close settled community in the next. Manitoba can look back for more than a century and a half to the Red River settlers, British Columbia for more than a century to the agricultural experiments of the Hudson's Bay Company and the miners' penetration into the interior. Even Saskatchewan, Alberta's nominal twin, had a substantial and relatively prosperous farming community that was as early as 1900 moving into a second and even a third generation. Like the rest of the west, Alberta was Europeanized after the revolution in communications that followed the triumph of the railway, the steamship and the telegraph. Unlike her sisters' slower growth, Alberta's transformation was telescoped into the two dramatic decades before the War of 1914 that brought spectacular growth to the west at large.

The drama of these two crucial decades should not obscure the importance of other stages in Alberta's development for changes in Albertans' attitudes to their own society and to the larger societies with which Alberta has relationships. For the remote corner of British North America which was, in 1882, to become the District of Alberta, the decisions that determined its future were essentially imperial decisions, decisions made in London. The outcome of the Seven Years' War with France placed it within the orbit of British power, the American Revolution and the War of 1812 did not displace it. The union of the fur trading interests of the St. Lawrence and Hudson Bay in 1820–21 ended the anarchy that had threatened not only to bankrupt the fur trade but also to plunge the northwest into social, economic and political chaos. The union introduced a period of relative prosperity for the fur trade, and relative peace and order in terms of relations between the native peoples, the European newcomers and the growing population of mixed bloods who stood somewhere between the European and the native societies.

The maintenance of a political boundary, vaguely defined though it was, ensured the separate future of western British North America. Had the United States frontier been able to move northward as freely as it did westward, the western heritage, upon which the older British colonies to the east were so heavily to depend after 1867, might have been dissipated before the latter were in a position to assume the burden of colonization. Certainly the threat of a political confrontation between Britain and the United States, precipitated by a breakdown of order in Britain's western territories but involving all her territories in northern America, was a major factor in the complex negotiations that issued in the British North America Act of 1867 and the subsequent transfer of the Hudson's Bay Company's territories to the new Dominion of Canada.

Henceforth the decisions that affected what was to be Alberta were essentially Canadian decisions, though the line between the Canadian and British interest was not to be easy to draw. The establishment of the Mounted Police at Fort Macleod and Fort Saskatchewan brought what was to be Alberta into the new Canadian colonial system in the process of elaboration by John A. Macdonald, by his colleagues and supporters, and by a reliably partisan civil service. Of the social, economic and political structures of the system the symbols were the Mounted Police, the Canadian Pacific Railway and the governments of Manitoba and the Northwest Territories. These institutions were intended to secure for the west peaceful and orderly administration, and development in accordance with the best of British tradition. They were also to ensure that the development of this western hinterland served the interests of the metropolis. To these ends control of the lands and natural resources, not only of the Northwest Territories but also of the province of Manitoba, was reserved to the federal government. The position of British Columbia was rather different. As a British colony she entered confederation on much the same terms as her eastern sisters insofar as her lands and other resources were concerned.

The reservation of the control of resources to the central government was intended to serve a lofty national purpose. Their development was to be the basis of a transcontinental northern American nation able to maintain itself against the pressure exerted by the United States. There was no intention that, once this national purpose was accomplished, these qualifications on provincial status should be maintained. The concession of provincial status to Manitoba, modified though it was, made it clear that western opinion could win concessions, though the process might be painful for both sides.

The fact remained that the Northwest Territories and the province of Manitoba were not colonies of Britain joining the Canadian confederation as equals, but colonies of the new Canada created by the central government and with a status inferior to their fellows. The people of the west were quick to recognize this status and to protest against it, but the experience of the North

West Rebellion of 1885 made it clear that the preponderance of physical force was with the federal government. Though many European settlers had been critical of federal policy, sympathy with its Métis and Indian victims died at the test of armed resistance. The indigenous elements were left to come to terms as best they could with the colonial structure or accept virtual exclusion from it, on their reserves, or on lands remote from the main lines of communication or regarded as agriculturally unpromising. There is little evidence that the presence of these alienated elements on the fringes of the new society caused much concern in the developing west in the next half century, but the consequences of the continuing isolation were to lay a heavy burden of unease on the conscience of the future.

The signal failure of armed resistance by no means implied that western discontent had been eliminated. It was, however, clear that changes in the structure could only be brought about by means that were within the law. The agitation for a fuller measure of self-government, with or without provincial status, and including control over lands and resources, was a continuing theme in relations between the west and its metropolis. Nevertheless the first objective of the territorial population, and especially of the dominant group within it, was not political emancipation but social and economic development. Though the Canadian Pacific Railway was to become the highly unpopular symbol of centralist domination of the prairie west, it was in 1885 the indispensable foundation for the material progress of the region. It could not have been completed without the indefatigable efforts of the central government and its promoters within the central Canadian business interest. The complacent acceptance by the territorial public of the national policy was scarcely surprising.

This complacency was supported in Alberta by the nature of its early settlement, especially of its southern area. Even before the railway, and not long after the arrival of the Mounted Police, it was apparent that much of the land was peculiarly suited to the ranching industry that was bringing such impressive profits south of the international boundary to, among others, investors from the United Kingdom. Ranching fitted in well with the social and economic planning of the Conservative governments of the 1880s, for, though American cattle could be welcomed to stock the range, American capital could be excluded by the leasing system adopted. Capital from the United Kingdom and from central Canada, and even from the Maritimes, brought settlers from the same areas, attracted not only by the prospect of profitable investment but by the romance of life on the open range.[1]

Though it would be possible to exaggerate the glamour and minimize the hardships of the ranching society of southern Alberta, especially before the turn of the century, the aspirations of this group of settlers created a view of the good life that was long to linger in the shadow of the Rockies. It was a view based on a romanticization of the values of nineteenth-century England. It placed great emphasis upon outdoor sports, especially on horsemanship, and it assumed a hierarchical ordering of society that recognized responsibility as well as privilege. It had a respect for institutions like the church and the school, and for service-oriented professions, which in Alberta could extend to cover the police.[2]

This view could appeal to the settler of middle or upper class aspirations not only from the United Kingdom but also from central and eastern Canada and even from certain backgrounds in the United States or continental Europe. As a social ideal it was acceptable to those who influenced the planning for the west of the central government and of those who were elaborating the structures that were supposed to be the basis of successful colonization, whether these were Mounted Police officers or senior civil servants like William Pearce. Pearce's twin passions for planning and for irrigation led him to elaborate schemes for southern Alberta's development that combined large land holdings and peasant villages complementing one another in an ordered society that might have done credit to Sir Thomas More or even St. Augustine. Though Pearce's name was anathema to contemporary populists like Frank Oliver, his emphasis on proper land use and adequate planning was discarded at a high cost to future generations.[3]

The ranching industry gave Alberta not only a view of the good life acceptable to a developing élite but an economic basis for a social structure congenial to the ideals of conservative policy makers and their supporters in central Canada. The whole district therefore entered the period of rapid population growth that began somewhere in the late Nineties with an élite firmly in place and enjoying a degree of acceptance by substantial elements in the population. Though that élite was not without interest in the greater degree of local autonomy provincial status would confer, relations between the élite and the central administration were on the whole cordial. Indeed much of that élite held, or hoped to hold, federal appointments or enjoyed, or hoped to enjoy, federal patronage. There were close links between the élite and the Canadian Pacific Railway. The cattle interest had excellent relations with Ottawa, and, as long as resources remained under federal control, every reason to maintain these even through a change of government.

The end of the nineteenth century brought marked changes to Alberta. There was a new government in Ottawa, a government much more open to a theory of western development that differed radically from that prevalent among those who had seen, as the primary objective of Canadian colonial policy, the creation of a peaceful and orderly society able, by its maintenance of British traditions and values and of close ties with central Canada, to resist the dangerous pressures exerted by a dynamic United States. Such a society provided ideal conditions for a controlled exploitation of the land and resources of the western hinterland by the enterprise and wealth of the older provinces and likeminded adventurers and investors from overseas. It could be relied upon to damp down any excesses of frontier democracy that might threaten to infect it from the south.

The policies of the Laurier Liberals, while by no means abandoning the concept of a separate Canadian identity, placed more emphasis on hastening the development of the west so that Canada as a whole could be placed in a competitive position with her neighbour. The building of new railways to the north of the Canadian Pacific and the more aggressive promotion of settlement would be much more effective in creating a new balance than the restrictive policies of the past, aimed rather at protecting existing investments than at promoting new ones. This change in the orientation of Canadian policy towards the west coincided with a change in the tides of overseas settlement, which, now that the desirable agricultural lands of the United States were settled, were beginning to flow towards Canada. Canada as a whole, and especially central Canada, had also begun to feel the quickening of the world's economic pulse after the doldrums of the later nineteenth century, and the west, as an area of settlement and as an area for investment, exercised a new fascination on those in the central and eastern provinces who sought broader opportunities.

For Alberta the quickening flow of settlement and the elaboration of the western railway network brought a shift of population northward as the newcomers moved into the park land areas of the central part of what was in 1905 to become a province with much wider boundaries than the old district. The prairie areas were by no means immune, for techniques of dry farming developed in the United States were optimistically applied by homesteaders who took up land opened under the pressure of a propaganda that saw the western future in terms of a sturdy farmer and his family on every quarter section. The ranchers retreated to their stronghold in the foothills or in lands still too remote or too ill-favoured in terms of topography or climate to attract even the most optimistic homesteader. Though the cattle industry remained a major factor in the Alberta economy, and some of the ranching companies survived as major landowners, the predominance that the rancher had held in the days of the open range gradually gave way before the more intensive use of much of southern Alberta's land for the production of crops, notably of wheat.

The rapid increase in the population of the southern part of the territories, and the prospect of the indefinite continuance of the boom conditions of the first decade of the twentieth century, made the attainment of provincial autonomy virtually an incident in the headlong development of the period. Neither federal party opposed it in principle, though there were differences in both as to the timing. The Laurier Liberals brought in the legislation but the leading advocate of the change in status was F. W. G. Haultain, a southern Alberta lawyer with a genteel Ontario background and Conservative affiliations. In spite of the latter Haultain had led the Territorial struggle for responsible government as a nonpartisan and continued this stance in his battle for autonomy.

The terms were a personal defeat for Haultain, for he stood out firmly for a single province, control of lands and resources by that province, and full control over education, which in effect meant control by the English-speaking Protestant majority. In the provincial elections of 1905 Haultain ran on a Provincial Rights platform in Saskatchewan and was soundly defeated, though less drastically than his Conservative counterpart in Alberta, Richard Bedford Bennett. The first Alberta election offered little evidence that the Alberta public was seriously disenchanted with the federal-provincial relationship as it was expressed in the autonomy bills.

The mood of buoyant optimism that characterized Alberta in 1905 carried the province through a period of steady growth that lasted almost unchecked until the recession of 1913. The Liberal government, though not the first Liberal premier, A. C. Rutherford, survived the scandal surrounding the proposals for the construction of the Alberta and Great Waterways Railway into the north. The public response suggested that it was not concern over the extravagance of the proposal but rather the possibility of corruption in government that dominated Alberta thinking. Government and people alike were preoccupied with the provision of an infrastructure that could sustain the increasing population.

The predominance of the English-speaking and Protestant element in the direction of provincial affairs continued. Though many of the new settlers came from the United States and continental Europe, they were too preoccupied with the hard work of establishing themselves on the land to mount an effective challenge. The predominant group was substantially reinforced by emigrants from the United Kingdom and from central and eastern Canada. Many of these shared the aspirations of the earlier generation of settlers and were quite prepared to accept the social structures and the way of life that they had put in place. Many of that earlier generation, having consolidated their resources in land, business ventures or professional skill, took advantage of the buoyant economy to extend their investments, often in agricultural land, often in urban real estate. The growing villages, towns and cities, where the booster spirit flourished and optimism knew no bounds, served them as a base.[4] These rising urban centres offered amenities not available in a rural setting as well as opportunities for investment. They also attracted many of the new immigrants from the more easterly provinces and the United Kingdom, especially those who had access to capital or marketable skills, even if the latter meant only a better than average education in a society in which the average was not particularly high.

Urban development spread the influence of the élite, from its original base in the ranching country of the south, throughout the province, even into the north, where it could link hands with congenial elements in the fur trading society of the pre-Confederation past. Its outposts in the smaller towns could establish links with the rural hinterland through settlers whose social or economic privilege enabled them to evade or to minimize some of the deprivations of frontier pioneering. Social congeniality was perhaps even more influential than economic advantage in building these manifold connections and maintaining communication within the structure. Thus, although the élite might be predominantly English-speaking and Protestant, it could accommodate Roman Catholics when they shared its aspirations. The French element, though small in the province as a whole, even organized its own élite, based in Edmonton, which managed to maintain generally harmonious relations with its English counterpart.[5] The French were, at least to some extent, insulated by their separate schools from the most severe pressures towards assimilation to the Anglo-Protestant norm. These pressures, consistently exerted through the educational system, fell relentlessly upon immigrants less well placed in terms of ethnic and cultural heritage.

By 1914 the influential minority, and those who shared its aspirations, had used the two decades of rapid material growth to develop the facilities that gave to their way of life its peculiar flavour, and were indeed its symbols. These facilities were concentrated in the two larger cities, especially in Calgary,[6] but they served the urban centres generally, and even had their counterparts in thriving communities like Lethbridge. There were shops that consciously catered to the carriage trade, though by 1914 some of their customers might arrive in motor cars; there were tailors and dressmakers who could produce reasonable facsimiles of London and Paris fashions. Hotels like Braemar Lodge in Calgary prided themselves on their gentility and were certainly far from the image of the frontier hostelry derived from stereotypes of the American West. Men's clubs, modeled on those of eastern Canadian cities but with a tradition that looked across the Atlantic, pretended to an exclusiveness few of the multitude of women's organizations could emulate. Private schools for boys and girls borrowed heavily from the same sources. The arts were not neglected, though largely the preserve of the amateur. The popularity of amateur theatricals made "putting on a play" a useful means of raising money for good causes, and concerts serving the same purpose could draw on a considerable reserve of musical talent. Before the boom collapsed in the prewar recession of 1913 many small centres had "opera houses," halls that served a multitude of social purposes. Calgary, Edmonton, and even Lethbridge had well-equipped theatres, "The Grand," "The Empire" and "The Majestic," names that reflected the tradition which provided the travelling companies, many of them actually from England, who kept the hinterland in touch with what was still the heart of English-speaking theatre.

Thanks to the swelling tide of immigration this was still a youthful society and it sought diversion in a variety of social activities. The more pretentious of these were faithfully chronicled by the ubiquitous local press, whose development was an important aspect of the period. Entertainments of the grander sort had a trans-Atlantic model, a further, if to some eyes frivolous, reinforcement of the British tradition. They served, perhaps not altogether consciously, as a means of establishing degrees within the social hierarchy. In an immigrant society, where people from a great variety of backgrounds sought to find their place in the larger community, organized social occasions offered a means of defining an individual vocation for association with a particular group. They were also productive of a degree of social discomfort. Bob Edwards, a highly effective social critic, ridiculed the pretensions of Calgary's social arbiters and aspirants. His writing reflects his ironic appreciation of the absurdity and the pathos of the immigrant society, locked into a struggle between the two traditions of hierarchy and equality and at the same time preoccupied by the necessity of material advancement as the condition of survival.

Closely related to its dances, card parties and picnics was prewar Alberta's élite's preoccupation with sports. Though well established by the earliest generation of settlers as an individual and local activity, organized and competitive sports advanced rapidly in the two decades before 1914. True to their strong orientation towards the United Kingdom model, the early arrivals had played as much cricket as baseball, but, although cricket survived with the support of new immigrants from the British Isles, in popular appeal it quickly gave way to the American game. Football was played widely, but appears to have had less appeal to organizers and spectators than hockey. Skating, thanks to the Alberta climate, was an obvious winter pastime, and women's hockey teams, like women's cricket, appeared. Lawn tennis was introduced to Alberta soon after its invention in North Wales. Tennis courts could easily be improvised. The equipment was not elaborate or very expensive, and it took only two to make a game. Though by no means the preserve of the well-off, tennis had a certain *cachet* as a game, rather like clerking in a bank as an employment for young men.

Though all these games had a part to play in the integration of new communities and in promoting the healthy spirit of competition so much admired by the booster of the times, in terms of defining the good life for Alberta they must yield place to the activities that so early connected the development of a provincial élite and the long love affair of the upper classes with the horse. Southern Alberta afforded especially favourable conditions. The importance of the horse to the Indian, the mounted police, and the rancher needs no emphasis. For none was the horse simply a useful beast of burden. He could be ridden for pure pleasure, jumped, raced, shown competitively, and, in tournament, gymkhana or polo match, made the indispensable collaborator. Interest in such activities and, especially in the frontier phase, participation in them was by no means the preserve of the privileged. The horse, indeed, was an important factor in the integration of the pioneer community.

An interest in horses and horsemanship extended far beyond the ranching country and was by no means confined to southern Alberta. The relationship between the horse and his rider was rooted in the British rural tradition that formed the aspirations of many an immigrant. This relationship flourished under the ideal conditions provided by the open range in the early days of ranching but it survived wherever the tradition penetrated. In the circumstances of Alberta's settlement before 1914 there were few parts of the province, and almost none of its urban centres, in which those nurtured in this tradition, or one of its many variants, did not attempt to establish themselves. As population increased after the turn of the century, equestrian sports became more elaborate in their organization. Though a saddle horse was still, for many, in-

Alberta 1905—1980: The Uneasy Society   201

Crack-the-whip on Skates, ca. 1915. The "rink" in this and the accompanying picture of the Hillside hockey team was a spring-fed tributary of Sheep Creek. The site of the rink was just below Riverside, the ranch of James Rodgers's bachelor brothers.

Hillside Hockey Team ca. 1915. "Hillside" was the home of the Rodgers family, the children of vivacious Irishwoman, Maude Hull Pinkerton, by the first of her three marriages, to James "Dublin" Rodgers.

dispensable on the grounds of utility, race horses and polo ponies came to involve considerations of money and leisure, though these could still be found by the dedicated. An affection for horses and a respect for horsemanship could help to integrate an immigrant society, for they knew no barriers of race, class, colour or creed. A view of the good life based on land ownership and the essential rural pursuits which involved the horse were equally innocuous as long as there existed for the majority a reasonable prospect of material advancement. There was a widespread confidence, at least until the prewar recession, that such a prospect did exist for Albertans generally, and that they could proceed in harmony under the leadership of its influential elements.

The War of 1914–18 dealt a shattering blow to Alberta. As the last of the provinces to reach a degree of close agricultural settlement, a high proportion of its recent immigrants were of military age. Within that group a high proportion came from the United Kingdom or from the eastern Canadian provinces where the traditions of loyalty to the British connection were strongest. Enlistments were understandably early and numerous, and casualties proportionately heavy. The effect of the experience on those who returned is a matter for speculation but there is some evidence that the level of confidence in Alberta's future was lower. Whatever four years of war did to the individual, its dislocating effect on the society of the province was obvious. Families were broken up, women were forced into new roles. Severe labour shortages occurred, not only on the farms but in services like nursing and teaching. The acceptance of women's suffrage and prohibition were manifestations of changing attitudes. The idea of the war as a maturing and consolidating experience for Canada as a whole had little application in a province where economic and social structures had passed through a period of rapid improvisation and growth and then been strained by a challenge that came before they had time to settle into the mould of an indigenous tradition. As the recession of 1913 had revealed the vulnerability of Alberta's economy, so the war showed the inability of its social institutions to maintain their services under adverse conditions.

Dissatisfactions generated by war and recession were manifested in the political decision taken in 1921. Though the Liberal party in its later years of power in the province sought to contain the farmers' movement, candidates backed by the United Farmers of Alberta carried the vast majority of seats in both the federal and provincial elections of 1921, seats they were largely to retain until the even more decisive Social Credit sweep of 1935. Though the triumph of the U.F.A. was at the expense of the parties to which the élite were affiliated, it was less a repudiation of the local élite as a class than an attempt to escape from the domination of interests that Albertans saw as adverse to those of an economy and a society based on agriculture.

In the still fluid state of Alberta society after the War of 1914–18 not all of those with qualifications for membership in a provincial élite had identified themselves with the two traditional parties, parties which were seen, by the Albertans who voted for U.F.A. candidates in 1921, as identified, in the last analysis, with the national interests of business and finance. The vote in the Alberta provincial election of 1921 was not against the domination of an élite but rather against the use of that dominant position to further interests that were not those of the Alberta farmer. The way of life that characterized the élite was, in the circumstances of Alberta between the war and the depression, not conspicuously extravagant or ostentatious. It was indeed more a matter of manners than magnificence, less a matter of what people consumed than of the way they consumed it. Though the prairie populism of Henry Wise Wood may have aroused a mild distaste among the politically conventional, his apparent rejection of the Marxist view of class and his emphasis upon group action gave room for an accommodation between the élite and the farmers' government. The former, his anti-Marxism, was reassuring to the property owner, the latter, his emphasis on the group, was at worst a recognition of the basic reality of politics in a province dominated by the farm vote.

The U.F.A. government, led for the greater part of its existence from 1921 to 1935 by the moderate lawyer J. E. Brownlee, found no insuperable difficulties in working within the Canadian structure. Indeed its major achievement, one surprisingly little noticed at the time, was the transfer in 1929 from federal to provincial control of what remained of Alberta's natural resources. Viewed from the vantage point of fifty years on, the elevation to first-class status of the three prairie provinces was an act of the Mackenzie King administration as important as its tentative approach to basic social change, which also owed something to pressure from the west. By 1929 most of the west's promising agricultural land had been taken up. With this apparent closing of the agricultural frontier the national purpose of using western land to promote settlement seemed to have been accomplished. Neither of the traditional political parties had ever committed themselves to the indefinite maintenance of qualifications on provincial status. Politicians and public alike accepted the transfer without much enthusiasm and with even less concern about what it might mean for the future. There appeared, as the Twenties drew to a close, to be no disposition, not even as much as in 1905, to question the fundamental terms of Alberta's relationship with the federal government, whether among the élite or among the general public.

Insofar as an élite had developed by 1914, it was not a rigid caste but rather an influential minority with a widely spread measure of support and acceptance throughout the province. Though it could make itself felt in provincial politics, after 1921 it no longer dominated the legislature. Only in the two larger cities could it still deliver the votes to elect members to the House of Commons. Its direct influence at the federal level was thus diminished and it was more and more restricted to executing the will of the federal government. It could count on senior federal appointments and the bench was still its preserve, though the English-speaking bar's monopoly had long been breached to accommodate members of the French-Canadian élite.

The war of 1914 had eroded the base of the Alberta élite and postwar immigration did not provide reinforcements. In what was still a predominantly agricultural economy, employment opportunities elsewhere beckoned the educated and the talented. The close personal associations of the advantaged elements with their friends and relations in central and eastern Canada, and abroad, still sustained a network of communication that stretched from one end of Canada to the other, and reached into the British Isles and parts of the United States. This at once maintained the British orientation and the sense of a vital part in the Canadian structure. Even so, and important as these associations were to the élite, especially as a means of defining itself, the contacts beyond Alberta's borders were more and more the contacts of cousins and friends rather than the more intimate contact of parent and child, and of brother and sister. The maintenance of these contacts did not necessarily make the intellectual cast of Alberta's society less provincial, but they at least promoted the salutary recognition that it was provincial. Though the strongly trans-Atlantic orientation of prewar days was severely shaken by the diminished prestige of metropolitan Britain, the latter, at least for the élite, had not been replaced by the United States as the centre of the universe and the model for the good life. Cities and towns, with Calgary in the lead, continued to offer the services, even if they did not assume the aspect, of the English country town.

The high farm prices of the later war years and degree of prosperity the province enjoyed in the Twenties enabled the non-English speaking agricultural settlers to establish themselves and to begin to move into new roles in the province. There is some evidence to suggest that the ethnic groups were using the educational structures, quite frankly intended to assimilate them to the Anglo-Protestant norms of Ontario, as a means of escape from the rural agricultural ghettos. The normal school and a period in teaching could open the way to a university and a more prestigious profession.

The United States settler also flourished. As he was not usually handicapped by a language barrier, he began to have an impact on politics as the medium by which American agrarian protest was transmitted to Alberta from the United States. The powerful influence of Henry Wise Wood was a current in Alberta thinking about politics as powerful as any that flowed out of the radical tradition of the British Isles. Not all United States settlers shared Wood's innovative views. Many were socially and economically intensely conservative. They often based their economic and social attitudes on a rigorous Protestantism foreign to the less puritanical Anglican or Presbyterian attitudes so heavily represented among the élite. Though the numerical preponderance of churches that looked overseas or eastward rather than southward remained, their efforts to serve their adherents, especially in rural areas, never fully successful before 1914, were undermined by the dislocations of the war years. In the years between the wars they failed to make much progress in extending their influence to the ethnic groups. Denominations like the Latter Day Saints and the Lutherans had of necessity looked to the United States for spiritual and intellectual support. The continuing availability of the familiar American model did not dispose those American immigrants to an enthusiastic acceptance of a life style so oriented to British upper middle class permissiveness as that still favoured by the Alberta élite. Thus, although often qualified by ability, means and education for élite status it was not always easy for American immigrants to feel comfortable in it. Books, magazines and newspapers, and, as radio became increasingly a part of western Canadian life, broadcast programmes were more likely to be acceptable to this group if they followed American models rather than the British or central Canadian ones still more acceptable to the élite and those who shared their values.

The decade of depression that preceded the renewal of world

war in 1939 affected Alberta less drastically than its sister province of Saskatchewan, for its economy was marginally more diversified and the drought less widespread in its effects. Even so Alberta knew a dire poverty, the more damaging because for so many, especially in the rural areas, it wiped out all the material gains of years of hard work and seemed to postpone indefinitely, if it did not destroy, the prospect of security offered by the ownership of land. Neither the provincial nor the federal government seemed able to make any creative or imaginative response to the tribulations of the increasingly despondent farmers and of those who depended for a living upon a prosperous agriculture. The appeal of Social Credit doctrine, especially when presented by a publicist as skilled in the arts of persuasion as William Aberhart, proved irresistible to the Alberta electorate in the elections of 1935. In 1921 Alberta voters had aligned the province with the forces of discontent that criticized the traditional structures of Canadian politics, but that discontent was expressed on a national basis, though only faintly heard outside the prairie provinces. In 1935 Alberta seemed to be prepared to move outside those structures altogether.

The election of 1935 and the years that immediately followed emphasized conflicts within the provincial society that the depression experience had done much to sharpen. On the surface the clearest divisions were between the "haves" and the "have-nots." Few of those who saw themselves as having a secure material stake in the established order voted, or at least admitted to having voted, for the new movement. Aberhart and his devoted followers were bitterly, even venomously attacked, both in public and private. The dismal failure of government, both federal and provincial, had moved some of the relatively secure to take a liberal, even a left-wing, view of government responsibility for social intervention. Voters of this persuasion either failed to perceive or were unmoved by Aberhart's genuine concern for the disadvantaged, and were among his most persistent critics, emphasizing his disposition to dictatorial tactics and his disregard of Canadian realities. Aberhart's supporters responded with equal vigour. Beneath this mutual vituperation lay, on one side, a sense that those who had directed Alberta's affairs had failed completely to appreciate the plight of the majority and, on the other side, an uneasy fear that the Alberta voter could all too easily be persuaded to support reckless, irresponsible and ultimately destructive policies.

Aberhart himself came to accept the limits the Canadian structure placed upon provincial activities and was able to restrain his more impetuous colleagues. Though improvement in the economic climate came with painful slowness, Alberta inched its way out of the depression. His administration gradually won the grudging acceptance of the business community, though scarcely its enthusiastic support. Full reconciliation came after the succession of Ernest Manning. By that time the outbreak of war had substantially changed the mood of the province and had at least temporarily reduced the pressure of its most urgent economic problems. By the time the war was over Manning was securely established as the protector of the poor and the defender of the privileged against the danger of socialism.

The depression had tended to isolate Alberta from Canada as a whole; the War of 1939-45 brought it back into the Canadian experience. The shared misery of the Thirties had not proved a reinforcement to patriotic fervour, especially when the misery had not appeared to be equally shared between the Canadian regions. In contrast Alberta after the war had some reason to feel confidence in the value of its contribution to the national effort. Individual tragedies and deprivations could be balanced against the collective goal. War service gave a generation of Albertans a physical experience of Canada that, while not always agreeable, was one that had been previously reserved to the relatively well-to-do, or to those driven to it by economic necessity. There was at least some sense of doing, as Canadians, great things together. Though this experience did not necessarily mean that inherited prejudices were forgotten, it did enhance an awareness of Canada. For the perceptive, the contrast between the devastation that war wrought on civilian society and the security and prosperity of Alberta made the prospect of nuclear war more than a distant alarm, and Canada's international role a matter of concern.

War and its prosperous aftermath greatly increased mobility within Alberta's society, especially for the ethnic groups whose concern for cultural integrity was less compelling than the desire to take full advantage of opportunities for what was perceived as material advancement.

Class distinctions expressed in cultural terms as matters of attitude, taste and manner, rather than in crudely and explicitly economic terms, became increasingly inconspicuous as affluence permeated ever deeper into Alberta's structures. To win, and indeed to hold, a place in the influential minority, it was necessary to achieve some degree of material success. Though material wealth has traditionally lain behind bourgeois values, in an immigrant society like Alberta's this had often worked in the opposite way. Inherited bourgeois values had been a passport to privilege in a society where affluence was exceptional and social congeniality an important asset in resistance to the homogenizing tendencies of the frontier. The newly pervasive affluence succeeded where the egalitarian frontier had failed and made the primary measure for admission to the élite success in the achievement of material wealth and the power derived from it.

Generational change and the weakening of attachment to roots elsewhere supported the assimilation to a new norm of life styles, and the cultural values that lay behind them. The new models for the good life were drawn from the United States rather than from Britain or from central Canada. Britain's old predominance, attenuated in the period between the wars, had disappeared. Central Canada itself was hard pressed to resist the penetration of ideas and attitudes fashionable in the United States. Alberta, still in the process of assimilating the disparate elements in her earlier settlement, was even more open to these influences. As television replaced radio and the press as the major force in determining fashion, the visual impact of the American way of life reinforced earlier impressions derived by many Albertans from their origins or from the ease of travel southward. With a cultural stock less mature than that of central Canada, and so many elements in it only partially absorbed, the material aspect of Alberta life underwent a steady homogenization, embracing the models provided by the United States economy at its most buoyant.

These changes, the direct result of a steadily increasing level of material prosperity, made remote any possibility that the Alberta élite, always fluid and remarkably open, would settle into a caste rigidly circumscribed by ties of blood. Most of the material benefits that had been available to the old élite were now widely dispersed. As time passed the aspirations of many Albertans were substantially realized, or seemed, if no disaster obtruded from outside, to be likely to be realized. Enough Albertans had obtained a stake in the existing order to be vitally concerned. Conservation of that order became a primary objective. An open élite that could so manage the affairs of the province that this objective was achieved could count on wide support. It would best serve this purpose by recruiting on the basis of ability and, of course, sound commitment to the established order.

The continuing attachment of Albertans to a society shaped in a conservative mould was strengthened by a new tide of immigration from the United Kingdom and from continental Europe. This time the tide flowed not into rural areas but into the cities, already expanding as a result of a movement from the rural areas to the urban centres of the province. The new immigrants from overseas were often professionals or skilled tradesmen with much to offer a growing society hard pressed to meet the demands for the services they could provide. As many of those from the continent had been displaced by the war, they were often disposed to see government intervention as dangerous, a view frequently shared by emigrants from the United Kingdom, whose enthusiasm for the welfare state was decidedly lukewarm. At the same time they were accustomed to a higher level of social services than generally obtained in North America and accordingly found those provided by the Social Credit administration a happy compromise between supportiveness and regimentation. They were also accustomed to a more developed cultural life than Alberta had traditionally afforded and played an important role in the development of the arts. This especially affected the quality of life in Edmonton, where the staid Scotch-Irish tradition of the influential element had been less diluted by English frivolity than that of Calgary. Much as the new immigrants enriched the province they did not alter its predominantly conservative temper, for like an earlier generation of newcomers they too sought to better their material condition and were distrustful of an excess of government intervention.

Manning's moderate policies and his reputation for an unshakeable resistance to corruption in government met the needs of a prosperous province in a prospering Canada. Though agriculture ceased to dominate the life of the province as it had before the war, and the population became predominantly urban, agriculture prospered sufficiently to wipe out the deprivations of the country-dweller. Indeed rural life began to seem so attractive that some affluent city dwellers began to set up as country squires, a reaffirmation of Alberta's long-standing tradition that the good life was based on land ownership. The manufacturing sector also developed, but was far outstripped by resource development, and the buoyant revenues were sustained by the levies on oil and gas.

The slow development of secondary industry was Social Credit's Achilles heel. Oil and gas were finite resources and even at the limited output dictated by high costs of production relative to other producing countries, the day would come when Alberta's supplies would be exhausted. Even before that technological changes in the primary industries created problems of unemployment particularly worrying in a newly urbanized province. Considerations like these lay beneath the campaign of Peter Lougheed to revive the somnolent provincial Conservative party. Alberta had replaced its Social Credit members at Ottawa with Conservatives in the Diefenbaker sweep and provincial Social Credit faced the difficult question of the succession to Manning.

Lougheed had all the attributes of the traditional élite, as had a number of the other young men who associated themselves with him. He had an education and business background that appealed to those in the business community who found the muted development policies of the old regime unduly constricting. He was also prepared to throw himself into provincial politics with an enthusiasm unmatched by any young man with his qualifications since Alberta had committed herself to third parties.

Lougheed also had a style that appealed to Alberta voters, whom prosperity had made more conscious of such matters. He and his followers made a notable contrast to the dowdy and old-fashioned image which Social Credit presented in a North American society whose attitudes were so largely formed by television advertising. Again urbanization had its effects, and the Conservative appeal was strongest in the larger cities. His victory seemed to bring Alberta into a new era.

In the euphoria of Lougheed's honeymoon period, Alberta's society seemed at last to be at ease with itself and with its situation within the Canadian structure. The new government would at once conserve the inheritance of the individual Albertan and make a contribution to the national prosperity on an equal footing with the provinces that had traditionally exploited the less favoured regions. This comfortable prognosis did not reckon with the decision of OPEC. Alberta suddenly found herself, not respectably prosperous but vulgarly rich. The central provinces, and especially Ontario, found themselves sinking into recession as energy costs mounted. To what extent should Alberta accept curbs on her buoyant revenues to ensure a long-term national benefit? In the conflict of loyalties that now engulfed the province, the values of a society that gave the defence of its acquisitions the highest priority offered little prospect for an easy future. The élite had moved from its rôle as agent of the central government in the creation of a national economy to the rôle of advocate of regional economic autonomy. Could such an élite find a compromise at once acceptable to the people of the province and consistent with the future of Canada as an undivided nation?

Notes

1. The impact of ranching on southern Alberta is admirably demonstrated in David H. Breen, "The Canadian West and the Ranching Frontier, 1875–1922," Ph.D. dissertation, University of Alberta, 1972.
2. My views on the early social development of Alberta have been much influenced by my association with the preparation of a local history. *Our Foothills*, Millarville, Kew, Priddis and Bragg Creek [Alberta] Historical Society, 1975.
3. For an account of Pearce's activities, see E. A. Mitchener, "William Pearce and Federal Government Activity in Western Canada, 1882–1904," Ph.D. dissertation, University of Alberta, 1971, especially pp. 225ff and 246ff.
4. Lewis G. Thomas, "Okotoks: From Trading Post to Suburb," *Urban History Review*, VIII, 2 (October 1979): 3–22.
5. Edward J. Hart, "The Emergence and Role of the Elite in the Franco-Albertan Community to 1914," in *Essays on Western History*, ed. Lewis H. Thomas (Edmonton, 1976).
6. Lewis G. Thomas, "The Rancher and the City: Calgary and the Cattlemen, 1883–1914," Royal Society of Canada, *Proceedings and Transactions*, 4th ser. 6 (1968), pp. 203–215.

Conclusion

THE "Golden Age of Ranching" in Alberta began in the early 1880s when the first large ranches were established and the CPR reached Calgary. When that age ended is more difficult to determine. Some historians have suggested the early 1890s, when the generous land leases which the government had provided to wealthy cattlemen were cancelled; other historians have pointed to the early 1900s, when thousands of homesteaders poured into the West and began subdividing, fencing, and farming rangeland that had once been the domain of livestock. In L. G. Thomas's opinion, the "Golden Age of Ranching" ended in 1914 with the outbreak of the Great War for Civilisation. Or, to be precise, 1914 marked the end of the golden age of the privileged ranchers of southern Alberta.

The First World War, Professor Thomas has written, was a "cataclysmic experience" for Alberta's influential minority: it had a "traumatic effect on the western institutional structure which the privileged settler had done much to create and which encapsulated the values to which he subscribed."[1] Those structures, "hastily erected" by emigrants in the 'eighties and 'nineties, were just beginning to take hold when war was declared. When immigration came to a halt, when the outside capital which had buoyed local economies dried up, when the young settlers left for the battlefields of Europe, the social edifice they had erected in southern Alberta began to falter.

The effects of the war were especially pronounced in small ranching communities, in those anglophile hamlets nestled in the foothills of the Rockies. In 1914 most of the men in these communities "were still of military age; many were single, most were British born; many of them were sons of families with a tradition of military or naval service. The proportion of enlistments was exceedingly high. Many never returned."[2]

Millarville, near Lewis's boyhood home, is a good example. Over seventy men, from a community numbering no more than one hundred and fifty families, enlisted for active service: twenty-one of those men were killed and an unrecorded number physically maimed and wounded.[3] Of the survivors who returned to the district, several had been transformed and psychologically devastated by their experiences in the trenches. Likewise, the families who had been left behind—the wives, the children, and the parents of Millarville's soldiers and sailors—were seared by the war. Few of them were inclined to carry on with the social activities that had enlivened the Edwardian years; most had to struggle with labour shortages and rising prices in order to maintain the family stock-farm; not a few, on hearing of the deaths of loved ones, moved away from the district, in sorrow. As Professor Thomas declared in "The Rancher and the City" [Chapter 2]—in a phrase that must rank as one of the most evocative in Canadian literature—"Life for the ranchers and their friends was not again to be the gay and decorous picnic of the golden generation before 1914."

But it was not just the genteel ranching communities that were shattered by the war: virtually every community was affected by the high casualty rates among the province's youthful recruits. The heavy casualties, Professor Thomas has argued, "drastically affected the structure of the age group of Alberta which might have been expected to provide the leadership in the middle years of the twentieth century."[4] Its pool of potential leaders reduced, the province stumbled through the next two decades, dispirited, disheartened, apparently without direction. After 1918 few Albertans felt, as many had felt only a few years before, that they were a vital part of a dynamic system.

The social fabric and focus of Alberta also changed because of the war. When immigration from the United Kingdom declined,

Cottonwoods Ranch, Okotoks, Alberta, ca. 1935. The house is little changed in appearance fifty years later, and is still occupied by L. G. Thomas's sister, Gwynydd M. Kelson.

the ranks of the province's influential minority were depleted: no longer could the established elite depend upon a steady infusion of youthful reinforcements from the Old Country. Moreover, as the "unquestioned centrality of Britain" faded in the public mind, the province's "trans-Atlantic orientation of pre-war days" gave way to an attitude that was decidedly more regional. In the process, many of the features which had distinguished Alberta from the Western United States became blurred. American influences became more pervasive, as the province succumbed to what Professor Thomas termed the "homogenizing forces" of modern industrial society.

Unquestionably, then, the First World War is a crucial element in Professor Thomas's view of Western Canada; in fact, along with his theory of social contiguity, the impact of the Great War is one of the most dominant themes in his writings. This is not surprising perhaps, from an historian who was born in 1914 and who spent his formative years in communities that were still reeling from the world conflict; though personally untouched by the horrors of the war, he was sufficiently close to it to experience its effects. Few other Canadian historians have been in such a position; consequently, few of them have been able to write about the subject with such perception and sensitivity. Certainly no other historian has described so poignantly the repercussions the war had on Calgary, Millarville, High River, and other congenial communities which had basked in the rancher's Golden Age.

Lewis G. Thomas has, however, never been one to cling to the wreckage of the past. Ever cognizant of contemporary realities and of the forces which shape modern society, he has continued to expand his scholarly horizons and explore new fields of study. Even so, and as must be apparent from the chapters in this book, Professor Thomas has always respected what he once called "the gentler tradition of Western Canadian history." His appreciation of that tradition is evident in the closing lines of his M.A. thesis, the pioneering study which launched his career half a century ago. We may conclude with his words on the ranchers' legacy:[5]

> In retrospect, the ranching period seems a Golden Age. In its economic aspect ranching in southern Alberta was a temporary adjustment of agricultural enterprise to the needs of a new country. As a dominant industry it has been destroyed; perhaps, present conditions suggest, hastily and unwisely, but nevertheless irrevocably. It will never again be more than a convenient method for the utilization of otherwise useless lands.
>
> In its social aspect it may have a longer life. It was, from this point of view, a not unsuccessful attempt to synthesize the customs and prejudices of Victorian England and those of the new West. The ranchers nourished a tradition of simple and gracious living which even the War, which destroyed many of the concrete realities of their period, was unable to eradicate.... Such a tradition, if it has vitality, should have its place in Western Canada. A renaissance of the ranching industry itself seems improbable, but we may at least hope for the continued life of its spirit: it will live, a grace-note in the Western symphony.

Notes

1. L. G. Thomas, "Privileged Settlers" (chapter 8 supra), Introduction to James E. Hendrickson, ed., *Pioneering in Alberta: Maurice Destrubé's Story* (Calgary: Historical Society of Alberta/Alberta Records Publication Board, 1981), p. xix.
2. L. G. Thomas, "The Shires Transplanted—Millarville" (chapter 4 supra).
3. Ibid. See also L. G. Thomas, ed., *Our Foothills* (Calgary: Millarville, Kew, Priddis, and Bragg Creek Historical Society, 1975), pp. 24-26 and passim.
4. L. G. Thomas, Introduction to Roger Motut and Maurice Legris, eds., *Ordinary Heroes. The Journal of a French Pioneer by Marcel Durieux* (Edmonton: University of Alberta Press, 1980), p. xviii.
5. L. G. Thomas, "The Ranching Period in Alberta," unpublished M.A. thesis, University of Alberta, 1935, pp. 171-72.